Rajesh Pandey

Rajesh Pandey was born on 15 June 1961, in Lalapur, Prayagraj. He completed his MSc in Botany from Allahabad University and was a recipient of both the Junior Research Fellowship (JRF) and Senior Research Fellowship (SRF) in Botany.

In 1986, he was selected for the Uttar Pradesh Police Provincial Service, and in 2003, he became an Indian Police Service (IPS) officer. He retired on 30 June 2021, after a distinguished career in law enforcement.

During his tenure, he served as the Superintendent of Police (SP) in six districts, including Lucknow, and as the Senior Superintendent of Police (SSP) in five districts. He later held positions as Deputy Inspector General (DIG) of Bareilly Police Range and Inspector General (IG) of Zone. Additionally, he served as IG Election at the DGP Headquarters.

He was part of the Special Investigation Team (SIT) that investigated the Ayodhya bomb blast on 5 July 2005. As one of the founding members of the Uttar Pradesh Special Task Force (STF) and the Anti-Terrorism Squad (ATS), he played a key role in tackling organised crime and terrorism. In 2016, he was posted as SP - ATS.

During his United Nations Peacekeeping Force deputation in 2008-2009, he worked with the Kosovo Police as an advisor to the Director General of the Border and Boundary Police. He also received training at the Royal Institute of Public Administration, London, in 2010.

Between 1999 and 2016, he was awarded the President's Police Medal for Gallantry four times, a remarkable honour. His other accolades include:

- President's Meritorious Service Medal (2005)
- United Nations Medal for Peacekeeping in Kosovo (2008)
- Silver Commendation Disc (2018)
- Gold Commendation Disc (2020)
- Platinum Commendation Disc (2021)

During his United Nations deputation, he visited several European countries, including Germany, Kosovo, Greece, and Serbia.

Since 2021, he has been serving as the Nodal Officer at the Uttar Pradesh Expressway Industrial Development Authority (UPEIDA).

Email: rajeshpandey61@gmail.com

FROM RAJESH PANDEY ABOUT SIDHARTHA

The book is translated into English by Sidhartha (BSc., Company Secretary, MBA (USA), LLM), a senior corporate professional with over two decades of rich experience. He is a product of the London School of Economics and a seasoned Fraud Examiner professional. He possesses a deep understanding of creative writing about investigation and crime.

My association with Sidhartha is beyond professional bonding. I am impressed with his dedication to translating this book and making it a delightful experience for the readers.

I acknowledge his hard work and wish him all the best in his personal and professional journey.

FROM SIDHARTHA

My special thanks to Sir (Rajesh Pandey, IPS (retd.)), who gave me this extraordinary opportunity to write "Varchasva" in English. Throughout the book writing, I was deeply moved by the commitment and determination it takes for a police officer to handle the system and bring the criminals and mafias to the book. In the process of writing, I realized that no matter how glamorous and attractive a police officer's job seems to be, it's challenging and rewardless since the police are always at the receiving end of public frustration.

Through this book, I pay my immense respect to all the police officers who have devoted their lives to their duty.

I am very thankful to my family and friends for supporting my book writing, as I always did at odd hours and on holidays. On this account, I am guilty of ignoring my family's many innocent requests and invitations to social events to complete the book on time. Nevertheless, this was an immense learning experience from all accounts.

My thanks to all the readers of this book.

Your comments and suggestions are always welcome, and I can be reached at sidbook9@gmail.com.

VARCHASVA

The Absolute Power

A true story about an era of crime in the state of Uttar Pradesh.

Rajesh Pandey

English version written by

Sidhartha

KAVYA
PUBLICATIONS

Publisher:

SDR INNOWAYS INDIA PVT. LTD.
667, Rajaward, Kulpahar, Mahoba - 210426

Imprint:
KAVYA PUBLICATIONS
Abhinav R.H.4, Awadhpuri, Bhopal - 462002

Centre
Kavya Publications
(Maxel Electronics) 8, 3rd floor DSIDC Shed SCHEME-1
Okhla phase -2, Delhi - 20.

Mob. : 7905266820, 9918801353
Website: www.kavyapublications.com
E-Mail: editor@kavyapublications.com

ISBN : 978-93-6431-592-0
Price : 999/-
Year : 2025
Edition : First

This book is printed at MTL and published by Ajay Agrawal, CEO of SDR Innoways India Pvt. Ltd. Kulpahar Mahoba with its imprint and centre, Kavya Publications Delhi.

First Book.

Dedicated to found memory of: -

My Mother Late Ram Kumari Pandey

My Father Late Chandra Prakash Pandey

Contents

AN ERA OF CRIME

The incident was shocking and terrified everyone. This incident can be marked as the beginning of an era of crime that later established its roots in northern India, stretching to Mumbai, Maharashtra, the financial capital of India. The incident was the brutally killed rail minister was none other than Late Lalit Narayan Mishra, who was bombed to death on 3rd January 1975 in the Samastipur district of Bihar amidst his supporters. Lalit Narayan Mishra was popular and fondly called "Lalit Babu" by everyone. His brutal assassination gave birth to new apprehension in the minds of the common man. The apprehension translated into a paralyzing threat that even an influential person could be murdered... that too in his hometown and amidst his thousands of supporters. Nothing can be more shocking and horrifying. Although the context is different, the brutal assassination of Prime Minister Late Indira Gandhi by her bodyguards further established the insecurity and threat in the minds of the commoner. The commoner was convinced that now, no one is safe anywhere.

This insecurity of the common man that anyone and anywhere can be killed became the turning point in the crime ecosystem, which made the criminals of Bihar and UP bold and dreadful. They posed a ruthless challenge to police in the decade of the 1990s. This period witnessed many criminals walk scot-free even after committing heinous crimes, as there was no internet, no CCTV (Close Circuit Camera & Television), no mobile, and no GPS location tracker. The modus operandi of the crime were traditional; the investigation and crime analysis, including the court procedure, were manual, slow, and highly susceptible to manipulations. Complainants used to bring their witnesses, and in more than 90% of cases, the witnesses were turning hostile, leaving the case flat in the courtroom. The remaining 10% of witnesses were killed or snubbed to maintain silence. It sent a shiver down my spine even while thinking about that era, but this was true, as it was the era of the 1990s and the period before.

This system emboldened the criminals, and there was no fear of punishment left in their hearts. The criminals of Bihar and UP had already started organizing themselves. By the 90s, they were so merciless in execution that they were rolling down the windows of their cars and firing from their sophisticated weapons without any hesitation on anyone whom they considered a threat. On 25th March 1996, a three-time MLA from Gorakhpur Vidhan Sabha, UP, Om Prakash Paswan, was bombed to death in his constituency in front of his thousands of supporters. Much earlier to this incident, in the same fashion, in the Samastipur district of Bihar, Lalit Narayan Mishra and several others were bombed to death; the pattern was starkly the same.

In the 90s, when political murder was at its peak, politicians were murdered frequently and in broad daylight; even bhaubali politicians were terrified of sudden attacks and getting killed. The phobia of being killed also paralyzed them, and the worst outcome was that this made the budding, righteous, patriotic leaders reluctant to join politics. It was shocking to see the politics go into the hands of rapists, killers, and scamsters, perhaps too scary as well.

Courageous and adventurous youths became more inclined towards crime. So politicians either maintained a low profile in active politics or compromised heavily, accepting it as the only path to their survival.

This was the time when notorious history sheets were glorified by society at large. This was the beginning of the era of the criminalization of politics or the politicization of crime. Like any blockbuster movie, it had glamour, wealth, and sophisticated weapons to display and even demonstrate their firepower wherever they wished. Whenever any don cum politician drove through the road, the entire highway turned deserted in fear. Same brand, same color, and exact model convoy of cars, with flaunting weapons from the car window, when passed through the cities blowing its hooters, the dumbfounded public stared with adulation and trembled with fear. This seems to be straight out of a Hollywood crime thriller. Some men in the crowd even bowed and saluted the passing convoy; the notorious history-sheeter inside the car might have smiled at this welcoming and admiring display of gesture from the public. People watched with bated breath as the twelve black boleros passed through the broad streets of Lucknow, scared and fascinated simultaneously. All these cars had the same number, although registered in different cities. From Shabuddin, who had killed one person by drowning in acid, Mukhtar Ansari, known for incessant firing at his will, Atique Ahmed, Brajesh Singh, Dhananjay Singh, and Hari Shankar Tiwary to Virendra Shahi, they all achieved high success in the same way. The modus operandi were not a secret.

The era of the 90s will be known when criminals coined the term "Bhaubali" (strong man) for themselves. These criminals were goons of the politicians who nurtured them for booth looting in elections, but now they were forcefully capturing the reins of power from their mentors. The mentors were eliminated, and the goons themselves became white-collar politicians. The point was that the criminals got the taste of politics and power flowing from it only because they were being used for illegal booth capturing and election rigging by the politicians. Still, suddenly, the table turned upside down. As a result, from an illiterate to educated youth, everyone started dreaming of marching into the corridors of power and politics by brandishing country-made pistols, which were later replaced by AK 47, and some even succeeded in it.

One day, the world witnessed the uproar and skirmishes in the UP Vidhan Sabha. That day, some of the bhaubali MLAs of UP Vidhan Sabha demonstrated their wild side and created unforgettable and shameful mayhem. They attacked co-MLAs with broken mikes and furniture. It was then realized that more than 2/3rd of the total MLAs had criminal backgrounds, and more than 1/3rd had serious charges of murder and rape pending against them. There was apprehension that if this continued, one day, any notorious criminal would become CM of UP and would have pushed the state into total anarchy. By then, the infamous state guest house scandal had happened, which shook the base of the leading political coalition government, and had it not happened, it would have changed the face of the political landscape forever.

During those days, there was a notorious criminal, Shri Prakash Shukla, whose terror gave sleepless nights to everyone in Bihar and UP. Shri Prakash's mentor cum Godfather was based out of Bihar, who later even became MP. Shri Prakash got sophisticated weapons from there and learned to exploit the situation after committing the crime. He was fast and forceful; he was merciless and lustful. He had a passion for two things: one was crime, and the other was women. He never had regard for anyone; he was devil incarnate, and he had committed almost a dozen murders in a week in Gorakhpur for setting up his cable business.

However, it is said that nature's wealth is unmeasurable; the night before dawn is the darkest, and the higher the heat is, the higher the possibility of intense rain. The crime was increasing at a fast pace, and the common man had almost surrendered before the criminals, as even the police were helpless; suddenly came EVM (Electronic Voting Machine) and mobile phones. EVM pulled the carpet beneath the politicians' feet, and those politicians who had always looted the booth and ballots were seriously affected. EVM made a historic contribution in checking such malpractices and tightened the rein around the corrupt parties of politicians to win the elections. EVM made the election process fast and efficient, which lasted for several days earlier, by making it transparent and reliable. EVM made a significant contribution to curbing election-related crimes.

The second big revolution of the 90s was the mobile phone. It changed the world drastically. No one thought people could talk while commuting, which could fit inside their small pockets. The true beneficiary of the mobile revolution was the police. It had solved many complicated problems for police, which otherwise gave them an endless run. It not only solved the police issues but also helped police locate the hideouts of big criminals. Specifically, for those fashionable criminals using sophisticated weapons and adopting modern technology, technology made committing crime even easier and faster. Those criminals who immediately adopted technology for committing serious crimes like murder, loot, rape, etc., didn't realize that slowly they have started walking on the path of self-destruction. They never realized that they were giving the police clues about their location.

The same thing happened with Shri Prakash Shukla. He never understood how police were able to crack his location. He was suspicious and restless about how the police got his location information, but he could never know that the same mobile continuously gave the police his location information. It was due to this mobile only that a terror like Shri Prakash Shukla was encountered by UP police's STF (Special Task Force) in Ghaziabad near Delhi.

This book revolves around this subject; the entire encounter story is captured in detail. The book is based on the actual information of Shri Prakash Shukla's much-publicized encounter. The book captures all the elements of the encounter to show that the workings of the police are complex and painfully detailed. It shows how police must maintain self-composure and focus in extreme testing situations. Police are aware that the commoner does not respect the police but still works with patience for the safety of the public at large. Even when police are looked down on with disgrace, they cannot shy away from their responsibility even though the system does not empower them to fulfill the public's expectations.

The readers might question the authenticity of the scores of information shared in this book and how the police knew that information. With due respect and courtesy, I confirm that every detail of the book is correct. Police have a system of finding information through informers. One thing is important to note that police had caught many informers of Shri Prakash Shukla's gang before and after his death. Shri Prakash's encounter, other criminal encounters, the genesis of crime, and other related crime story analyses can be heard on the YouTube channel "Kissagoi" since 2021. The same can be said of me on Facebook, also.

Then, the ADG of UP Police (Law & Order), Ajay Raj Sharma, conceptualized UP STF, which led to its birth. My mentors, the

Director General of Railway Arun Kumar, Ex-DG BSF Rajni Kant Mishra, Ex-DG Subesh Kumar Singh, and scores of several other senior and subordinate police officers, can never be forgotten. The book contains references to all of them at relevant places. I am indebted to my wife, Srimati Minu Pandey, whose support and encouragement enabled me to handle several criminals successfully in due course. I acknowledge my daughter Krati and son Aashey, who faced stress and threats as a child of a police officer when I was in STF and ATS and especially when we were involved in the operation related to Shri Prakash Shukla.

This book is not a personal memoir but an accurate account of the dark crime era of UP, and while recording the events of that time, I have paid attention to the fact that it should not harm anyone. However, an error may inadvertently happen, and if any such statement hurts anyone, I beg pardon for the same. One more fact without which the book will be incomplete: I was DIG and later IG of Bairelly range, and the onslaught of COVID happened, which led to incessant death all around. When everything around me was dark and gloomy, I felt intense restlessness within. The dilemma of whether or not to do anything gave rise to the feeling that I must record the most critical phases of my career. Since I was not a writer, I wrote only to the extent required in my work. Then I met Mohd. Usfaque was an expert typist who typed at the same speed as I used to dictate. I started calling him at my residence from 24th October 2020 till 25th December 2021, and the book was born. I am indebted to his contributions.

FROM HAPPINESS TO TERROR

Lucknow is known for its pleasant evenings, but now the evening was stained with blood. This was January 13th, 1997, and the cold was at its peak. Even in the heart of winter, the evenings in Lucknow remain just as romantic and engaging. This evening belonged to a city renowned for its etiquette and sophistication. Lucknow adores me, and I am passionately in love with her. Unfortunately, and tragically, it was decided by someone to fill the evenings of Lucknow with terror and fear.

Around 8 pm, the wireless beeped with the message that a person had been shot dead at Latos Road, Kaiserbag, of Lucknow. At the time of the broadcast of this message, Rajesh Pandey was on his way to Kaiserbag from Wazirganj; he hurriedly rushed to the crime scene. There was a huge crowd, and a person's dead was lying in a pool of blood. The person was hit with several rounds of bullets, and the constable present at the crime scene was busy collecting the empty cartridge shells. Rajesh Pandey was immediately informed that the body belonged to Vivek Srivastava, one of the oldest and most prominent lottery businessmen.

Rajesh Pandey was confused to see the bullet wounds on the dead body. He was unable to understand the background of the case. Rajesh Pandey was wondering why there were so many bullets needed to kill this man. The second question that flashed into his mind was how a person could fire so many rounds of bullets in such a busy city locality. Finally, the procedure started, and the body was sent for postmortem. The deceased family was contacted, and the case registration process was initiated. This matter and this incident ended up here.

Only the date changed; the month and year were the same. The same month, on the 24th, in Lucknow's super busy area of Tedhi Pulia, Titu Sardar and his men entered a chamber and murdered another person. This incident too happened at around 8 pm, and the workload on police was increasing. At the same time, two murders had rocked the city. The government and Police Commissioner released several instructions and orders, and the pressure on the police mounted. Meanwhile, all the empty cartridges collected on the spot were sent for forensic examination as part of the police investigation process.

For the next two months, no murder or any other significant incident was committed. The police force, journalists, and pro-police politicians started commenting that an outsider gang might have committed the murders. It will take some time before police will eventually find out. It was said that police informers are passing on the information, and the culprit gang will be identified soon. Then, on March 31st, 1997, an incident happened in the Indira Nagar in the Trans-Gomti area of Lucknow, a decently developed and considered very peaceful locality. The spring season was witness to this heinous crime.

It was around 9 am, and the Sprigdell School was going to declare the results of the primary section students. So, the kids were accompanying their guardians for the results. Many guardians visiting the school parked their vehicles outside the gate. Young primary section children in their school uniform either came out of the school or went inside it, holding their parent's finger. Hearing the continuous gunshots, people were confused and tried to discover what was happening. A man wearing a white kurta pajama was lying on the road facing down. A lady and a young child walking with this person ran ahead to save their life. The three killers were firing continuously on the back and shoulder of the person lying face down. After shooting several rounds, the three assailants started walking away, and suddenly, after walking for around ten steps, they turned and came back to the lying victim.

The tall, strong, good-looking guy came closer to the victim. The tall assailant wore jeans, a t-shirt, and expensive sports shoes. He had a revolver in both his hands. He tried to turn the victim face up, who was wet with his blood and lying face down, by his feet, and when he was unable to do so, the second assailant too joined him. They both ruthlessly turned the victim face up. Standing there, they both changed the magazine of their weapons with rare calmness and confidence. The short-height assailant, who appeared robust and quick, changed the magazine of his Sten gun.

The tall assailant started abusing the victim in a loud voice –

"Mother fucker... He used to stare a lot! "

After saying this, he again pumped five more bullets each into the victim's eye.

This horrific incident was watched by over a hundred shocked kids and their parents from the other side of the school boundary. While the bullets were pumped into the eyes of the victim, there was little movement in the body. Seeing this, the tall assailant shouted that he would survive this time, too. Where is his heart, on the left or right side? Hearing this, the shorter assailants pumped ten to ten bullets into both sides of his chest. Now, their second magazine was also empty. The tall assailant loudly abused the dead person and spat on him. After that, they both walked briskly to their car, parked at a distance of a hundred steps, and conveniently left. They both had a desire to touch the height of terror.

The brutally murdered man was no one else but the most significant Bahubali mafia of eastern UP, Virendra Pratap Shahi. Neither the police nor the men of Virendra Pratap Shahi had ever thought that he would be murdered in such a way. The news of his murder spread like wildfire in the entire UP, and once again, pressure on the police mounted. The police team who reached the crime scene started collecting the empty cartridge shell for hours at a stretch. The police team tried talking to several persons present at the crime scene, but the people were so scared and shocked that they refused to speak. They all were dumbstruck. Virendra Shahi's body was sent for postmortem. The Lucknow was already working under severe pressure.

During the cremation ceremony of Virendra Shahi, there was a massive crowd of his supporters, family members, police officers, and many politicians cutting across the party lines. Heavy police deployment was done at the cremation site, and the senior police officers were monitoring the police deployment from their chambers. They were also trying to find out if there was any lead about who had killed Virendra Shahi and why. Most people generally guessed that another local mafia might have eliminated him – Hari Shankar Tiwary's men. Twice on earlier occasions, Virendra Shahi was attacked near the Golghar of Gorakhpur. His car was fired several rounds of bullets, but he narrowly survived. This incident was also credited to Hari Shankar Tiwary.

One of the relatives of Virendra Shahi, who was present at the cremation site, disclosed to his known police officer that the gang was from Bihar. The bone of contention was railway tender, and someone Shri Prakash Shukla had threatened him on the phone for the last 6 months. He was constantly repeating; I will kill you before the Holi festival. He confidently said that no one in the Hari Shankar Tiwary's gang is so aggressive that he will kill Virendra Shahi so brutally and then escape easily. When Rajesh Pandey came to know about this information, he called and tried to coax the name of the relative who gave so seriously relevant information from the police officer, but he didn't budge. Rajesh Pandey deployed all his policing techniques, but the constable didn't budge the name or any other information about it. All he kept on repeating that –

"The killer is a hard-core criminal, and he will kill anyone who will give the information."

For the first time, Shri Prakash Shukla's name appeared in the police records. The Gorakhpur police then inquired about Shri Prakash Shukla, who he was, and where he was from. After intense investigation, it came to light that Shri Prakash Shukla was a 22–23–year–old young man who was very fond of arms and mostly lived in Bihar. No further information could be found.

In the postmortem report of Virendra Shahi, there were 126 bullet marks. All the marks were of the bullet entry and exit. The killing of Virendra Shahi was a significant incident in the crime world, and this became a big challenge for the police. Virendra Shahi was a known name in the eastern UP and the neighboring districts of Bihar. Gorakhpur was the headquarters of the Eastern Railway, so

A large part of Bihar was under the northeast railway, and Gorakhpur was the headquarters of the northeast railway. Gorakhpur was also the center for the UP East railway tender and all railway-related activities. The contract work of railway tenders was a significant way of making big money quickly. When the tendering of the government work started, the tenders were either taken by Virendra Shahi's men or Hari Shankar Tiwary's men. Immediately, these tenders were assigned to their men / contractors at the margin of 10% – 15%. Slowly, this tender pooling started in all the departments, such as the public construction department, irrigation, Nagar Nigam, forest, mining, and several other small departments. All the tenders of these departments, be it construction, maintenance, or supply, went to either Virendra Shahi's men or Hari Shankar Tiwary's criminal.

Due to these government tenders, so many broad daylight shootouts and murders were committed, leading to total anarchy in Gorakhpur and the neighboring areas, so much so that Gorakhpur became notoriously called the "crime capital" of India. The then CM of UP, Vir Bahadur Singh, was from Gorakhpur and became very disturbed by this increasing crime. This was the first such trend in the history of eastern UP and Bihar when the entire crime polarization was being done based on caste. The Thakur caste criminals were protected and patronized by Virendra Shahi, and the Brahmin caste criminals were protected and patronized by Hari Shankar Tiwary. Vir Bahadur Singh introduced the UP Goonda Act to stop this mafia gang war. This resulted in a slight improvement in the situation, and some control over small-time goons was observed. Only some Bihar mafia gangs started interfering in railway tenders during this time. They used to come to Gorakhpur with their caravan to snatch the tenders forcefully. Vir Bahadur Singh offered maximum resistance to these Bihar mafias, and shootouts were shared outside the government offices of Gorakhpur.

Surajbhan Singh was a Bahubali of Bihar. He was a resident of the Mokama district of Patna and used to bid for railway tenders.

Immediately after getting the railway tenders, 10-15% was paid as commission, after which the profit was reduced. In such a situation, Surajbhan Singh stayed in Gorakhpur and started searching for any possibility of connecting with another influential person in Gorakhpur who could effectively counter Virendra Shahi. On one such day, Surajbhan Singh failed to win a tender at the railway headquarters in Gorakhpur. The MLA of Faizabad Pawan Pandey, Sattu Pandey, Ghanshyam Pandey, Anand Pandey, and Sudhir Tripathy were also there to forcefully snatch the same tender. At the gate of the railway headquarters, both the gangs met with Virendra Shahi's gang, and Virendra Shahi's gang started firing incessantly at both gangs. Surajbhan Singh and his men ran away to save their life. Pawan Pandey and his men, too, ran for their lives. Surajbhan and Pawan Pandey met while escaping from the Virendra Shahi's men.

Surajbhan asked Pawan Pandey – from where you all are?

The reply came from Pawan Pandey – I am MLA from Ayodhya.

Is the rest of the team also from Ayodhya?

Yes, they are my friends.

He is Sattu Pandey; He is Anand Pandey.

Surajbhan asked, what brings you here?

We came here to get the tender to supply stone pebbles (chips) in meter gauge conversion to broad gauge.

Surajbhan said, “Oh! I also came for the same purpose."

Then Pawan Pandey replied, "This motherfucker will not let any Brahmin get the railway contract. Some arrangement needs to be made for this."

Surajbhan said, "I have also been troubled by his hooliganism for the last 6 months. For the last 100 years, the railway workers have been from outside: George Babu, Ram Vilas Paswan, Nitish Kumar, and Jagjivan Ram, all from Bihar. Still, none of the Bihari contractors had got the work of Bihar tender from Gorakhpur. We get the work done, the railway ministers are ours, the budget is ours, and all the business will go to Shahi and Tiwari. How long will this go on, and I will tolerate it?"

Hearing this answer, Pawan Pandey said, "Suraj Bhai, you have said what is in my heart. He gets tenders based on his goonda power, and without doing any work, he makes crores of rupees and distributes the contracts to small contractors. Both of them are rascals."

Surajbhan asked, "Who is the bigger rascal among the two? We have to deal with him first."

Pawan Pandey replied, "Tiwari ji adjusts with everyone but this Shahia! Mother fucker doesn't even let me touch it."

Surajbhan replied, "Pawan bhai, you are also Brahmin, so you say that Tiwary ji adjusts to everything. I tried my best to see, these two are like mother fuckers." Talking, everyone reached the hotel.

Pawan Pandey called Surajbhan below the hotel and said, "If you have a phone number, give it to me; we have to work together."

Surajbhan said, "Come, let's sit and talk."

Pawan Pandey hesitantly said, "We will talk some other time. If possible, then we will come to Mokama."

There is also a tender for the expansion of five small railway stations. The total tender is more than a hundred crore rupees. Hearing this, Pawan Pandey signaled his people, and they all came inside the hotel, sat in the same room, and started talking.

Pawan Pandey replied, "Nine mm pistol, one ten, the rest are 315 bore rifles. There are no small weapons available right now."

Surajbhan said, "It's impossible to overcome Shahi with such weapons. The sound and blow of an AK-47 can make the opponent unconscious. The opponent will not be able to touch his weapon for at least ten minutes."

Pawan replied, "We don't get any AK47s here, and in fact, I have not even seen one in my life."

Surajbhan said, "We will give you four AKs. Only on the condition that Shahi should not be alive until the next tender." Pawan Pandey said, "Okay, but where will you get it from?"

Surajbhan said, "Come with me right now. I have kept it in my house in Mokama."

Pawan Pandey said, "Tomorrow, I have my relative's wedding. I can't go right now, but definitely before the next tender, I will come to Mokama."

Surajbhan gave his landline number and said, "Call this number before coming. Tell whoever picks up the phone that I want to talk to Dada. Ashok Singh is calling from Gorakhpur."

Pawan Pandey noted this number in his diary and asked, "I don't understand why you should use the fake name of Ashok Singh."

Surajbhan said, "Pawan Bhai, just think you are an MLA. People know you. If we tell our name, people around us will also start using their brains and try to speculate."

Pawan Pandey said okay and left with his convoy of five vehicles. Even Surajbhan left in half an hour for Patna with his convoy.

Four days later, Pawan Pandey, Sattu Pandey, Rajan Tiwari, Shri Prakash Shukla, Anand Pandey, and Sudhir sat at Pawan Pandey's residence.

Sattu Pandey asked Pawan Pandey, "Bhaiya ji, the man we met at Gorakhpur on the day of the tender, was talking about AK 47. Do you think he was trying to create an impression that he owns an AK 47? Even if we leave aside his ability to use it, we have not even seen an AK 47 in our entire lives, and that guy was talking about giving four AKs to us?"

Pawan Pandey replied, "Listen, I am not a foolish person who will get carried away with fake claims and talks and will go to his home only because he is asking me to come. I have also made my discreet inquiry in this regard from local people. This man is well known, and there is nothing wrong with it. Now, how many AK 47 he has, we will know only when we go to Mokama."

After looking at it, Pawan Pandey took his diary from his pocket and said, "He had given us his number. Let's talk to him and ask when we should come, simple? The question here is not about four AK 47s. The question is about how to get the tender worth a hundred crores. Once we get the tender, then all the AK-47s and machine guns will be with us."

Sattu said, "Okay, bhai, but I won't be able to speak so politely. Let's have Shri Prakash talk to him." Pawan Pandey replied, "Okay." Pawan Pandey began reading the number loudly from the diary while Shri Prakash Shukla wrote it on his hand so he could dial the phone. The call was from Pawan Pandey's office; the phone was answered immediately, and the person on the line said, "I am Ashok Singh, calling from "Faizabad. Can you please put me through to Dada?" After two minutes, Surajbhan came on the line, and Shri Prakash handed the phone to Pawan Pandey. Pawan Pandey asked, "Brother, when should we come to Mokama?" After receiving a reply from the other side, Pawan Pandey said, "Okay," and hung up the phone. After the call, Pawan Pandey said,

"He is calling the day after tomorrow. There are two vehicles. Sattu will bring one more vehicle, and then we will leave for Mokama the day after tomorrow." After three days, all these people reached Mokama. After necessary checking was done on these people at three places in Mokama and after this, Surajbhan's men brought all the people home. After the conversation, Surajbhan gave a signal, and his man got a big black cricket bag. Surajbhan took out four AK 47s individually and showed them to everyone. Stunned and impressed, everyone took turns to see the AK-47 in their hands.

Surajbhan said on a serious note, "There is no benefit in lengthy discussion. Let's talk about the issue. Right now, I will give you two AK 47s. It's evening, and the river Ganga flows behind my house. Have your meal and then come with me on the banks of the Ganges. I will also explain how to use it in ten minutes. You all take away two AK 47s; I will bring two on the tender day. If the work is done before the tender, I will give you these two AK 47s forever, and if the work is not done, I will take both of them back with me. After that, I will return all four AK 47s for the job whenever you ask me. Keep in mind that the work has to be done at all costs.

" One more thing, Pawan Bhai," Surajbhan said in a decisive tone: "Ensure that only courageous ones are given the AK 47 to use it."

Pawan immediately said, "This is Shri Prakash Shukla, who spoke to you; we trust him." We will give one to him and another to Anand Pandey.

Surajbhan asked while looking around and trying to find, "Who is Shri Prakash Shukla?"

Shri Prakash responded in a pleasing tone, "Dada, it is me. I called you by the name you told us to use when we called."

Surajbhan said in an enquiring tone, "Ashok Singh?"

Shri Prakash confirmed, "Yes, dada."

Surajbhan smiled and remarked, "Your name is too long. I am not comfortable calling you such a long name. From now onwards, I will call you Ashok Singh only, and whenever you want to call me, make the call by this name."

Pawan Pandey took both AK-47s and 100 cartridges, leaving Mokama in all three vehicles. Along the way, Shri Prakash asked, "Which routes would be best to avoid checkpoints?" The entire convoy chose a route and navigated accordingly to their destination.

Then, it was decided that everyone would go to Pawan Pandey's residence in Ayodhya first and then go to their respective places. The next date of the railway tender was postponed by three months, and it was fixed for October 24th, 1996, leading to a long waiting period. Meanwhile, Shri Prakash Shukla and Anand Pandey were looking for an opportunity to use AK 47, and then came the auction of liquor shops in Faizabad. This event will turn into a new era of high-profile shootouts at UP.

47 BUST

The liquor shop auction was to be scheduled on March 31st, 1996. Now Pawan Pandey and his brother Rakesh Pandey were keen to take the contract for the liquor shops in Faizabad. Satyendra Singh alias Langad of Faizabad was a ruling terror, and he was known for threatening people who were going to the district court for participating in the auction of liquor shops. It was then decided that Satyendra had to be killed before this year's liquor auction. Otherwise, there was no chance of anyone else taking the auction this year, too; like in earlier years, Satyendra would forcibly get tender, take commission, and distribute the shops among his contractors.

Anand Pandey had insight into the matter through his sources, and he informed everyone during the meeting, "Nowadays Satyendra Singh is traveling in a gypsy, he keeps a 9 mm pistol. Three of his men occupy the back seat of the gypsy carrying a 315-bore rifle and a double-barrel shotgun, threatening anyone who tries to overtake him. Satyender Singh himself drives the gypsy, and the person sitting next to him is also an armed weapon."

Anand Pandey apprehensively said, "Bhai, his firepower is good. His goons will not betray him at any cost! Everyone depends on Satyender alias Langad for survival; we must work very cleverly and secretly."

Sudhir Tripathi added, "When he drives on the road, he does not allow any vehicle to overtake him. If someone tries to overtake him, his goons sitting in the back seat of gypsy scare him by showing their weapons. If someone is known, the boys tell him to give him the way."

Shri Prakash thought momentarily and said, "This is even better."

Anand said in a determined tone, "We will try to overtake him; we will kill him the moment we get an opportunity to overtake."

Listening to such a plan pissed off Shri Prakash, and he said, "This is a completely foolish plan; if you try to overtake by hook or by crook, the goons sitting behind with 315 guns will pump you with bullets. Always remember, the one who fires the first bullet is the king in the field. We will fire the first bullet in any case. Dada's AK 47 will be tested on Langad. It's final; he has to die."

Shri Prakash devised a plan and said, "Let's go to Lucknow to get a VIP siren installed in our Maruti car from Aminabad market. When the VIP siren sounds in the vehicles coming behind, Satyender takes his head out and turns back to see whose vehicle is trying to overtake him. If it is an officer's car, he lets it pass, and if it is any politician's car, he doesn't let it pass."

Pawan Pandey asked, "What will happen with this?"

Shri Prakash explained, "He goes on the bypass road every day. Sarai Rasi is a deserted area. We will take our car closer to him and blow the VIP siren. Immediately, he will peep out of his vehicle's window to check our vehicle and look behind us. By the time he understands who is blowing the VIP siren, I will pump the entire magazine of AK 47 in his head."

The gang decided to go to Faizabad only in the Maruti car and trace him. Satyender was to be attacked at the deserted stretch on the bypass road.

Pawan said to Shri Prakash, "You will go with only one AK 47. Anand's AK 47 will remain at my house, as there is a risk of taking two AK 47s. Sudhir will take one stun gun; the rest will carry small weapons."

After this planning, the gang went to Faizabad and started keeping an eye on him. After three days of effort, finally, on February 22nd, 1996, Satyender alias Langad was being followed by Shri Prakash's car. Once Satyender's car turned towards Sarai Rasi, Shri Prakash followed him.

Dheerendra was driving the car, and Shri Prakash was sitting in the front left seat with an AK 47 while others were in the back seat. The white car where they were sitting had black film on its windows, making it difficult to see the occupants. As soon as the Shri Prakash's car came near the Gypsy, Langad's guards sitting in the back seat signaled him not to overtake.

Shri Prakash told Dheerendra, "Speed up the car and bring it parallel! Speed up the car and sound the siren."

Dheerendra obeyed and sped up. As soon as he took the position to overtake Langad's vehicle and took his car near the jeep, he blew the VIP hooter. As the hooter sounded, Satyendra alias Langad immediately tried to stick his head out from the side and saw the car trying to overtake him; the speed of both vehicles was around 100 km/hour. As soon as Langad stuck his head out, Shri Prakash fired from his AK-47. About 20-25 bullets pierced Langad's head directly, and immediately, Langad's head blew off. Blood spatter spread on the front glass, steering, and side mirror. Langad's jeep, which was moving at a speed of more than 100 km/h, overturned on the side of the road, screeched for some distance due to high speed, and tumbled down into the ditch at the side of the deserted stretch of the road. All the people sitting in the back seat of the gypsy also fell straight into the ditch. They were stunned by the sudden event that blew Langad's head and toppled the vehicle.

Shri Prakash, Anand, Sudhir, and Pawan Pandey ran towards the overturned jeep with their weapons. Langad's men sitting in the back somehow re-collected themselves, pulled themselves out of the overturned gypsy, and ran away, leaving behind their weapons. Shri Prakash's gang chased them and snatched away their weapons. Shri Prakash and his gang took all the weapons, including 315-bore rifles, kept them in their car, and fled from away. From there, they went straight to Pawan Pandey's Shiv Sena office in Lucknow's Kaiserbagh. They kept all the weapons there and congratulated each other that this year's liquor contract for the entire Faizabad was in Pawan Bhai's name. Now, no bastard dares to enter even inside the liquor auction pandal of Faizabad Collectorate. Meanwhile, Shri Prakash took this as an opportunity to update Surajbhan; he called him from the PCO at Kaiserbagh crossing.

Surajbhan picked up the phone.

Shri Prakash said, "This is Ashok Singh. Is Dada speaking?"

Surajbhan said, "Yes, tell me Ashok!"

Shri Prakash was thrilled to inform, "Dada, I have done the testing of AK 47; it's wonderful in execution, and the first prey is dead. Now we are waiting for October 24th."

Dada praised him and said, "Okay, there is a lot of time for October 24th. Come back to Mokama if you get a chance."

Days passed, and now it was May 4th, 1996, in Muhaddipur, where Om Prakash, elder Bhaiya of Shri Prakash, lived with his family and had an altercation with Ramshankar Srivastava. Shri Prakash killed Ramshankar on May 4th, 1996. After this, Shri Prakash developed evil confidence in killing and never looked back; subsequently, on April 29th, he shot Gorakhpur University student leader Naveen Singh in the NC hostel of the university, but he survived. Then, on September 24th, he shot dead a rising leader, Vivek Singh, in the cantonment area of Gorakhpur. All these killings gave him horrible notoriety in Gorakhpur, and people started to recognize Shri Prakash Shukla in the league of Virendra Shahi and Hari Shankar Tiwari.

Finally, October 24th came. Surajbhan visited Gorakhpur with his entire entourage for the much-awaited railway tender. Shri Prakash, Anand, and Sudhir had already made arrangements for the hotel. Surajbhan and his men came straight to the designated hotel. They discussed the issue of Virendra Shai's interference, and it was decided that every effort would be made to win the tender today. It was the general perception of all present there that Shahi himself would not come to bid for the tender, as he was fully confident that now no one would be there to oppose him. Virendra Shahi was to travel to the Gol Ghar area of Gorakhpur for a program known to Surajbhan and Shri Prakash. From there, while going home or coming towards the railway tender office, Surajbhan and Shri Prakash decided to kill him on the way. Then, the tender will be postponed, and the next date will be announced, so the tender can be won without any hindrance. Near Chandralok Lodge, two cars were taken from the lodge's parking; Shri Prakash's team occupied one car, Surajbhan's team in the other car; they sat with two AK 47s each and the rest of the weapons.

They all waited there, and after some time, Shahi was seen coming from a distance with his driver in his Ambassador car. Then both cars started. When the Ambassador came near, both cars started crawling in the same direction, trying to run parallel to Shahi's car. The plan was to overtake him from both sides, ambush him, and escape. Three cars belonging to Shahi's armed men were behind him as his security.

According to the plan, Shri Prakash's car overtook Shahi's car from the left and Surajbhan's from the right. Surajbhan's car slowly started moving and was trying to overtake. Suddenly, a truck appeared from the opposite direction; though all efforts were made to stop it, it went ahead, and due to this confusion, Shahi's car went far ahead. Shri Prakash was successful in overtaking him from the left, and as soon as he overtook, he opened burst fire from his AK 47. The area echoed with the deafening sound of AK 47. A volley of bullets hit Shahi's car, and by then, Surajbhan's car also came from behind. All other cars on the road stopped there due to the deafening and scary sound of gunshots. Though plenty of bullets hit Shahi's car, his driver, showing exemplary courage, sped ahead. Meanwhile, Shahi's security cars also reached the spot. Seeing the crowd increasing, Shri Prakash and Surajbhan's cars fled in the direction of whatever they found.

The next day, the newspaper blared with the headline that one of Shahi's gunmen had died in the fatal attack. Shahi's driver was hit with one bullet in his hand. Shahi ducked his head under the seat and raised his legs and hips. Shahi, too, was hit by bullets in his hip and thigh. This was the first serious attack on Shahi in which AK 47 was used. Shahi was discharged from the hospital for a long time and returned home. One of these days, Shri Prakash Shukla called him and threatened, "I am Ashok Singh, and I will kill you before Holi at any cost."

Shahi first ignored such calls, but Shri Prakash continued threatening him by the name of Ashok Singh. Surajbhan was depressed for not being able to kill Shahi. Surajbhan called Pawan Pandey and asked,

"Shahi was not killed as earlier promised, now return both of my AK 47."

Pawan Pandey told this to Shri Prakash. Shri Prakash immediately called Surajbhan and requested, "Dada, trust us! For sure, we will kill Shahi before Holi at any cost."

After thinking for a while, Surajbhan replied, "Ashok, I am witness to your courage; no doubt you are a courageous man, but you have left an injured lion, and now he is more dangerous. He will plan diligently; he will plan deadly attacks. Now, he will carry more weapons; now, it will take time for us to kill him. I am sure that I will not be able to get any railway tender for at least a year. I was planning that if I had got 100 crores of tender, I would have bought a house in Gorakhpur and built an office for you. All these are distant dreams, so return the AK, and let's wait till Holi."

Shri Prakash strongly agreed, "Dada, I will return it."

Shri Prakash was upset by this and devised another strategy. He called some local boys to watch Shahi's activities and bribed them a little for any meaningful information. One day, Shri Prakash got information from a boy that tomorrow, Shahi would be going to Lucknow by the morning train for a meeting.

Shri Prakash immediately contacted Pawan Pandey and said, "Can you Find out where the meeting is in Lucknow? And where will he stay?"

Shri Prakash told Anand Pandey and Sudhir Tripathi, "Ask any of our four / five boys to go to the station in the morning and spy on Shahi; boys need to inform us about the compartment he boards; when will he get down? Ask them to call us from the station when the train stops for two minutes; he will keep informing Pawan Bhai by telephone. Meanwhile, we will reach Lucknow by road before taking the train. Since Pawan Bhai would have received all the information, he will send someone outside the station to tell us Shahi's location, along with the details of his pickup vehicle, and then we will strike him, then and there only."

As per the plan, the boys sat in different train compartments and observed that Shahi was traveling along with ten armed men in the seventh boogey from the engine of Gond Lucknow Express. Shri Prakash kept calling Pawan Pandey from the highway side PCO. It seems that it was a reserved compartment. Meanwhile, Shri Prakash Shukla was continuously in touch with Pawan Pandey from the highway side PCO to get the latest information. Shri Prakash Shukla and his gang arrived before time at the station. In some time, the train arrived, and his boys got off from it.

The boys told Shri Prakash, "Shahi has left at Gonda railway station."

As a part of the plan, one boy followed Shahi. This boy had informed a little while ago that three vehicles were parked outside the station when Shahi reached there. Shahi boarded the car, and all the vehicles moved towards Lucknow by road. Shri Prakash, Sudhir, and Anand noted down the number of vehicles, and disappointed, everyone reached Pawan Pandey's office in Kaiserbagh. Shri Prakash said to Pawan out of frustration, "Bhai, do you know where the meeting in Lucknow is going now? If we had found out, we would have surrounded him there and killed him. At least now, send someone to find out where the vehicles have stopped. Today, I am seriously in a terrible mood. I am determined to kill him either here or while going back to Gorakhpur."

Pawan made several calls to get the lead of Shahi while sitting in his residence along with Shri Prakash Shukla and informed his men of the numbers of the three vehicles in which Shahi was traveling; he also told them to find out where all these vehicles were parked. After about an hour, Pawan Pandey got the information about the Shai's three vehicles, which were now parked in the VIP guest house parking lot on the slope in front of the Sugarcane Institute in Hazratganj. Shri Prakash and the entire gang sat in the car and reached the turn of the slope in front of the Sugarcane Institute. Shri Prakash, Hemu Gujar, Anand Pandey, and Sudhir Tripathi remained inside the Maruti car. A Gulmohar tree is at the turn, where the slope starts and the car is parked right under it. It was a clear line of sight, and the parking and portico of the guest house were visible. The team was ready to make the kill.

Shri Prakash commanded the team, "No one will even think of getting down from the car; Shahi is there with ten to twelve people in three cars; if anyone recognizes us, for sure, we all will be killed."

Turn by turn, Shri Prakash and his gang were watching the three cars parked in the parking lot and on the portico through the car's glass. The wait was getting longer; two and a half hours passed, and Shahi did not come out. Meanwhile, Anand Pandey became restless and opened the car door. Shri Prakash reacted aggressively and immediately pointed his loaded pistol towards Anand Pandey and said, "If you get down, I will kill you." Anand Pandey was nervous and said, "Bhai, I just wanted to urinate; pls allow me to go for it." Shri Prakash ordered, "No one will go down; whoever wants to urinate, there are empty Bisleri bottles lying in the car; use that."

As the evening rolled into darkness, the cloak struck half past six, and it was dark by seven.

Shri Prakash looked the darkness around and said, "It's dark now, and staying here is not advisable. These bastards will not be able to recognize Hemu Gujar and Syria Pehlwan, so they both can stop here. Call Pawan bhai for a car; we will go back. If Shahi comes out by midnight, Hemu Gujjar and Syria Pehlwan will inform us, and we will come here again."

The gang obeyed and dispersed, but Shahi did not come out the whole night. The next day, too, the gang sustained in the car on Bisleri water bottles, murmura, and roasted grams and waited, but Shahi did not come out. On the third day, Shahi had to reach Gorakhpur by evening to inaugurate a shop owned by one of his men. Shri Prakash got wind of this plan from his informer from Gorakhpur and became ready for it. At six in the morning, Sudhir Tripathi, Anand Pandey, and Shri Prakash came and took position under the same tree. After half an hour, suddenly Shahi was seen coming along with his men towards the cars; unfortunately, at the same time, a state minister reached the State Guest House with his big convoy. This didn't deter Shri Prakash, but then he became reluctant owing to the massive loss of life that it may cause and advised that there was a lot of crowd there, and many people might get killed, so he decided to follow him quietly. From there, Virendra Shahi moved and reached Indira Nagar at a female's house, and Shahi got down alone from that house a little while ago. Shahi sent his car and security back to the guest house. There, too, Shri Prakash, along with his shooters, waited the whole day for Shahi to come out as they were not sure into which house he had entered. This was because Shri Prakash, his team, Shahi, and his team were all from Gorakhpur, and there was the probability of Shahi identifying Shri Prakash and his accomplice. This was not the case for Hemu Gujar and Syria Pehlwan, as they were not from Gorakhpur. Since Gujjar and Pehlwan were not there, Shri Prakash and his accomplice didn't come out of the car to avoid possible detection. The wait was again long, and when Shahi didn't come out, and it was night, they returned to Kaiserbagh.

Meanwhile, at another parking location, Hemu Gujar and Syria Pehlwan were watching Shahi's car and his security people at the state guest house, thinking that Shahi would call for the vehicle whenever he had to leave. But the car stayed at the guest house. At around eight in the morning, Shri Prakash saw that Shahi, a woman, a man, and a small child left the woman's house on foot and went inside another house at a distance of about fifty steps. There was no security person there and no other person either. Immediately, Shri Prakash drove the car as far as it could go and parked it on the road which was way to exit from that location. They left the car with the engine running, and then they all stood near the school boundary, trying to mix in the crowd of school parents. They all three waited for Shahi to come out. The wait of Shri Prakash was like a tiger lurking to pounce on its unaware victim.

The wait was not long. An hour thereafter, Virendra Shahi, the woman, and the child came out of that house and again started going towards the woman's house from where Shahi had come out. Shri Prakash pounced on Shahi from the back and shot him dead. Then he calmly searched Shahi's lifeless body. Shri Prakash took out Shahi's licensed pistol and the blood-soaked INR 20,000 from his pocket. Shahi's murder shook the city, and it was a disturbing big incident for the state police, and the pressure started mounting on the police. For a few days, everyone was trying to find out the details of the matter.

Shri Prakash sensed the police movement and said, "Since the police will raid various locations in Gorakhpur and Faizabad to get him, going to these places is not right. Even Pawan bhai's hideout is not safe now. The police will raid there as well. So, let's rent a house in Lucknow."

Anand said, "But how do you search like this?"

Shri Prakash said, "Just check the newspaper. There are many advertisements for renting out houses. Speak to them. Then we will go and see it. It's best if we get a house in Gomti Nagar. There are lots of beautiful ladies and girls in this area. We can enjoy the beauty in the morning and evening."

Anand browsed through the newspaper and pointed to one of the advertisements: "There is a house in Vishal Khand. The telephone number is also given. I will talk to him." They went to a nearby PCO in the afternoon and called the given number. He said, "I am Ashok Singh, Town Area Chairman of Jahanganj town of Bihar. I need a house in Lucknow for the education of my nephews."

The landlord said, "I will rent this house only if you stay with your family."

Shri Prakash replied, "I will bring my entire family. My Bhabhi and wife will come, and as soon as I get my children's results in July, I will bring them along, too." Then, the deal was finalized, and the rent was fixed. The next day, a house visit was planned. By coincidence, Shri Prakash Shukla met Mrityunjay Shukla, son of a former minister of Pratapgarh, in that area.

Shri Prakash told his gang, "Mrityunjay is from this area, and he knows many influential people. Tomorrow, we will take him with us; if the landlord asks too many questions, Mrityunjay Shukla will mention his IAS father and sway the landlord." As planned, they all arrived at the designated house behind IAS Akhand Pratap Singh's bungalow in Gomti Nagar the next day. Mrityunjay Shukla also took the lead in conversation with the landlord. The matter was settled.

The landlord asked about Shri Prakash's family, "In how many days will they come?"

Shri Prakash said, "The family is expected in a week." The landlord asked, "Bring your family with you, and then you can use the house and the premises." The gang moved from there; then, everyone started cracking jokes at Shri Prakash. From where will he bring his family?

Shri Prakash suggested, "Let's go to Kanpur tomorrow and bring Manju from Barra-3. Let her stay with us for ten days. Once the landlord is satisfied, we will drop her back."

The next day, they all went to Kanpur. When Shri Prakash spoke to Manju, she first rejected the proposal, but Shri Prakash insisted, and later, she agreed. She also agreed to get another girl, Usha, along with her. Thereafter two days later, Shri Prakash brought Manju and Usha from Kanpur. The vehicle they traveled in, was an Ambassador and a Gypsy with red lights. Once he reached the rental premises, he called the landlord and introduced Manju as his wife and Usha as his sister-in-law. The landlord was satisfied and immediately executed an eleven-month agreement. The landlord happily told Shri Prakash, "You all can bring your things, and you can start residing here." Shri Prakash replied, "We will bring our belongings in a few days."

Since the landlord lived in another locality, he handed over the keys and left. Shri Prakash, Anand, and Sudhir went inside the house with the two women. Shri Prakash asked Anand, "Get five mattresses, sheets, pillows, and some kitchen stuff from the market." Anand returned the mattresses, sheets, and some kitchen stuff by evening.

Shri Prakash was also sexually aggressive and was found of multiple women. He asked Anand to make his bed with Manju and Usha in one room and asked Anand and Sudhir to stay in the other two rooms. He warned Manju and Usha, "There is no need to talk to anyone here.

Let me know if you need anything. Anand or Sudhir will get it. If you want to go out, then I will take you all."

As time passed, Shri Prakash visited Ayodhya several times to meet Pawan Pandey. Pawan Pandey had forcefully taken possession of a house in Jiyamau, Hazratganj, and captured the plot next to it. Then, he also built a small house there, which he was using. Shri Prakash was not aware of Pawan's house in Jiyamau. Gradually, Shri Prakash got the information that Pawan had a home in Jiyamau, and he used it whenever he came to Lucknow.

One day, while looking for Pawan Pandey, Shri Prakash reached his house in Jiyamau. Pawan Pandey and his wife were present there. Shri Prakash got attracted to his wife, and he started looking for the opportunity to seduce her. Shri Prakash hatched a plan: he used to find out from his people where Pawan Pandey was at that time, and then he visited his house in Jiyamau and befriended her. He started taking her out for shopping and established a physical relationship with her. Slowly, Pawan Pandey also learned about this illicit relationship. The tide of time was against Pawan Pandey; he had lost the election, and many sworn enemies were after him. When Pawan Pandey became aware of this relation, he tried to discuss it with Shri Prakash Shukla and put better sense in him.

Shri Prakash, in his typical attitude, said, "If I see you in Lucknow ever again, I will pump the entire bullet of AK 47 in your mouth."

As time passed, Shri Prakash came to know that Pawan Pandey was at Chinhat to meet his acquaintance; he was furious, so he went straight to Chinhat. Pawan Pandey saw Shri Prakash coming, and he hid inside the house because of fear. Shri Prakash chased him inside the house and thrust his AK 47 in his mouth. Shri Prakash roared to Pawan Pandey, "I had warned against showing up in Lucknow, now just see, I will pump entire magazine down your throat."

Pawan Pandey trembled at the thought of consequence, fell on Shri Prakash's feet, and begged, "I will leave Uttar Pradesh forever. Spare my life this time, I promise you"." After that, Pawan Pandey left for Mumbai within a week.

RANSOM OF CRORES

Shri Prakash began to explore Lucknow University to connect with the boys from Gorakhpur. At that time, a pager service was introduced in Lucknow. Shri Prakash took advantage of the pager services and provided pagers to several dozen people from Gorakhpur. The method was straightforward. The Gorakhpur boys were tasked with gathering information about wealthy businessmen, doctors, politicians, and others, in exchange for some money, favors, or sometimes to impress Shri Prakash. In the criminal lingo of UP, this information was referred to as kundli. One key target was Moolraj Arora, the richest and most prominent builder in Lucknow.

Moolraj Arora was an influential contractor in Lucknow and was worth billions. In his early career phase, he constructed multistory flats in phases 1, 2, and 3 of Ayesha Apartment in Lucknow. The apartments were in demand and sold at high prices. In his business empire, railway contracting was one aspect. It was Moolraj Arora who constructed the building for Lucknow's narrow-gauge railway station. Boys from Gorakhpur conducted reiki for Moolraj Arora, and his kundli was sent to Shri Prakash. After that, the telephone at Moolraj Arora's house rang, and the entire household went into shock and tension.

The caller spoke in an unfamiliar language and in a rude tone, "I have been following you for the last two days. I just want to inform you that I could have killed you when you got down near the Civil Hospital to get the medicines from the medical store, as I was right behind you. No one was there to protect you. If I wanted, I could have easily shot you dead. I need money; arrange for crore rupees."

Moolraj Arora didn't understand the gravity of the situation and refused out rightly, saying, "I don't have much money."

The next day, Moolraj again received a call from Shri Prakash, who said, "I know you have the money. Give it without much tantrums, or else I will recover it in my way. I will give you comfort to begin with. Give it in small amounts, I will send my person. Give him fifty lakh rupees right now."

Moolraj was also adamant; he replied boldly, "I don't have it."

Moolraj made a strategy, and he stopped taking any calls, so whenever Shri Prakash called, his daughter took the call and informed him that her father was not at home. Shri Prakash, as he was given to carnal pleasures, started talking obscenely to Moolraj Arora's daughter. After that, the daughter also stopped calling. Then the servants began taking phone calls and refused to hand over the call to Moolraj. After a week, Shri Prakash changed his strategy and asked the Kundali boy to pass on the information on Moolraj's location for the entire day on his pager. The kundali boy informed that Moolraj was in his office at this time.

On May 13, 1997, Shri Prakash, Anand, Sudhir, and two more boys reached Moolraj Arora's office in Hazratganj, in front of the Civil Hospital, by car. While entering the office, Shri Prakash was stopped by a guard. Then, Anand and Sudhir immediately took out their pistols, overpowered the guards, and snatched their guns.

Shri Prakash entered Moolraj Arora's chamber, threatened him with his AK 47, and loudly asked him, "You idiot, stand up immediately and follow me; you thought that you could escape if you stopped taking my calls? And Moolraj was told to walk down to the car quietly. Shri Prakash further threatened that – "If you try to play tricks on me, I will kill you in no time. And then I will go straight to your house and kidnap your daughter." When Moolraj tried to show some resistance, Shri Prakash pointed the AK 47 on his chest, and Moolraj trembled. Moolraj started walking with Shri Prakash. Shri Prakash kept the AK 47 in his backpack and, pointed the pistol at Moolraj's waist, and again threatened.

While executing the kidnapping of Moolraj Arora, Shri Prakash locked the office door from outside. He took Moolraj down in the lift and made him sit in his car. From there, the entire gang took Moolraj to his own house, and there he made Moolraj sit in the middle of his Ambassador and replaced the red light from the Ambassador with a blue light. He left his Maruti at home and drove towards Faizabad in the Ambassador.

Anand reluctantly said, "Bhai! You will be recognized by the blue light." Shri Prakash cracked the joke, "You fool, no one checks the vehicles with blue and red lights in India. Just wait and watch; wherever you find a post, the police will salute you and also let the vehicle cross." Anand became silent. Shri Prakash was sitting in the front seat, and Dheerendra Singh was driving the vehicle. Surprisingly, as Shri Prakash had predicted, all the policemen standing at the Chinhat barrier, Barabanki, and Raunahi police check post saluted the occupants, without any search of the vehicle, saluted and opened the barrier to let the Ambassador, with a blue light, pass. Finally, everyone reached Mokama with Moolraj. Surajbhan arraigned Moolraj's captivity stay in one of the houses of Surajbhan Singh. kept in a house in Mokama town itself. Then the ransom negotiation started, and Lucknow was stirred. It was also known in Lucknow that a call was received from someone named Ashok Singh, who had carried out this kidnapping. Moolraj Arora's elder brother was a very high-ranking officer on the Patna railways.

Moolraj said, "Whatever money you need, let me talk to my brother. I will get it for you. But don't harass my daughter by calling her." Because Shri Prakash kept calling Moolraj's house and his daughter used to pick up the phone in anxiety to find out where her father was, Shri Prakash started talking obscenely with her. She felt outraged and disgusted.

One day, Shri Prakash threatened Moolraj and said in a humiliating manner, "I kiss your daughter on the phone every day. Get me my ransom in a couple of days. Otherwise, I will kidnap her and bring her here and rape her to my heart's content, that too in front of you. After that, my boys will rape her." Moolraj got petrified and started crying and pleading and begged, " Pls let me talk to my brother, I will get the money arranged for you." The ransom deal was fixed at fifty lakhs, and fifty lakhs were immediately given to Surajbhan's men in Patna. After getting the money, Shri Prakash terrorized Moolraj Arora again and, to his shock, said, "Only fifty lakhs have been given to me; rest of the fifty lakhs is pending; arrange for it soon."

Helpless, Moolraj wanted to get released from his captors as soon as possible, and hence, he meekly agreed, as disagreement would have gotten him killed.

Moolraj was in a hurry to get released; realizing the threatening situation, he agreed helplessly.

At the time of release, Shri Prakash again warned Moolraj and said, "As soon as you reach home, entire policemen will gather around you and will try to influence you. They will trouble you with all sorts of questions like in which direction you were taken, someone will ask for the destination of your captivity, someone will ask for details of the kidnappers, details of weapons used, details of ransom paid, etc. These idiots will not let you sleep for many days. Even the big big officers will try to counsel you and give you long lectures. Don't get carried away and start telling them the truth. You are a wise man, and hence, I expect you to act accordingly. If you dare to disclose, then one thing is clear: the police cannot even touch me. On the contrary, the same officer will call and will give me information. Now you must have understood this much that the police cannot even touch me, so you are smart, understand this." Moolraj Arora returned to his residence in Gokhale Marg peacefully. As he had committed to Shri Prakash, he kept misleading the police with fake information and false narratives. Police, too, sensed that Moolraj was not cooperating. So the police tapped Moolraj Arora's phone lines and started scanning all the calls made to or made from them. The next day after Moolraj's arrival, Shri Prakash called to check the status of police pressure and enquire. As usual, his daughter took the call, and the familiar voice asked her, "Ashok Singh, this side, did Moolraj reach safely." The daughter replied back, "Yes. Let me make him speak to you," Moolraj immediately came on the line, and Shri Prakash asked, " Police must have surrounded you like bees, isn't it?"

Moolraj replied in fear, “Yes.”

Shri Prakash re-confirmed, "Did you have any problem?"

Moolraj said, "No."

Shri Prakash told him, "Remember your commitment. I know the police will keep smelling you for any clue. They even tap your call and might be listening to the phone now. I don't care. I will talk to you after a week or ten days."

On 21st June, it was the birthday of one of Shri Prakash's brothers. The weather was extreme, hot, and sweaty, making people restless. Trees and plants had started withering out without water. Shri Prakash had told his people that he would go to Gorakhpur on his brother's birthday. Do let me know if there is any work. Anand informed Shri Prakash, "Ravi Rai and Ashok Dwivedi have become police informers these days. It is necessary to show them a trailer. Otherwise, the police will create more informers."

They all arrived in Gorakhpur on 21st June. Shri Prakash called his brother to another place and gave him two boxes of sweets and new clothes, which he purchased from Lucknow, as his blessing. After an exchange of pleasantries, he made his brother leave. Then he asked Anand, "Where are Ravi Rai and Ashok Dwivedi?"

Anand said, "Ashok Dwivedi was in Hydel Colony an hour ago." Shri Prakash, Sudhir, and Anand drove the blue light-fitted jeep and went straight to Hydel Colony. They entered Ashok Dwivedi's house and shot him dead; he was hit with several rounds of bullets. Deen Bahadur, who was with Ashok Dwivedi, was also brutally killed on the spot. Shri Prakash learned that Ravi Rai had just left there on his motorcycle some time ago. So Shri Prakash and his companions went to the city searching for Ravi Rai in the same jeep. Ravi Rai was spotted on his motorcycle near Prem Chand Park. As soon as he saw Shri Prakash on the jeep, he got petrified; in order to escape his chasing in the jeep, he left the motorcycle and started running in the opposite direction. Unfortunately, he was chased and pumped with a volley of bullets; he died on the spot.

THE ERA OF MOBILE

The era of mobile phones arrived in the UP. The UP-East was declared a telecom circle, and the mobile network started on March 30th, 1997. It marked the beginning of a new era. Telecom towers were installed in Lucknow, with two mobile operators: Essar and Usha.

At the same time, after the murder of Virendra Shahi, his dominance faded in railway tenders soon after his murder. Some petty criminals tried to get the tenders, one of them being Bhanu Mishra from Gorakhpur. Shri Prakash threatened Bhanu Mishra twice and warned him against coming to the DRM office, but Bhanu Mishra took it lightly.

Shri Prakash was fascinated by this technology and purchased a mobile phone immediately after it was launched in UP East. Shri Prakash got information that Bhanu Mishra had checked in Lucknow for a railway tender and was at Dilip Hotel in Hussainganj. Shri Prakash, Anand, and Sudhir all barged into the Dilip Hotel in a Maruti car.

At the hotel's reception, Shri Prakash asked, "Which room is Bhanu Mishra staying in?" The receptionist pointed towards the stairs and said, "Go upstairs; he is in room number 102."

While going upstairs, they got hold of a waiter who was coming down; Shri Prakash placed the pistol on his waist and said, "Knock on the door of room number 102 and have it opened." The waiter trembled at this unexpected gesture from a guest, anticipating what would happen next moment.

The nervous waiter knocked on the door of room number 102, and promptly, it was opened by the unsuspecting inmate. There were four people inside the room at the time. The door opened, and immediately, Shri Prakash burst fire AK 47 on all occupants of the room. This was completely unexpected to the inmates, who were aghast by the sudden attack. All the bullets hit the walls and roof of the small, average, standard-lit room, leading to fog-like air mixed with cement and sand dust, and the strong smell of burnt firecrackers filled the room. Petrified and unnerved, the inmates tried to take cover by falling over each other and trying to hide behind whatever they could find first. The room had bare visibility, and the nerve-cracking sound of AK 47 was enough to melt even the brave hearts. They tried to crawl under the bed and tried to get inside the bathroom. So much dust fell on all four that it is not impossible to recognize them.

Shri Prakash roared with every gunshot – "Where did Bhanu @#&#@ bastard have gone?

The sudden bang of firing brought out the occupants of other rooms. In the wildest dream, they would not have thought what was happening. The aghast public stared in all directions to find out what was happening. Shri Prakash noticed the crowd and signaled to move out. The ward off the occupants of other rooms, he flashed his AK 47 and pistol, and in no time every, one disappeared into their rooms and bolted the door from inside. Leisurely, he and his men came down and threatened the receptionist, who was still panting because of such a scary attack.

Shri Prakash warned the person sitting at the reception, "Don't call the police, or else you will also get killed." Shri Prakash took a pause to check around to see if everything was ok, then he put the bag on his shoulder and walked out of the hotel in a calm, composed manner. Although the Dilip Hotel was in a very crowded area of Hussainganj Chauraha in Lucknow, many had heard the gunshot and the commotion. They also saw three men walking out of the hotel and one man carrying a sports bag on his shoulder. None could even think that these were three men who had unleashed an unspeakable horrific attack a moment ago.

Once Shri Prakash and his friends had left, the unnerved and scared people hiding inside their hotel rooms waited another 10 – 15 minutes to check whether the criminals had left or were still there. Post all this, the person sitting at the reception did not have any courage left to inform the police about this incident from the reception phone. Such was the terror of Shri Prakash that the reception person went to a nearby PCO with trembling legs and a pounding heart to make the phone call to the police and inform the Kaiserbagh police station.

In a trembling voice, the information to the police station was given - "Some people had come; they fired in a room of the hotel and went away after firing."

In a quick span of time, Rajesh Pandey, Circle Officer (CO) Kaiserbagh, Satyendra Veer Singh, SP City, Sudesh Kumar Singh, SSP, and a large number of policemen reached the spot. Police cordoned the area and started collecting the blank cartridges, marking the gunshots, collecting blood samples, taking witness statements, and trying to guess who came from where.

The fatality was a young boy due to bullet injuries. Bhanu Mishra had bullet wounds in his hand, and the other two had bullet wounds in their hands and legs.

This was the first attack by AK 47 in Lucknow. The city panicked. The news of high-profile gunshots spread like wildfire.

Ironically, the Legislative Assembly was near the Dilip Hotel and in session. When the news reached there, the legislators registered their protest by desk-thumping in the assembly.

Shriram Arun- DG Police and ADG Law & Order also reached the spot. The Lucknow Police, which was reeling under pressure, came under more pressure due to this incident. It seems that with every passing day, the police were demoralized, and the public was losing confidence in the system.

Shri Prakash called the landline number of Bhanu Mishra's home. Bhanu's brother picked up the call, and Shri Prakash said, "I have killed @#$%@ Bhanua, bring shroud and collect his body at Lucknow."

Bhanu's shocked brother informed SSP Gorakhpur, "Such calls have been received."

Thereafter, Bhanu's brother called SSP Lucknow and asked the person on duty, "Has any such incident been reported after quickly describing the phone call?" The constable on the phone said, "No such incident has taken place as per my information." The constable was completely unaware.

Though assured by the constable, Bhanu Mishra's brother left Gorakhpur immediately with his entire family as he was extremely scarred by the call. Bhanu Mishra had survived but was shaken to the backbone, and his hand was wounded by the gunshot, yet he was lucky. All the police officers also interrogated Bhanu turn by turn to find out who had shot him or at least about whom he was suspicious. Bhanu was puzzled as Shri Prakash had used the name Ashok Singh on the call; Bhanu said, "A person named Ashok Singh kept calling repeatedly, but the killer was shouting that enmity with Shri Prakash Shukla would prove fatal."

In the evening, a high-level meeting of senior police officers was held at DG Police Headquarters, and it was decided that the top priority of the police right now must be to finish off this entire gang. The meeting concluded with the issuance of instructions to form small action teams and to arrest all the criminals as soon as possible. Police started intensive interrogation of Bhanu Mishra and his family members with the hope of extracting information about the deadly gang. Though Bhanu Mishra was also a resident of Gorakhpur, the police hoped that Bhanu Mishra might provide some important information about Shri Prakash and his gang, but the police were wrong.

Then, the course of interrogation turned towards Bhanu's brother and the phone call. When Bhanu's brother was asked about the call timing, police were puzzled to know that there was barely a difference of five minutes between the time he told and the time of the incident. The five minutes was not only a minute in this case, but it also opened a new dimension of the investigation. It was assumed that the call had been made from a PCO located around five hundred meters from Dilip Hotel. The police, though that may be a PCO operator, might be able to provide concrete information about the caller. The entire night, all the nearby PCOs were searched and scanned to find out the landline number of Bhanu Mishra's house on any PCO as there was culture to note down the number before calling, but no such call number was found in any of the registers of any PCO, police were down with disappointment and the roadblocks it was facing.

Now, in the investigating style of police, for the first time, the numbers of all the PCOs were noted, and the General Manager's Telephone was contacted to extract the information from the billing system of all the PCOs to ascertain from which PCO Shri Prakash Shukla had made this call to Bhanu Prakash's house. This was going to be a revelation for the police. Anxiously, police waited, and by 11 am the next day, the telephone officials informed that the call had not been made from any such PCO, as no PCO was within a radius of five minutes from the incident site. The nearest PCO was at a distance of ten to fifteen minutes. Meanwhile, the telephone officials informed, "In Lucknow, Usha Phone has launched its operations, though the calls are maturing and landing through the telephone exchange and Usha Phone's tower, but the information about this number can be found only from the mobile phone switch which is with Usha Phone."

The technology was too confusing for the police, and they didn't know where the mobile switch was. But everyone was worried about the divine switch, which is controlled by God as a ray of hope in this matter. On enquiring, it was found that the switch of Usha Phone is in Shriram Tower and it can provide some information. Rajesh Pandey, CO Kaiserbagh, was given the task of contacting the mobile company and trying to find out the details of the number from where the call was made. Due to the launch of the service, a new office set up of the mobile company was inaugurated, and Rajendra Kumar Singh was head of the office and was based out of the same office. When CO Kaiserbagh checked with him, he assured him that he would consult his technical team and revert.

Two days later, the much-awaited call from Rajendra Kumar Singh (RK Singh) was received by CO Kaiserbagh that the information had been received, and he requested them to come to the office. CO Kaiserbagh and SSP Rajnikant Mishra reached the office. The information that RK Singh revealed to CO Kaiserbagh and Rajnikant

Mishra took the ground beneath their feet. RK Singh said, "Currently, the switch only gives the message whether the call is incoming or outgoing, the duration of the call, and the total charge of any SMS sent". What RK Singh informed was the billing-related information. The switch engineer in Delhi of Usha Phones was asked to extract the information; all the relevant information about the landline number of Bhanu's house in Gorakhpur was obtained, including the mobile number from which the call was made, the time and duration of the call was obtained. RK Singh also told, "The address available in the mobile service provider's office was of Vinay Khand Gomti Nagar, Lucknow. The house was of the daughter of former minister of Pratapgarh Ramnaresh Shukla and by taking out the call records from the time this number was purchased till now, the people in contact with the mobile holder and his movements can be found out". Both the officers were amazed at the advancement of technology.

Thereafter two days at 5 pm, RK Singh again requested SSP Lucknow, "Please come to my office; the complete details of that mobile number have been received." Eager to know how mobile numbers can disclose information about a specific person's movement, contact, and location, SSP Lucknow Rajnikant Mishra and Area Officer Kaiserbagh reached Shri Ram Tower on Shahnazaf Road at SSP residence. RK Singh had an idea bout the person who is being investigated and so he had requested to come in plain dress rather than in police uniform. When both the officers reached RK Singh's office, only his technical head, Mr. Sarkar, was present to maintain the highest level of confidentiality. A twenty-five to thirty pages print out was referred by Mr. Sarkar, who informed that the number in the first column is the number from which the call was made, and the second column contains the numbers who had received the call, the letter 'O' in the third column is marked for outgoing calls, the letter 'I' is for incoming calls and the letter 'S' is indicated for SMS and the last column is for the cell ID. This turned the investigation in completely unknown territory. Mr. Sarkar further explained that the cell ID is the location, name, and address of the towers where our towers are installed, which means the call-receiving and forwarding tower. He further explained that in the report, some numbers are written in place of the cell ID, which means the names of the places were not available. The towers are being installed in Lucknow and are in process. The list was available for the calls made through the operating towers.

In a short while, RK Singh provided a list of forty-fifty pages for extracting the information that the police needed. SSP Lucknow reached his home with this list, and SP City Satyendra Veer Singh was called there, and its study started around 10 o'clock at night. This study of call details and its investigation started a new wonder of endless surprises. The name and address of every number and every landline number were searched in the telephone directory or by calling the telephone exchange, and then details like from where the call was made...etc, were found out. The distance between two telephone calls was noted, and then the possible route he might have taken was identified. As more and more such information was extracted, everyone was surprised. Hours rolled by, and the process of removing the information was so engrossing that it was already 4 o'clock in the morning. A new dawn was about to start; the night melted in a reddish-orange sky with a new sun on the horizon. After so much relevant information was pulled out, the investigating team concluded that the name and address on which this mobile phone was taken would certainly be connected with Shri Prakash Shukla. At least hope was there.

The next day in the evening, the investigating team gathered again and a thorough study was done about all the numbers that featured in the call details. The line of movement of Shri Prakash emerged; this was the most important breakthrough the police got. Shri Prakash and his gang had made several trips to Bihar. There were many such numbers of PCOs in Mokama, Bihar; on speaking all such numbers, it was found that all these numbers were located in and around Surajbhan's house or Surajbhan's places of stay. Many numbers of Patna and Muzaffarpur were also found in it, most of which were of political persons. The call detail report also revealed that Shri Prakash and his place of stay in Bihar was mostly in Mokama. Apart from this, numbers of Gorakhpur, Lucknow, and Banaras were also found, but until then, very few numbers of Delhi were found there. An entire pattern of activities and communication had emerged, which other cases were impossible to detect and even more difficult to establish. SSP Lucknow again talked to RK Singh of Usha Phone and tried to find out if it is possible to get any information immediately apart from the telephone bill from the switch.

RK Singh said, "Though our billing cycle is fifteen days, we can still tell you. We try to tell you the location as soon as possible, though the mobile number gets only after fifteen days." The next day, RK Singh informed, "For three days in the last week, his location has been Vinay Khand Gomti Nagar, Lucknow continuously."

Everyone decided to raid the address in Vinay Khand, Gotami Nagar; it was the same address found on the mobile connection address proof; the police team said we would find it there tonight, too. SSP Rajnikant Mishra said that he himself will go in this raid. Satyendra Veer Singh and Rajesh Pandey believed they would handle it, but Rajni Kant Mishra insisted on accompanying them. A party was sent to first inquire about that address. Everything turned out to be the same, the house name, the house number, etc. on which the mobile connection was availed.

The time for the first raid, in this case, came. It was dead of the night. A night that was dark and ominously still. It was around 1.30 am in the night when the entire team of raiding party wearing bulletproof jackets and bulletproof helmets slowly moved towards the house. The house was locked from the outside. On quick reiki it was concluded that there was no other option but to surround the house from all sides and jump over the wall to go inside. Rajnikant Mishra, Satyendra Veer Singh and Rajesh Pandey led their team and were armed with AK 47. The rest of the team had taken position outside the boundary with AK 47, too, and two constables jumped from the terrace of adjacent houses and came onto the terrace of the target house. The constables tried to hear any sound, and then the door was knocked, but no sound came from inside. The night was disturbingly dark, and silence was deafening. The raiding party thought that Shri Prakash and his gang might be holed up inside, so the door was not opening. The entire raiding team was on high alert, and all the guns were pointed toward the possible shooting points from which bullets could be fired at the raiding team. When there was no response to the knock on the door, it was decided to break open the door. As soon as an attempt was made to break the door, the light inside the house was switched on, and a woman responded from inside.

Rajnikant Mishra immediately replied, "I am SSP Lucknow; please open the door."

The woman kept on questioning why she needed to open the door. This infuriated Rajnikant Mishra, who responded in a loud voice, "Open the door." After a while, the door opened, and the woman was holding a landline phone in her hand.

She said, "Here they are; talk to him." Rajnikanth Mishra asked, "Who is it?" She took the name of a prominent Congress leader. Then he said, "First, we will search the house and talk to someone."

With this, everyone entered the house. Every room was thoroughly searched. No one was found there except two girls. On further inquiry, the woman said that both of them were her daughters. After getting complete information from the woman, everyone left from there empty-handed. The entire raiding party walked away with a heavy heart for not getting Shri Prakash.

SHORTAGE OF PHOTO

The police team was doing a continuous investigation, and after weeks of rigorous efforts, after scanning all the information received from the pager office, the chat generated from the page numbers and the people with whom Shri Prakash was talking; the raiding police started getting information, although in small fractions, about Shri Prakash Shukla and his gang. This information was not sufficient for taking any action, but it helped the police in deciding the course of the investigation. It was surprising that even though police picked up nearly 100 people, none of them were able to provide any information that was either reliable or relevant. Nothing worthwhile was achieved despite all the meticulous work the police were doing. Police had a couple of important pieces of information; one of them was that Shri Prakash had never shaved his beard himself. Shri Prakash was visiting all the high-end saloons in the city for shaving; the problem was that there was no fixed time for a visit. Another tip was that he sometimes visited Hotel Taj, a newly constructed property, which was a newly built property, to get his beard and haircut, and he heavily tipped the barber who did the job for him. Another vital piece of information was that he had tipped the guy who had shaved his hair with a thousand-rupee tip. This was the huge tip. So the saloon staff liked him so much that they used to leave their work and attended to him first. To check the authenticity of the information, it was decided that all the information brought by one team shall be verified by another team and vice-versa. Another critical information was that he used to go to the stadium early in the morning wearing a tracksuit for running, but instead of running, he used to sit on the stairs and watch the women players playing. Being a compulsive womanizer, he derived pleasure in ogling at girls. Another piece of information was that he was parking his car in front of the primary school and watched people come and go until the school started. Though strange and disturbing, this behavior was mysterious and threatening. Later on, it was found that he was interested in watching the young mothers dropping their toddler kids to school. This was an unimaginable reason, but then he was a man given to brutal and extreme emotions.

Janpath market of Hazratganj is known as the heart of Lucknow, the capital of UP. The place is upmarket, bustling with activities, and frequented by many girls and females. Shri Prakash was found roaming casually from one shop to another; the purpose was to stare at the girls and note the shops doing great business for identifying targets for extortions, which in the future he did. Sometimes, he sat at the Chhedilal Juice Wala shop or a small Woodland shop for his lustful girls' gazing activities. It was also found that he noted the car number of beautiful girls.

Now it was time for verification, so policemen in plain clothes were sent to Hazratganj crossing, Woodland shop, Chhedilal Juice Wala's shop, and other shops on Janpath to verify all this information. The shopkeepers were instructed to inform police if they found any guy of similar description roaming here and there and ogling at girls, but the greatest challenge was there was no photograph. None of the persons related to Shri Prakash had confessed to having a photo or could provide one.

Meanwhile, police contacted an old Shri Prakash accomplice, Ghanshyam Pathak alias Ghannu. He informed that after the killing of Virendra Shahi, his men were planning to avenge his death but could not identify him. So they found a photographer who had claimed to have a photo of Shri Prakash, and he sought time from Shahi's men to pull out the negative and develop the photograph. Somehow, Shri Prakash got info about it, and he killed the photographer in front of his shop. Coincidentally, the deceased photographer was having issues with his neighbor, and police acted against his neighbor. Shri Prakash's name didn't come anywhere.

After this incident, Shri Prakash, after finding out the name of the photographer at such functions where there was a possibility of his photo being taken, threatened him that if the photo came out, he would be killed inside the shop like Saini. Almost everyone in Gorakhpur knew about this; even if someone had a copy of the photo in his shop, he refused to give it to him. Virendra Shahi and

Harishankar Tiwari's goons tried hard but could not get any picture of Shri Prakash.

When a team arrived at the Taj Hotel's salon to verify some information related to Shri Prakash, the salon owner became nervous. He said, "Yes, sir, a good-looking young man comes here. He tips generously. In fact, once, I hesitantly asked for his name, and he told me it was Ashok Singh. He also mentioned that he is a contractor from Bihar, currently working as a road contractor in Lucknow." The salon owner noted that his accent sounds like Bihari.

It has been confirmed that Shri Prakash Shukla has been visiting various high-end salons and male grooming parlors to get his hair and beard trimmed; even now, he must still be going. The verification team that went to check the authenticity of the information regarding the Taj Hotel salon continued to meet with and warn all the high-end salon owners, instructing them that if he came again, they must inform the SSP, SP City, or CO Hazratganj using the provided numbers. Meanwhile, police teams were patrolling the entire city to determine if a person matching certain descriptions had visited them at any time. Despite roaming all day from one salon to another, the police team could not find even a single witness or clue about his visit; practically, there was no confirmation.

The police team was under immense pressure. The scale of pressure on the police was unimaginable; it was losing confidence in front of its superiors and respect in front of the public. One criminal had brought the entire system to a standstill. In the words of Dushyant Kumar, 'If you tell the truth with courage and conviction, people feel bad and challenged, but we do not have the habit of crying and presenting facts after sugarcoating them.' Finally, the DGP summoned the entire Lucknow team, including the IG Zone Lucknow, DIG Lucknow, and SSP, to the DGP headquarters. The DGP was furious with anger and pressure. First, he allowed us to give him an update patiently, and after the discussion, he wanted to know how far the police had progressed. The DGP then questioned the police's role in the Dilip Hotel murder case. Everyone updated him on their activities regarding this matter. The next logical question was about the photograph of

Shri Prakash Shukla; the DGP asked to see Shri Prakash Shukla's photo for himself. Everyone present there found themselves at a loss for words. It felt as if a blooming flower had suddenly withered away. The DGP lost his cool and raised his voice to express his dissatisfaction. Suddenly, he became angry and said, "All these are fake and nonsensical stories. When the police have failed to obtain even one photograph of Shri Prakash Shukla, how can they expect someone to tell them when Shri Prakash is seen, who can identify him, and inform the police? Furious, the DGP warned of taking action against all the erring officers present." After the DGP's reprimand, everyone returned with the same consensus: without a photograph, it was nearly impossible. The following strategy was discussed again at the SSP's office. Most of the attendees agreed that the DGP's statement was correct; information could not be obtained by just describing their situation appearance.

No one except the saloon owner of the Taj Hotel confirmed his appearance. It was unanimously agreed that the police needed to get his photograph at any cost. A team was dispatched to Gorakhpur. The police then contacted all the individuals killed by Shri Prakash Shukla regarding the weddings he had attended and attempted to obtain details from the wedding photographers. When contacted, these photographers outrightly refused to provide any photographs. Such was the terror of Shri Prakash that even remotely, people were unwilling to share any details about him.

When the police collated all the information from Gorakhpur, another relevant detail came to their attention. Kishori Lal and Nilendra Pandey, close friends and professional smugglers, were involved in smuggling goods from the Nepal border and had several smuggling cases pending against them. Nilendra Pandey had ordered an attack on Kishori Lal with an AK-47. Somehow, Kishori Lal escaped, and when the police contacted him, a reference to Subhash Tripathi surfaced, who was the brother-in-law of Shri Prakash and lived somewhere near the Dairy Crossing of Hazrat Ganj. Subhash Tripathi was a big lottery dealer and had become a multi-millionaire overnight. At his behest, Shri Prakash Shukla had killed Vivek Shrivastava, the biggest lottery dealer in Lucknow. Whenever Shri Prakash is on the run from the police and comes to Lucknow, he visits them. Although Subhash Tripathi's daughter is his niece, Shri Prakash harbored lustful intentions toward her. On one pretext or another, he keeps giving her expensive gifts.

Kishori Lal told the police, "Shri Prakash had a photograph taken with that girl in one of the studios in Lucknow. Although Harishankar Tiwari and Virendra Shahi's men tried their best, they didn't get even a single photograph of him. While it may be impossible for the police to find Shri Prakash's photo in Gorakhpur, if they try Subhash Tripathi's location, there is a high probability that they will either get the photograph or learn the name of the studio where it can be obtained. In fact, Shri Prakash is a very cheap and low-character guy; he spends all day running around after girls with lustful intentions. He is addicted to brand-name clothes, shoes, and watches and tries to show off to impress women. He makes his chance at impressing females by entering big shops frequented by high-profile girls and women. In a loud voice, he orders and buys expensive items and gifts, intentionally flashing his cash so that the women present would notice him. All this he does to give the impression that he belongs to a very rich family, and in this way, he has ensnared many attractive women to satisfy his sexual urges."

The information was so crucial that the team relayed it immediately to the SSP Lucknow via telephone. The SSP then promptly summoned Satyendra Veer Singh and Rajesh Pandey, informing them that there was now no hope of obtaining a photograph of Shri Prakash Shukla in Gorakhpur. Additionally, the instruction was to verify Kishori Lal's information on the ground. Meanwhile, another sensational tip arrived from a different source, stating that some vehicles carrying large bags had stopped at a hotel on Faizabad Road in Lucknow.

SSP Lucknow told Satyendra Veer Singh, "You go to Faizabad Road with your team, and Rajesh Pandey, you leave for Subhash Tripathi's place to search for the photo. If any photo is found there, they will directly take it to Satyendra Veer Singh." Both teams left for their respective destinations. The police team surrounded Subhash Tripathi's house in Hazratganj, and then the door was knocked, and his name was called out. Subhash Tripathi peeped from the upper floor and was taken aback when he saw many vehicles parked there. There was no escape route either from the upper part of the house or from the ground floor, so there was no option except to open the door. The police team entered the house and started the search operation. All the members of the house were questioned about Shri Prakash Shukla, but everyone blatantly denied and refused to accept any relation with him. When the questioning intensified, very reluctantly, they admitted that he was a distant brother-in-law and they don't have much relation with him. He had visited only once and that too in the distant past. The entire team was looking for the photograph, and the team was aware of every development. Each team member tried to unearth the photographs in their own way. One of the constables, Rantendra, started interacting with the teenage daughter of Subhash Tripathi, the same daughter on whom Shri Prakash had nurtured his sexual desires. In a seemingly casual way, he asked her, "When is your birthday"? The girl fell for the trap and replied about some date.

Rantendra proceeded in a very calm and cunning manner - "Who took the birthday photo?"

The naïve girl replied - "We have our own camera for such purpose."

Rantendra targeted his question towards the most coveted information - "Where is the camera"?

She showed the camera. It was an expensive Nikon camera.

Rantendra prodded further - "This is an expensive camera; it must take very good photos."

The girl said, "Yes, uncle, it takes perfect photos."

Rantendra now played master stroke and said, "Son, let us see what kind of photo it takes; if you have any photo, then show it to me."

The girl ran and brought her album. In one photo of that album, that girl and a young man were with her.

Rantendra asked, "Who is this?"

The girl fell silent and said, “I don’t know.”

The cat was out of the bag. Police, after herculean efforts, had unearthed the most vital information in the form of the first-ever pic of Shri Prakash Shukla.

Rantendra rushed to Rajesh Pandey, who was in a different room. Rajesh was determined and pensive to extract the truth from Subhash Tripathi. Rantendra whispered in Rajesh's ear that the girl was not saying anything about this photograph; he flashed the photograph before Rajesh and added that the girl had turned pale. Probably, he is Shri Prakash Shukla.

When Subhash saw the photograph, he trembled, and blood drained from his face. He appeared pale, and visibly, he started sweating. His face turned white, and fear was evident. He could not speak, and even if he tried, he only trembled. The police team was jubilant at this first significant breakthrough. The entire police team pounced on him and started applying all sorts of police pressure to make him tell the truth. The police team pressured Subhash in multiple different ways, and after some time, he gave up and faintly nodded yes. At least there was now a face to the terror. The date written on the back of the photo was three months ago. Soon, the entire family realized the blunder they had committed. Subhash’s daughter and wife began crying and pleading with the police team once they realized the gravity of the situation. If Shri Prakash Shukla saw the newspaper photo, he would immediately figure out where it was clicked. The entire family was profusely explaining that Shri Prakash was extremely merciless and cruel. The police team assured them that the photograph would not be published in the newspaper. The family continued to cry and express their fear.

Subhash Tripathi, out of sheer anxiety, said that he had already read in the newspaper that the police didn’t have the photograph of Shri Prakash despite all his efforts. So the DGP had expressed his anger and dissatisfaction with the entire team. He further added that now, when the photograph is published, the whole family will be killed by Shri Prakash Shukla. After much assurance, the police convinced Subhash of his family’s safety and returned. While returning,

Satyender Veer Singh was contacted from the car's wireless, and the police team informed him that they would be meeting him in the next fifteen minutes.

Satyendra Veer Singh also informed that the report of Gorakhpur's numbered vehicles on the highway was incorrect.

He expressed his desire to meet them at the SSP's office. The entire police team gathered at the SSP's office, where they were shown the photograph. Everyone was satisfied with the breakthrough. The SSP was informed that the person from whom the photo was recovered feared for the safety of his entire family from Shri Prakash Shukla. The SSP became thoughtful and suggested that if we could change the background and remove the girl from the photograph, no one would be able to identify where it was taken. However, Satyendra Veer remained doubtful; he feared that Shri Prakash, being sharp, would recognize details of the photograph and the incident from his clothing.

The SSP was puzzled and said, "You all guys figure out how to remove any other identification mark? You people check I am going to the administration office for an important meeting." Satyendra Veer took the lead and said, "All the photo studio shops are in Hazratganj itself. Rajesh, since you have been CO Hazratganj, can you please get his photograph printed and published in the newspaper by tomorrow."

Rajesh started wondering how to get the photo in a way that makes it difficult to recognize the story behind the photo. After continuously trying to think it over, Rajesh came up with the idea that a photograph of any hero is picked up in the same position, and both the photo's face is replaced. Can this serve both the purpose of hiding the background story of the photograph and satisfying the investigation requirement of the police? There was a place in the corner of the verandah in front of Coffee House and Universal Book Depot at Hazratganj crossing where postcard pictures of all the actors and actresses were sold. Someone from those pictures may have a similarity with the photograph of Shri Prakash, which can be used to replace the face of the actor with the face of Shri Prakash. Rajesh tried to match several of the photos with Shri Praksh's photo, and after several failed matching attempts, his eyes got fixed on one of the photographs of Sunil Shetty, which could be a potential match. Now Rajesh started scanning each of the photos with respect to the height and pose. Ironically, this was the work a police officer least expected to do, but suddenly, his eyes fell on a photo of Sunil Shetty. There was a striking resemblance with respect to the height and pose. Rajesh immediately purchased four of his photos and rushed to the biggest photostat shop next to Hazratganj police station, the owner of which was known to him. The match was so perfect that when Rajesh showed both photos to Bunty Bhai, the owner of the photostat shop, he immediately responded, "If Sunil Shetty's head is replaced by his head, no one will even notice any mismatch."? Such was the level of accuracy by which the actor's photo was picked up. Slowly, the day was melting into a satisfying evening for the police.

Bunty replied in appreciation, "You have picked up really nice matching pics; let me make it for you right now."

Bunty Bhai was also scared, and, in fact, he was so scared that he had requested a minimum of ten times. No one should know where the photo was taken, or else his entire family would be murdered by Shri Prakash Shukla. Bunty bhai went to the rear room of his studio, a part of Sunil Shetty's head was removed with scissors, and the head of Shri Prakash's photo was pasted on it, and then colored printout was taken and pasted in it. Then its color photocopies were made. Only a hard-core film enthusiast or a very sharp observer could know that the whole photo was not of Shri Prakash;

(Recreated photo of Shri Prakash Shukla.)

only the part of the head was of Shri Prakash. Rajesh got five such photos prepared and went to the SSP; when the SSP saw the photo, he was highly impressed with the innovation and execution of the entire process till the final photo. SSP approved the photo and asked to get it published immediately by calling a press conference. He was very hopeful about the results it might produce. For the first time in the entire journey of crime and investigation involving Shri Prakash Shukla, his photo appeared on the front page of all the newspapers in the state and across the country. The moment the photo was published, information began flooding into the Lucknow Police Control Room from multiple sources, and calls also poured in on the phone numbers of various officers whose numbers were printed. The police were working with a very systematic approach, and to sort through all the information received, they formed specialized teams solely for the verification process. All the information was reported individually in the evening at the SP City Satyendra Veer Singh office in Kaiserbagh. The police verified ten to fifteen pieces of information daily, but ironically, the results were nil. The pressure on the police increased every moment, which negatively impacted their efficiency. The pressure on the police headquarters and the district officials to stop these crimes was also evident in their daily work. Every number the police obtained from the telephone exchange was significant, as Mr. Prakash had spoken on these lines, so the police arranged to monitor these calls. This task was very challenging. The senior management of the telephone exchange had to instruct the junior telephone operators that it was necessary to listen to all the calls. At that time, outgoing calls were charged at Rs. 17 per minute, and incoming calls were charged at Rs. 10 per minute, as mobile services were very expensive. Only registered addresses were used to obtain mobile connections.

The DP boxes were installed on the telephone poles, and most landlines were monitored by tapping into a parallel line extending from the DP box. In case there was a reliable office or house nearby that facilitated the listening of telephone calls, the said office or house was utilized by drawing a wire from the DP box to maintain confidentiality.

As for the technology, it was the most primitive method and was widely employed by the British.

Following the Dilip Hotel murder case, eight such telephone numbers were monitored on parallel lines. Of these eight numbers under police surveillance, no office or house was adjacent to serve as a cover; tents were used for surveillance, presenting the scenario as if repairs were being made to damaged telephone lines.

The plain-clothed policemen listened to the telephone conversation of the suspected person who used to sit on the ground or on a small stool in the midst of the equipment used for digging the telephone. High caution was needed in this exercise. When the target's phone rang, the parallel set kept for listening rang, too. Now, if the target picked up his phone first and the policeman listening picked up his phone later, then the target would also get the knocking sound of the cradle, giving a suspicious sound to the target. The modus operandi were so sensitive that even a slight sound from the policeman's side would create suspicion and revealed the setup of phone tapping. To avoid this danger of being caught, the mouthpiece of the telephone set, which the policeman used for listening, was either removed or covered with strong cellotape.

There were large numbers of newspaper publications in Lucknow, and so there were many journalists; soon, this news got published in the newspapers, and police started tapping the phone lines of Shri Prakash Shukla's acquaintances. There were evening meetings scheduled to review the progress made during the day. Even after intense discussion and scanning of all the possibilities of news leaks of phone tapping to the news reporters, it never became known as to who disclosed it or how the reporters got wind of it.

In the list of telephone numbers tapped, there were several Mritunjay Shukla whose address Shri Prakash Shukla had bought his mobile. Shri Prakash called in the evening on the same number under surveillance.

Puzzled, Shri Prakash asked Mrityunjay Shukla, "Is my photo printed in the newspaper?"

Mrityunjay replied, "Yes, bhaiya, your photo is printed in all the major newspapers."

Shri Prakash became cautious, "Is it colored or black and white?"

Mrityunjay Shukla replied confidently, "It is colored as well as black and white."

Shri Prakash became thoughtful and again asked, "What color shirt is in the colored photo?"

Mrityunjay said, "It is a denim jacket of jeans."

Now, Shri Prakash was pretty sure that it was not his photograph and said, "Can't it be my photo? I never wear a denim jacket!"

Mrityunjay said, "Can't say, I don't know this."

Shri Prakash was known for his shrewdness. He said, "Very few people wear denim jeans jackets. If I roam around wearing denim outfits, I will be easily recognized in the crowd; that's why I don't wear them."

Although Mrityunjay disagreed, he said, "But bhaiya ji, the photo is yours."

Shri Prakash wanted to reconfirm and asked again a little louder, "Have you seen it properly?"

Mrityunjay replied, "Common bhaiya ji, will I commit an error in recognizing you? The photo is yours".

Curious and confused, Shri Prakash instructed Mritunjay, "Put all the newspaper cuttings in a big envelope. Tomorrow morning, around nine o'clock, you will find a boy at the Gomti Nagar Mithai Wala crossing who will be waiting, and the identification is that he will be wearing a black cap. Approach and tell him that your name is Ram Narayan Dwivedi, and handover the envelope. It will be delivered to me."

Shri Prakash could not come to terms with the fact that the police had got his photographs; he asked once again, "Are you sure that the photo is mine?"

Mritunjay replied immediately, "100%."

In an attempt to reassure himself, Shri Prakash said, "Note one thing for sure: to date, no person ever has been identified only based on photographs. You can identify in the photograph if you have seen a person but not vice versa. These mader@#%d policemen can never identify me even if I pass by them".

Mrityanjay tried recollecting and then said, "Yes, bhaiya! Newspaper has reported that the Lucknow policemen will carry a photograph each with them and have been told to search for this person."

Shri Prakash's temper started rising, and they arrogantly said, "I will come to Lucknow soon, and I will search every policeman on the way I see; if I get the photograph in the pocket of a policeman, I will kill him on the spot, and after that, no policeman will ever dare to keep my photograph. Just see".

Subhash Kumar Singh had his origin in Bihar and was the Senior Superintendent of Police – Lucknow then. RK Singh used to collate all the details of the mobile numbers and handed over to Subesh singh, a weekly exercise it was. Then, the information was verified to evaluate its truthfulness. All the numbers were of Uttar Pradesh and Bihar. The discussion in the SSP's chamber was around the motive of the call and possible relation with Shri Prakash. Sometimes, the discussion was so intense and engaging that the whole SSP's office spent the entire night in the office itself.

The efforts of the police intensified, so it became almost a routine that someone who was connected to the numbers on which Shri Prakash had either made a call or received a call was picked up and questioned by the police to get more information. Hence, information too flowed in volumes. Verification of all the received information was promptly initiated. Now, police started roaming and searching for Shri Prakash by visiting all the high-end saloons. It became common for the policemen to patrol the markets of Hazratganj and Janpath almost every day. The police were targeting all the bag packers and bag holders, be they big, medium, or small. Police intelligence sources informed Shri Prakash that he never goes out in the city without his AK 47, which he keeps in a big cricket bag. He was seen many times in front of small children's schools in the morning and the evening. He was frequenting Janpath as well during the evening. Further, he was also spotted in front of Karamat Girls College in Mahanagar, Lucknow, St. Francis, and Cathedral Schools in Hazratganj. Shri Prakash lusted for girls; it was his way of deriving satisfaction by lustfully staring at girls.

FIRST SACRIFICE

One day, Anand Pandey asked Shri Prakash Shukla, "Bhai, are you interested in kidnapping children? We should focus on the children; they would immediately give us a significant amount."

Shri Prakash Shukla replied after a bit of introspection, "Just see, you should never get one should never get engaged in the kidnapping of kids' even with a slight error, the entire matter comes to light, and you understand they are so well dressed early in the morning, and they apply a small pinch of vermilion so that it remains hidden in their groomed hairs. The purpose of coming so well dressed early in the morning is that people see them, and such women get trapped very easily. Why would one get ready early in the morning just because they want to get they want to get the attention of the males? "

Anand said, "Oh, now I understand the lady who comes from Muhadipur and another from Indiranagar; they are both married." After saying this, both of them burst into laughter. Anand became serious again and tried to warn Shri Prakash, "Every day, we stand in front of the same school, and it's not good. I've felt that someone has been following us for the last couple of days."

Shri Prakash assured him by saying, "If you suspect anyone, just show me, and I will gun him down then and there only; after that, no policeman will dare to come close."

The SSP had the news that Shri Prakash Shukla had been seen standing in front of some high-profile schools. During the evening meeting, SP informed all the team members about Shri Prakash Shukla's activity and asked to deploy policemen in civilian dress in front of every high-end school to identify any person who looks suspicious or who resembles Shri Prakash Shukla or if there is any suspicious vehicle movement. The policemen were instructed to wireless the information, and the vehicle immediately would be surrounded from all sides. If he succeeds in kidnapping any children of a prominent businessman and politician, then there will be another issue in the police department.

The SSP further said, "Some officers should meet the management of all these schools and warn them to deploy school watchmen outside the school at the time of opening and closing of the school, who can keep an eye on the people coming and going. If a small child of a businessman or a political person is kidnapped, it will be a bigger problem."

It was 9th September 1997, pleasant weather and cool air made the day very beautiful. Outside the Kaiserbagh office, there were trees and lots of greenery; different birds inhabited those trees, and all were chirping as if everyone was trying to sing different melodies. A high-level meeting of all the team members was in progress in the SP City's office in the Kaiserbagh area. After the meeting, everyone was allotted the duty to visit the different parts of the city for checking. Inspector RK Singh, Satyendra Veer Singh's peon, and gunner Rantendra Singh left in Satyendra Veer Singh's Maruti 800 towards Janpath Market, the allotted area for checking that particular day. They traveled from Darul Shafa to Janpath side road and parked in the parking lot. All of them were in plain clothes and carried pistols tied to their waist, which were hidden under their shirts. It was the third consecutive day when the entire team had reached Janpath for the manhunt. Despite this, there was no success.

As a matter of patrolling and identifying Shri Prakash Shukla, RK Singh entered the Bombay Hair Cutting Salon- a high-end saloon for the affluent class of Lucknow, a shop located outside Janpath. The Rest of the team members were keeping an eye on the passersby and a couple of groups of people standing outside. The hope was that, like every day or at least informed by the police informers, Shri Prakash might turn up to get his hair trimmed in the salon. Some police team members were randomly checking the bags of the people crossing that particular spot on the Janpath. Satyendra Veer Singh and Rajeh Pandey were stopping suspicious-looking people and checking their bags, while Inspector RK Singh and gunner Rantendra Singh were standing on the other side of the corridor, at an elevated point to keep a sharp eye on the suspicious behavior of the persons who may react seeing the police checking. The entire scene was tense with anticipation and desperation to catch Shri Prakash, and considering that the place was fully crowded, Shri Prakash could not do any weird act to save himself.

Immediately when the police team returned from the gallery side after taking a full round of Janpath, the police team's eyes caught the sight of a short person coming from the front; coincidentally, there was a bag on his shoulder. The bag was now notorious amongst the police team.

The suspicious-looking big sports bag was on his shoulder and ended near his waist. Satyendra Veer Singh's eyes caught this view; he became alert. Although many times earlier such suspicion hadn't yielded any result, he stopped him from showing him the contents of the bag. The man was reluctant to open the bag and tried to avoid any pressure to open the bag; then, hesitatingly, he pulled the chain partially and inserted his hand inside the bag. For a moment, nothing happened, and then he thrust his whole hand inside the bag. His action was strange and threatening, even though the man was nervous. Sensing the volatility of the situation, Rajesh Pandey went ahead and, in quick action, pulled the chain of the bag completely, and immediately after that, he tried to run away in the opposite direction, pushing and elbowing the crowd who were there totally unaware of the events happening right in the midst of them. Satyendra Veer Singh caught him immediately and authoritatively asked, "What is it, what is it?"

Immediately, Rajesh Pandey looked inside the bag and noticed the AK 47. He shouted, “Sir, it is an AK 47."

The man carrying the bag was strong and an underworld's professional courier; he fought back and escaped Satyendra Veer Singh's grip. The man jumped ahead and started running inside Topandas's chikan cloth shop right next to it, as that was the only escape route he could figure out. But soon, he was caught after a brief chase. When Rantendra held him, the man started fighting and tried to escape again; this scuffle caught the crowd's attention, and the crowd circled to see what was happening. This circle of crowd made it difficult for the bag man to escape. The bag man didn't give up on his efforts; he tried hard to fight Rantendra and then tried to snatch his pistol. This was a risky situation in the public place, and sensing that it might run into casualties as the struggle between both increased, Rajesh Pandey sensed that if he succeeded in getting the pistol, there could be many casualties; Rajesh immediately pulled out his pistol and fired one shot on his leg to prevent him from escaping and thinking that he would let go of Rantendra's pistol. Rajesh's bullet injured him; he fell on the floor, but he didn't let go of the pistol. Rajesh saw this and pumped two more bullets at his leg, but somehow, he still managed to get up and run with the bleeding leg. The scene was intimidating to the onlookers. Again, he was overpowered and brought to the police vehicle parked there. The bag man was putting his extreme fight to escape. Again, in the police jeep, he tried to make his move but was prevented by a thick layer of crowd encircling the event near the police jeep and the fast action of the police.

In a short while, there was murmuring in the crowd that another criminal was killed on the outside road. The criminal was shot with several bullets. In the midst of the ongoing chaos, the gunshots fired by Rajesh Pandey were heard by the patrolling police team of Hazratganj; soon, several police vehicles arrived from the Hazratganj police station. The captured bag man was handed over to the Hazaratganj, and then the police team and Rajesh Pandey rushed to the front part of the Darul Shafa MLA residence. It was anticipated that the criminal the crowd was murmuring about was still there. Already, many bystanders had circled the spot, and a man was lying on the road, breathing lightly. When the police team looked carefully, they immediately recognized the person: RK Singh, Satyendra Veer Singh's office staff (peon). Shocked and horrified, the police team fanatically searched for the killer, thinking that he might still be there. The horrified team found that RK Singh was shot in the head from close range; beside him was the half-cut cord of his pistol, and the gun was missing. It took no time for the police to understand that the killer or the killers had snatched away his pistol as well after shooting him. The police team immediately rushed him to the hospital after putting him in the police vehicle; despite the swift action by the police, RK Singh died on the way to the hospital without receiving any resurrection process. To understand the chronology of the event, when the police team intercepted the bag man and got engaged in the fisticuff, which was one person against three policemen, RK Singh, who was standing on the right, saw three persons running in the opposite direction. RK Singh chased them, and at one point in time, when RK Singh, holding his pistol, was very close to the three running men, his leg got entangled in the wire of the parking platform and fell on the ground. The gun also fell apart. Although tied to the cord, RK Singh was helpless and in the most vulnerable position. The fall created a sound, and three men were just a few steps ahead; they heard RK Singh's fall thud and turned back. The three criminals took advantage of this; they snatched the pistol from RK Singh's hand and fired all the bullets of RK Singh's pistol into his head. This was a most unexpected development, and in the coming times, it would shake police confidence immensely.

Once the criminals escaped after killing RK Singh, the crowd swelled and were shocked to see a bleeding man lying on the floor in the pool of blood and his life slipping away. The crowd took it as a criminal was killed because both the police teams were in civil uniform. The death of RK Singh was a setback to the already shaken confidence of the UP police, as RK Singh was a valuable asset, and his contributions were immense. A workaholic, RK Singh, always sat with the team in the number analysis of Shri Prakash Shukla and made a systematic list of all the information whenever received from the control room. As a matter of routine, every day and evening post-meeting about the identification of the team with the allotted areas, information verification, and thereafter preparing the report of findings and then submitting it for review and guidance from the high-ups office, was 24 by seven assignment of RK Singh and he was on top of his duty.

RK Singh was interested in verifying the information received by the police as well. Whenever the police team was ready to go out to check the information, RK Singh always insisted on accompanying even though he was asked to accompany the next time as every team was going out for the information verification. RK Singh never agreed to stay back and was always accompanied by childlike zest, as the irony had it, on the fateful evening. RK Singh informed that he would be going to listen to the gospel narrated by His Holiness Shri Murari Bapu at Eldeco Park of Gomti Nagar, as he had been following him for a long. He joyfully announced that after completion of work, he would also go there that evening. Satyendra Veer Singh said, "You may call the police station in charge of Gomti Nagar, and he will arrange for two passes. Today, we all will go with our families to listen to His Holiness Shri Murari Bapu."

As fate had it, RK Singh was lying lifeless on the same evening when he was supposed to be in the holy company of the saint, as if God wanted to be in his company rather than in the company of any mortal. The entire police team's eyes were wet as pain beyond any words to describe it. It was humiliating to the morale of the police. The words of RK Singh were echoing in everyone's ears as just half an hour ago, he was all set to the holy company of a saint for listening to the gospel at the celebrated Eldeco Park.

On the other hand, many efforts were made to identify the slain criminal, i.e., the bag man, whether he was Shri Prakash or some other known person from his gang. Police started searching all the photographs available in the police records related to the Shri Prakash's gang was rechecked, and none of the pictures was helpful in identifying the deceased bag man. The cache was huge; two magazines and about 50 cartridges, along with an AK 47, were found in the bag, along with the cloth and diaries. From the diary, police concluded that the person was from Bihar. Police could not establish anything else from that. Police carried out massive checking in the entire city as police were anticipating that this work was of Shri Prakash Shukla and he must be one of the criminals who had escaped after killing RK Singh.

The back gate of Darul Shafa was well-lit, and the street lights were bright on the road between Darul Shafa and Janpath. The sequence of events was such that the three criminals who had attacked RK Singh were running towards the Darul Shafa gate, and when they saw that RK Singh had fallen on the floor, they came back quickly and kicked RK Singh. They snatched the pistol from RK Singh. RK Singh was in the most vulnerable position; he was helpless, and before he could understand even, one of the criminals sat on his back and pumped all the bullets from point-blank range into his head. All these happened in the center of one of the busiest markets in Lucknow, which was considered a shopper's paradise and boasts mouth-watering dishes and street foods. It seems that more than two – three hundred people have seen this ghastly murder.

One more angle to the scene was that a new cabinet was formed, and two to three MLAs living on every floor of Darul Shafa were now ministers. There were bodyguards assigned to each of the ministers, and these bodyguards were heavily armed with rifled sentries standing in front of each MLA's quarters. The entire incident happened in the full view of these bodyguards and sentries. Police station heads and constables from all over the district were gathered there.

SSP Subhash Kumar Singh was present on the spot; he asked all the teams to monitor the city's and markets' escape routes and check all the hideouts. He dispatched all the well-wishers and acquaintances of police personnel. A team of two deputies and four station heads was appointed only to find out in detail about the appearance, clothes, gait, and language of anyone who had seen the killers around here. He instructed that even the constables on sentry duty on each floor of Darul Shafa must be questioned.

Immediately, everyone went to work. After a short while, information was received on the wireless that a bag was lying near the block of Darul Shafa's stairs; the apprehension was that it probably contained weapons. All the officers rushed to the location of the bag, and very cautiously, it was opened; there was a carbine, two magazines of the carbine, and a few small weapons. Immediately, police tried gathering information from neighboring shops and passersby. After a quick inquiry, it was found that this bag was not there until half an hour ago. Police swung into action, and immediately, the entire force was deployed, and B side of Darul Shafa was cordoned off, but to utter frustration, nothing worth was found or caught. It seems that the criminals were favored by luck. Without losing time, all the visitors were questioned, and all the rooms of the MLA's residence were also searched. Still, no breakthrough was achieved. However, it was almost 1.30-2 am of the morning. The information broadcasted on the wireless was checked every half an hour, but it did not reveal anything, and everyone was simply disappointed.

The Gorakhpur resident family of RK Singh reached Lucknow.

As a matter of routine analysis, the police headquarters and the administrative wing of the government were asked about the incidents, and the officers involved in the operation were criticized. As usual, the police team conducting the operation had to face many frivolous and out-of-context questions. The questions were trivial and baseless; someone said, "When it was known that he was coming here, why did only four people go for checking"? Someone said, "Why was the checking done by standing in one place." Someone said, “RK Singh should not have followed them alone.”

The words of disgrace spoken for the police personnel involved in the operation were splashed as the front page news of the leading newspapers the next day. Many analyses and counter-theories were written against the police personnel. It seemed that there was no end to the declining morale of the police personnel, and the heart of all the officers was pitch dark and gloomy; it might take the light of even a thousand fireflies to light it up. Everyone reached the postmortem house early in the morning to get the postmortem done. Ironically, the postmortem of both the bodies was to be done, and a huge crowd swelled outside the mortuary. Hundreds of policemen were also there.

Sub-inspector RK Singh was the staff of the SP-City, and he was a very sober, gentle, and learned officer. His interaction was with all the policemen of urban police stations, and he had always maintained warm and cooperative relations with everyone. It was RK Singh's duty to assign duties of police officers for every event, festival, and VIP visit held in the urban area. Every police personnel, from constable to inspector, were in touch with and respected him. Finally, the postmortem started, and someone came out and informed that Shri

Prakash Shukla's photo, some money, and a small Hanuman Chalisa were in the purse of the Late RK Singh.

This became a matter of discussion amongst the crowd standing there. The presence of Hanuman Chalisa was not reported even in a single newspaper, but the presence of Shri Prakash's photo was reported by all the newspapers. It is important to note that Shri Prakash's photo in RK Singh's pocket was not at all a surprise, as the photographs were distributed to all the officers a few days ago. All the police officers had been provided with four or five passport-size pictures to show to reliable people in any hotel, lodge, market, shop, or salon, and if the need is felt, they should be given to them as well. There was no surprise or confidentiality in this because a couple of weeks ago, a press conference was held. Shri Prakash's photograph was distributed among the press people and later published in all the newspapers.

By the time the postmortem was over, the family, friends, and relatives were weeping hysterically. The doctor who had conducted the postmortem came out, and he took the senior police officials aside and informed them, "There are nine bullet injuries, and all were shot at close range. The shot causes blackening, tattooing, and charring of the skin."

One of the police team members said, "RK Singh Sahab used to load only nine bullets in a magazine of ten bullets; all the bullets in the magazine were fired on him before stealing the pistol."

Then, Late RK Singh's body was sent to the police line in a police vehicle from the mortuary, and the crowd followed. All the officers were walking together, followed by the huge crowd, but no one spoke a word. The only sound was the sound of silence interrupted by the sound of vehicles passing on the road. All the arrangements for the final salute and farewell were made in the police line itself. The cloak struck three o'clock in the afternoon. Entire families of all the police personnel living in the police line were all present there, totally taken aback by the ferocity of fate, and no one had any word to utter; such was the grief and shock. The body was kept on a pedestal, and the officers came forward, turn by turn, to pay their homage to the brave departed officer, the Late RK SIngh.

The guard of honor was given as a last salute to the slain officer. In the midst of this grief and pain, Rajesh Pandey noticed that the SSP Suresh Kumar stood on one side after paying homage; he was perturbed and thoughtful, his head bowed down, and he was facing the other side of the event. Rajesh said to Satyendra Veer Singh, "It seems that SSP sir is upset"?

Both of them rushed towards SSP Subesh Kumar, and when they reached there, they found that Subesh Kumar Singh was bitterly crying. It was difficult for both of them to stop their tears. There was a saying that SSP Subesh Kumar was a tough guy, and no one had seen his tears, but not only him; in fact, one thousand policemen there could not stop themselves. After some time, Subesh Kumar sat in his car and kept crying with a bowed head. As the moments rolled by, RK Singh's body was placed in a decorated police car and sent to his home district with due honor for cremation. Subhash Kumar left for his residence. The senior officers followed him as they wanted to talk, but he gestured for them to go.

The incident date was 9th September 1997, and it shook everyone. The crowd was still there. Someone on the next day, everyone assembled at Satyendra Veer Singh's office. There was absolute silence as no one spoke anything for half an hour. Everyone lacked the courage or the passion to start a conversation. The issues of lives were looking too irrelevant. This was a case of extreme emotional turbulence as the room and the chairs were the same, and the strategies were discussed with RK Singh.

After a long pause, with a heavy heart, Satyendra Veer Singh said, " He was wronged."

All those present supported Sayendra Veer Singh with silent and supporting gestures.

ONCE AGAIN

Following these developments, two more officers were inducted into the team. One was Indrajit Singh Tewatia, who, in previous postings, worked with Shri Satyendra Veer Singh on multiple occasions. He was both hardworking and courageous, and he was also a distant relative of Satyendra Veer Singh. He possessed impressive knowledge of crimes and criminals in western Uttar Pradesh. The second officer was Avinash Mishra, a sub-inspector stationed in western Uttar Pradesh. During his time there, Avinash Mishra executed several encounters that garnered media attention as well. However, he was later suspended due to legal complications arising from one of the encounters. DIG Kashmir Singh had recommended his inclusion in the team.

Avinash Mishra was also interested in joining this team on his own. Tewatia and Avinash Mishra used their contacts to get in touch with selected informers from western Uttar Pradesh, bringing them to Lucknow and putting them to work. The morale of the police was already low, and the killing of RK Singh further undermined it. There seems to be no relief as if sadness were cast in stone and darkness refused to be dispelled by the thousand fireflies' light. The police officers continued to motivate each other to maintain high morale and were inspired to take revenge for the late RK Singh's murder.

The police learned that after RK Singh's murder, the daredevil Shri Prakash fled to Bihar with his gang. By then, the criminal (bag man) killed during the RK Singh incident was also identified as Tuniya Ram, who was a henchman of Surajbhan Singh in Mokama, Bihar. Whenever Shri Prakash visited Mokama with his gang, Surajbhan arranged for their stay. Surajbhan also provided security for Shri Prakash, and Tuniya Ram was assigned to guard Shri Prakash's place of stay with an AK-47. Tuniya Ram had become very friendly with Shri Prakash and traveled from Gorakhpur and Faizabad to Lucknow.

Surajbhan had instructed Tuniya Ram to carry Shri Prakash's AK-47 but not to touch his own. Tuniya Ram was a sharpshooter and an expert in handling the AK-47. Now, his family members were at the Lucknow mortuary to collect his body after completing the necessary formalities. It was confirmed that Shri Prakash had escaped to Bihar after murdering RK Singh. The likelihood was that he was in Mokama, although that information was unconfirmed. The police could only gather information indicating that he was living somewhere near Raxaul, close to the Nepal border with Bihar. The police tightened their informer network, and gradually, information in the form of rumors and unverified tips began to pour in about his activities in Lucknow. It was discovered that he had gotten his Maruti car repaired at Gomti Motors in Nirala Nagar and had also taken his Gypsy there for repairs. The Gypsy had a tragic past; it was looted after the murder of the sitting MLA and minister of Meghalaya state government's brother-in-law in Gopalganj, Bihar.

On June 21, 1997, three murders occurred in Gorakhpur, and this Gypsy (vehicle) was involved in those murders. Gomiti Motors confirmed this information. For the first time, the police discovered he also owned a white Maruti 800 with tinted windows. Shri Prakash Shukla himself came to collect the car from Gomiti Motors just two hours before the murders. He signed in the name of Ashok Singh in the garage register, and everyone recognized Shri Prakash Shukla as Ashok Singh after seeing his photographs. In fact, the mechanic and other employees of Gomiti Motors referred to him as Ashok Bhaiya.

Police were in shock now as it was established that Ashok Singh and Shri Prakash Shukla were both the same people. Rakesh Agarwal, the owner of Gomti Motors, was summoned. Initially, he refused to budge, but then the police deployed their psychological trick to make him speak, and he disclosed that before sending the car for repair, he used to call me; he had also asked if the vehicles of the policemen also came here for repair. Rakesh became suspicious, but he kept silent due to extreme fear. Rakesh also said, "Sometimes he gossips a lot about irrelevant things and even calls without any reason." Police were interested in knowing about the pickup time of the Gypsy.

Rakesh checked the log records and informed, "On September 9th, Ashok Singh picked up the Maruti 800 around 5 pm He was alone at that time. Then, on September 13th, Ashok Singh sent someone else to pick up the Maruti Gypsy after speaking with him."

This was the first authentic and verified information received about Shri Prakash from confirmed sources. Immediately on the same day, a recorder was attached to Rakesh Agarwal's phone, and a constable was posted in the office of Gomti Motors to note the timing of the call from Shri Prakash. At the same time, Rakesh was instructed to engage him in conversation to track his location. The constable was trained and assigned to record the calls. Several teams were sent to different locations in Bihar to confirm his whereabouts, but no trace could be found. Numerous attempts failed, and the police were back to square one.

In the meantime, Surajbhan contacted Shri Prakash Shukla to have Chotan Shukla's gunner, Ajay Singh, killed. Ajay Singh, Chotan Shukla's private gunner, had killed him on December 5, 1994 in Muzaffarpur. One day, Anand Mohan and his party members were protesting against the murder of Chotan Shukla by demonstrating on the road with later's dead body. Coincidentally, it happened that the District Magistrate, Shri G Krishnarayya of Gopalganj, was going from Muzaffarpur to Gopalganj via Patna. On the way, the protesters surrounded DM and killed him in totally unprovoked violence.

Surajbhan, Chotan, and Bhutkan Shukla had a strong rapport. They frequently discussed their intentions to kill Ajay Singh. Surajbhan often delayed the plan by stating that Ajay Singh, the gunman, is currently in jail, and once he is released, they would carry out the act.

Surajbhan Singh introduced Shri Prakash, Anand Pandey, and Sudhir Tripathi to Chotan Shukla and Munna Shukla in Patna.

Surajbhan told Shri Prakash that Chotan Shukla was a very close friend of mine. He stood by me during all my difficult times. I need you to settle the score with Ajay Singh, who killed my dearest friend. Whatever you need, both Bhutkan and Munna Shukla will help you out.

Shri Prakash promptly agreed, and they all went to Lalganj, Bihar. Bhutkun and Munna Shukla told him everything relevant to killing the gunner Ajay Singh and said, "He comes to the court hearing with a lot of weapons. There is also police present in the court, and the job is difficult."

Shri Prakash confidently answered, "Bhutkun bhai, the one who fires the first shot is the actual don. We will kill him in police custody, for sure, and you don't worry about it."

Bhutkun and Munna Shukla deployed their men to find out the upcoming dates of Ajay Singh's hearing. At the scheduled day and time, Shri Prakash and all his accomplices sat in the car, followed the police vehicle of Ajay Singh on the way to court, and killed him in police custody. Munna Shukla and Bhutkun Shukla went to Surajbhan's house and thanked him for this work.

Surajbhan was also pleased with Shri Prakash and told him, "Ashok Singh, you have done a fantastic job. I, too, have some enemies; I suggest you kill them as well; I will give you one more AK 47." Surajbhan made arrangements for the stay of Shri Prakash, Anand, and Sudhir in a flat in Patna's Kankarbagh and also made them identify his enemies one by one for execution. In a ghastly crime, Shri Prakash killed five people; two were killed separately, and Manoj Singh, Ajay Singh, and Vijay Singh were murdered in a group in Mokama only. Now, there was heightened police movement owing to such frequent murders. Already, UP police were after Shri Prakash Shukla. So, for further execution, three more youths to work as contract killers were called from Gorakhpur, and they stayed at Surajbhan's place in Mokama.

Surajbhan told Shri Prakash, "Still, there are two more people left to be eliminated, but it's not right for you to go to Patna now. The police are hyper and very active, and the situation is critical. Even if you commit the slightest mistake, police will catch you and will destroy all of us by linking all the murders to you and me. I suggest that the three boys who have come today seem good. Let me try them now".

One of the guys was known as Gandhi; one day, Surajbhan sent these three shooters, along with his cousin Lallan Singh, and got one of his enemies identified for elimination near Gandhi Maidan in Patna. These shooters killed him after firing several rounds of bullets from their 9mm and 0.45 bore pistols near Gandhi Maidan at Patna and returned to Mokama without any trouble from any source. On hearing this news, Surajbhan was very happy.

Surajbhan praised them in front of Shri Prakash: "These boys are very courageous; even bigger work can be given to them. Now I will get them an AK-47; they will do the rest of the job, too."

Shri Prakash felt hurt and said to Surajbhan, "These three are idiots and spineless. Don't trust them. They will let everyone down."

Surajbhan said, "Do you know how efficiently they have worked today? They were all going in a car; our boys overtook them, surrounded them from both sides, and fired several shots, killing them on the spot. There were two weapons in their car. They snatched both the weapons too, and they didn't even get a chance to pick their weapons".

After discussion, Surajbhan got them to stay in another house and went to his house. After some time, both the groups ate together. But these three boys said, "We will not sleep in the room; we will sleep on the terrace."

Shri Prakash objected, "You should have asked Dada if you wanted to sleep on the terrace; this is Mokama, after all." But three sharpshooters did not agree and took their bedding and went to the roof. Shri Prakash, Sudhir, and Anand stayed in the room.

Shri Prakash said to Anand, "Surajbhan bhai is now downgrading us. These guys did just one job, and now, just because Dada made them do the work on the pretext that we may get caught in Patna, this is beyond my understanding and tolerance level. If these idiots get one or two more jobs done from these three, then we will be out of the race, and Dada may ask us to return the AK-47."

Anand said, "What should we do?"

Shri Prakash said, “These guys must have slept on the roof; let's engage them in talk and finish all three of them together even before anyone comes.”

Anand said, “Don’t even think of doing this. Suraj bhai will not let us go alive from here.”

Determined, Shri Prakash said, “Whatever happens, let it happen, I will see.”

Shri Prakash, Anand Pandey, and Sudhir Tripathy all three loaded their weapons and went to the terrace. Gandhi and his two boys were sleeping, totally unaware of the approaching death in the name of Shri Prakash Shukla. Being on the banks of the Ganga River, a pleasant cold breeze was blowing. Shri Prakash signaled to both, and all three fired five bullets each on the heads of the sleeping shooters; the area echoed with gunshots, and they sat there for a while to see the reaction; neither anyone came, or any sound there was completely confusing for all three of them.

Scared and nervous, Anand said, “Let's leave immediately from here.”

Shri Prakash said, “This is a nonsense idea. Do you think you will be able to get out of Mokama alive? There are informers of Suraj bhai all around on the terraces; they will inform Dada in an hour or so, and someone will come here. Since the time is less, wrap each body in the bedsheets, and let take them to the Ganga and drown them.”

Although Sudhir and Anand lacked any courage, they had no choice. Shri Prakash took the pistols of Sudhir and Anand and tucked it on his waist. They all three took bodies, each on their shoulders, and, along with the bed sheets, came down. The distance to river Ganga ji is not more than 100 meters. They somehow reached the bank of the Ganga; there was one boat there, but no one was there to row the boat. Hence, they put the bodies in the boat and rowed it to the middle of the Ganges River. They threw the bodies into the Ganga River and rowed back to the shore. The splattered blood in the boat was cleaned off by themselves. Then Shri Prakash removed his upper body clothing, which was soaked in blood, and tossed it into the river. He had his accomplices throw their upper clothing in as well. All three returned in jeans and trousers.

Then, at four in the morning, Shri Prakash found one of Surajbhan's men downstairs.

He asked sternly, "Where did the bullet was fired? Dada has enquired."

Shri Prakash said, "Since we could not sleep, we went to the bank of the Ganga and fired there."

The man left on hearing this. All the three went to their room and slept.

In the evening, Surajbhan summoned them to his other house in Mokama and said to Shri Prakash,

"Ashok Singh! You have not done the right thing."

Shri Prakash pretended innocence and said, "What happened, Dada? What thing do you think has not been done right?"

Surajbhan sternly said, "You killed all the three shooters at night and threw them in Ganga? How do you think that I will not be able to know it? I came to know everything early in the morning itself; the boat owner is also my person; he saw blood in the boat. I got that sunk in the middle of the river before sunrise, and the blood cleaned on the terrace. You are still very new; learn to trust."

Shri Prakash did not give any answer. Surajbhan asked again, "What had happened between all of you at night yesterday?"

Shri Prakash said, "Dada, you have already seen our work. Now, these people did a small job yesterday and started talking arrogantly. You know that I will never tolerate arrogance in any case. So I killed all three of them."

Surajbhan said, "Whatever you did is over now, and it should not be revealed. You don't know that where you stayed last night was my sister's house. If the family members of the deceased shooters find out about the killing that happened in my sister's house, it will unnecessarily drag my sister into legal complications without any justification. This will not be accepted, so let's forget the whole matter right here."

After sensing Surajbhan's anger and hearing his reprimand, Shri Prakash, Anand, and Sudhir decided to stay that night and leave tomorrow morning. The next day, Shri Prakash went to meet Surajbhan alone and said, "Dada, I know I made a mistake in anger yesterday. Now, I swear I will never do anything without asking you first. I just wanted to let you know that we're going to Gorakhpur today for a marriage function in my family this evening."

Surajbhan said, "Okay, but now don't go out to crowded places. There is a lot of pressure in Uttar Pradesh, as well as here in Bihar."

Shri Prakash said, "Dada, let me go to Nepal for a few days if you say so. It seems Pappu Dev has established himself in Viratnagar; these police dogs will not be able to reach there."

Surajbhan said, "Alright, you can head to Viratnagar and relax for a few days. Everything is going well since all the railway work has settled down. All the contracts from Bihar are now coming to us. In fact, I'm getting a share in all the UP tenders. It's better to stay calm for a few days. But one thing, Shri Prakash, you shouldn't have shot a police inspector in Lucknow. You must remember that once a policeman is killed, all the police officers unite, and their sense of revenge is much stronger than that of gangsters. So take some time to spend peacefully somewhere else where no one can pursue you." you."

Shri Prakash said, "Okay Dada."

Surajbhan once again said, "Now we have read a lot in the newspapers that the Lucknow police have obtained much information about you by tracking the number you dial from your mobile phone. At my house in Mokama, we also receive strange calls on our line. I know that these policemen are like dogs. All of them are police dogs; they must be sniffing around. I will also be out and about for a few days, and you should take a break for a few days, too. There's no need to communicate too much on your mobile."

Shri Prakash said, “Okay.”

Meanwhile, in Lucknow, a call came into the control room one day. The caller stated that the person you are looking for is at Surajbhan's house in Mokama. If a raid is conducted there right now, he could be killed on the spot. Immediately, this information was relayed to SSP Lucknow Subesh Kumar Singh. It was a strange time when politics had become criminalized, and crime had become politicized. Newspapers were filled with reports of kidnappings, murders, and ransom. Subesh Kumar Singh then called the number that had provided the tip about Shri Prakash’s presence in Mokama and had a lengthy conversation with the caller. He briefed the team members, saying, “I will give you the number of Mokama. If you call Ashok Singh at this number, he will answer the phone. Once he comes on the line, you will see that I am telling the truth."

Suresh Kumar Singh said, “If one of us calls him, why would he answer? Give me a name for which he would immediately pick up.”

The caller said, “You can tell him you are JP Singh, Block Pramukh from Gorakhpur." He stated that JP Singh is a resident of Gorakhpur and serves as the Block Pramukh. He was also arrested in the Virendra Shahi murder case. He will immediately connect on the phone line upon hearing JP Singh’s name. In the evening, when everyone was in the meeting, the SSP raised a point about verifying one piece of information: whether Shri Prakash was in Mokama with his entire gang. According to police informants, he was in Nepal.

Satyendra Veer said, “Sir, he has never stayed in one place after the Janpath incident. We are verifying all the information to ensure it is true. Not only this, if we get a location in Mokama, we will raid there as well.” SSP Subhash Kumar Singh said, “The caller who told us all this info has also given us a number and said that when you call on that number and whoever picks up the call, ask him to call Ashok Singh, and he will come on the line. However, the person who makes the call must disclose his identity to the person who takes the call; this must be done with the utmost caution and care. Only when he comes on the phone can it be confirmed whether he is in Mokama? That man has also said “If you tell the name of Gorakhpur's Block Pramukh JP

Singh, he will definitely come, but the problem is that there is no person from Gorakhpur in our team right now. Who can speak well in Bhojpuri and assure that it is JP Singh speaking? Maybe the phone will be answered by Shri Prakash Shukla's person only.

Satyendra Veer Singh said, "We all are from western Uttar Pradesh. We cannot speak that accent; however, Rajesh Pandey is from Allahabad, and he speaks a little Bhojpuri."

Suresh Kumar Singh was surprised, and he asked Rajesh Pandey in Bhojpuri, "So Pandey baba, did you learn the language?" Rajesh Pandey said in heavy Bhojpuri, "Yes sir, I have learned it a little."

Then Rajesh Pandey said again, "Sir, when we were inquiring about Shri Prakash Shukla, we learned that he speaks Bhojpuri and only threatens in Bhojpuri. Sometimes, he abuses the pure Bhojpuri language. After listening to the cassettes of his recorded calls from the landline telephone, I'm sure it can also be learned. Someone told me that to learn a language, if you listen to music or songs in that particular language, it comes to you naturally. On our way to Banaras, we always stopped for tea at a dhaba before Sultanpur. Now there's a paan stall owner who plays Manoj Tiwari's songs and keeps his cassettes in the stall. Every time after having tea there, I asked him for new Manoj Tiwari cassettes and listened to them in the car while traveling. Sometimes, I also listen to songs at home. Since Manoj Tiwari is a great Bhojpuri singer, I now understand the words better. I currently have about thirty to forty Bhojpuri cassettes.

Satyendravir Singh said smilingly, "Now I understand which song you listen to in the car."

Suresh Kumar Singh said, "This is great; you can call him on this phone number, but use a PCO. It is possible that the number may be of a PCO where there is caller ID installed."

There were four to five PCOs opposite the Kaiserbagh police station; everyone left from there and went to one of the PCOs. Rajesh Pandey made the call; immediately, it was answered, and the receiving person inquired about the name and address of the person making the call. Once satisfied, he enquired, "Who do you want to talk to?"

"Ashok Singh," Rajesh Pandey said.

"Call after half an hour," came the reply.

Everyone came into the office of Satyendraveer Singh and informed Subhash Kumar Singh about his location in Mokama. The team waited patiently for half an hour. Then, everyone reached the PCO. Rajesh Pandey made the call again.

Now Ashok Singh himself took the call and said, "I know your bail was not granted yesterday. From where are you calling today? Yesterday only, I spoke to Vakil Saheb Muktinath Mishra, and he told me that bail has not been granted yet." Rajesh Pandey said a little hesitantly, "Bhaiya, I came for hearing, thought of talking to you, I am into lots of trouble." But Shri Prakash immediately disconnected the call as he became suspicious.

Everyone went straight to the SSP and requested that he take action, as his location was only in Mokama. However, the way he talked suggested that he had some suspicion, so we needed to act quickly. Subhash Kumar Singh immediately spoke to the DG and Principal Secretary of Home, informing them that his current location was in Patna, Mokama. He requested a state plane so the entire team could reach Patna to make the arrest him.

After about half an hour of making calls, Subhash Kumar said, "Today, you all will arrive at Amausi Airport in an hour. From there, the state plane will take you to Patna Airport. I have spoken to the SSP of Patna; Mokama falls under the jurisdiction of SP Rural. SP Rural Murari Lal Meena is there. Connect with him, and he will help you arrange the raid, but don't enter Mokama without the local police."

Satyendra Veer Singh asked, "Sir, how many of us can go?"

The SSP said, "Only five people can go. I have discussed everything; you must take the AK-47 and the 9 mm pistol. After it is checked at the airport, the pilot will keep it in a box in his cabin and will hand it over to you once you land in Patna. Now, go and get ready immediately and leave."

We all brought our bags and arranged the weapons in them before leaving for the airport. At the airport, everyone was aware of the support we needed. After inspecting the weapons, around 5:30 pm, a small plane from the Uttar Pradesh government landed at Patna airport with Satyendra Veer Singh, Rajesh Pandey, Tewatia, and Avinash Mishra as the passengers who formed the team to lead the operation. Some local police officers were at the airport to receive the team with police vehicles that were not in good condition, along with an ASP. From there, we were taken to Shri Murari Lal Meena. Shri Meena listened to the entire situation and advised that it was not appropriate to raid at night and that the raid should be conducted early in the morning. "You all will stay in the Police Officers Mess; you will be sent in the morning with a capable section of police force." Furthermore, Murari Lal Meena instructed the ASP not to speak with the inspector of Mokama when he met them. Satyendra Veer Singh requested, “Sir, it would be better if we could have raided now.”

Murari Lal Meena said, “Mokama is caught up in an intense gang war. It becomes barren and quiet there as soon as evening falls. I don't want you all to go into those narrow lanes; someone might mistakenly identify you as a member of a rival gang and shoot at you. During the day, at least people will see that there are police vehicles." They all agreed.

As decided, an early morning convoy of five to six police vehicles set out. In one of the vehicles, all the Lucknow police officers were seated with their weapons, while in another vehicle, the ASP, a DSP, and the rest of the force were present. A local informer also accompanied the ASP. The convoy entered the notorious town of Mokama. It was surprising for the Uttar Pradesh Police to see that on the roof of almost every fourth or fifth house, there was a person sitting or standing, keeping an eye on the movement of people and vehicles. They immediately noticed that some individuals had disappeared from the roofs as soon as they saw the vehicles or were moving away suspiciously.

The driver of the vehicle carrying UP Police was asked, "What are people doing on the roof of every house so early in the morning?" He replied, “In Mokama, every house has one-night vigilante guard posted to track people’s movements and handle the activities of counter-gang members."

The informer signaled to stop the vehicles before entering a lane. ASP Sahab, along with two or three constables, turned toward a narrow lane and mentioned that he was heading toward Ganga. He believed they sensed the police were coming for a raid, as the watch guard at Surajbhan's house also moved away. Then, the DSP of Patna Police, who was also part of the raiding party, instructed the UP police team to go ahead on one of the roads and, through gestures, indicated that the house belonged to Surajbhan Singh.

A white Ambassador Isuzu car was parked in front of the house, and the door was open. As soon as the team cautiously entered, they found three bags lying there. A shaving kit was also on the ground, with a shaving brush that had fresh soap on it, still wet. It took no time to understand that the whole gang had just fled upon seeing the police. The raiding team immediately searched the bags and found a 9mm pistol and cartridges that had been looted after RK Singh’s murder. Keys for an Ambassador car were also discovered in one of the bags. Shoes and slippers belonging to at least three people were left behind, and a sports bag lay open, empty. It appeared that these individuals had fled in a hurry, barefoot but armed. Upon climbing the stairs, the team encountered a woman who began shouting. She was signaled to be quiet, but she did not comply. The team had to question her about who these people were.

She said, “I know Ashok Singh only; the other two guys, I don’t recognize by name, but they are also familiar. Dada had asked me to prepare breakfast for them, so I came in the morning. The watch guard came running from upstairs. All the three people ran away along with the watch guard.”

She also said, “This car was also brought by Ashok Singh.”

After hearing her, everyone was extremely angry. They broke the fridge and TV in the house. The woman also started misbehaving and got into a scuffle with one or two team members. Meanwhile, due to sheer carelessness, an AK-47 was accidentally fired. Thankfully, no one was hurt. Then, the Ambassador was thoroughly searched—it was examined and checked, and the team found it in perfect condition. Officers from the Patna Police were seated in it, and they followed the convoy back to Patna.

All the houses pointed out by the informers were searched, but no one was found. After a while, the team saw a boy, about 22 to 24 years old, riding away on a bicycle.

When enquired about the three youths running away, the cyclist got down and said, "There were three people; one of them had an AK 47. These people ran away and then boarded a boat; I was coming from the other side on a bicycle. A police officer and some policemen were also standing in the way. These three boys walked away with the AK 47 crossing them; the young man who was carrying the AK 47 pointed the AK 47 towards the policeman as if pointing him to fire it out, and then the policemen who were with the officer ran away. The officer's pistol also fell down. All three burst into laughter and ran away from there and boarded the boat."

When the raiding party ran in that direction, they saw ASP coming along with his three constables. When he was asked, "They had just crossed you with their AK-47. The entire team had weapons, but still, none of you tried to stop him. At least you could have fired once they had left; we could have gotten the signal and attempted to ambush them?"

Satyendravir Singh noticed that the ASP was carrying a Glock pistol and then said, "ASP, sir, you have a Glock pistol, too. It fires 15 to 16 bullets at once and is a deadly weapon. If you had fired it in the air, we would have received the signal. Do you know that the Uttar Pradesh police have not yet received Glock pistols? The people with us have never seen one." before."

The SSP said, "Sir, we are clueless about these guys carrying AK 47."

Then, the entire force took the Ambassador's car and went to Patna railway station from there. The entire matter was told to SP Rural Meena ji. He was requested, "Somehow send this car to Lucknow," and he agreed. After that, everyone came to the Patna railway station and boarded the train back to Lucknow.

After reaching Lucknow, all the papers of the ambassador's car were actually the documents found in the vehicle. In addition, a driving license in the name of Dheerendra Kumar Singh was discovered. He was a resident of Sultanpur, and the initial investigation revealed by the Sultanpur police at the address mentioned on the driving license confirmed it to be accurate. When the neighbors were consulted, it was found that he had been away from home for a long time and had begun living with history sheeters from Gorakhpur. Previously, he had connections with the Ayodhya MLA Pawan Pandey. This information was sufficient to suggest that he was the third person in Surajbhan Singh's house that day and had fled before the police arrived. It was reported that he was highly skilled in driving, and he also procured cartridges for Shri Prakash from Paramjeet alias Balli's shop, the owner of Punjab Gun House in Faizabad, located at Rakabganj, Faizabad. Subsequently, Paramjeet Singh Balli was apprehended in Faizabad, as there was ample incriminating evidence against him.

When strongly interrogated, Balli disclosed, "An hour ago, Dheerendra was at his friend's place in Rakabganj. I saw him there."

Half an hour later, Dheerendra Singh was found; he was drunk and staying at his friend's place in Rakabganj. The police apprehended him and brought him to Lucknow.

Dheerendra Singh disclosed information about Shri Prakash Shukla's house in Gomti Nagar, stating, "I have also stayed in that house. When the landlord troubled him too much about bringing his family, Shri Prakash used to call Manju from Kanpur to stay for a week or two, and then he would send her back to Kanpur."

The police raided the house in Dhirendra's presence. The lock was broken, and all of Shri Prakash's belongings found there were seized. A gypsy car with a red light was also discovered inside the premises, which had a fake license plate. The condition of the house suggested that no one had lived there for more than a month. Dhirendra informed the police about all of Shri Prakash's activities up until a week ago, including where he had gone and what crimes he had committed. However, he could not provide any information about where he had gone after fleeing Mokama.

Everyone was satisfied that the police received accurate information about Shri Prakash Shukla and his gang for the first time. Everyone felt that this work would now become easier. Following the police raid, during which they took Shri Prakash's Ambassador car and RK Singh's pistol, Shri Prakash, Sudhir, Anand, Anuj Singh, Satyavrat Rai, and Rajan Tiwari set off for Viratnagar.

Shri Prakash said, "We'll stay here for a few days. Mobile phones don't work here. Cell phones haven't made their way to Nepal yet. There are only public call offices; if anyone wants to talk, they can either go to Kathmandu or cross the border into Bihar. No one should make calls from the PCOs around Viratnagar because the police dogs are sniffing more than necessary. After arriving in Viratnagar, they contacted Pappudev, who booked four rooms in a hotel for them to stay in."

Pappu Dev said, "You can stay here comfortably with weapons. This is a policeman's hotel. Nepal police don't come here."

Shri Prakash and his companions were completely relieved. These individuals used to drive around in cars all day and often traveled to Kathmandu. Shri Prakash always insisted on making the trip to Kathmandu. On one occasion, Shri Prakash got Pappudev, Rajan Tiwari, and Sudhir Tripathi to drink alcohol at a bar because of a girl, yet he himself did not drink. After leaving the bar, they all realized that the three of them were very drunk and, while inebriated, insisted on returning to Biratnagar, even though all the weapons were left in the car.

Shri Prakash said, "No one is going to drive in a drunken state. Let's find a hotel here; we'll stay for the night and leave in the morning." Rajan Tiwari insisted otherwise, and Shri Prakash threatened him repeatedly, telling everyone to stay at the hotel. Rajan Tiwari and Pappudev were intoxicated and felt very upset by Shri Prakash's words. While having dinner in the room that night, Shri Prakash said,

“Look, our fight is for supremacy, i.e., complete dominance. Not all enemies are finished yet. Virendra Shahi's entire family is also searching for us, and everyone's eyes are on our shortcomings and mistakes. As soon as there’s a rumor that certain people enjoy alcohol, everyone will be in danger. Someone will inevitably invite them to a party under the pretense of alcohol, making them have a good time, and then the informers will have a field day. Until we eliminate all our enemies, we must not reveal our weaknesses.

The next day, everyone woke up early and began searching for Shri Prakash in his room. Shri Prakash was nowhere to be found there.

Rajan Tiwari said, “He was giving a lot of speeches last night; he must have seen some girl. He must be lying with her somewhere. Now, who will explain to him that in the fight for supremacy, a fondness for girls gives the most opportunities to informers?” All of this was happening when Shri Prakash entered.” As soon as he entered the room, he began to smile. Rajan Tiwari teased, “I can see where you’ve been. This very act of yours is going to get everyone killed one day.”

Shri Prakash said nothing as everyone settled into the car and left for Viratnagar. It had been a long time since they had visited Viratnagar, and both of them were spending freely. Shri Prakash remarked, “We’ll need to take on some big job again; the money has run out.” Anand Pandey replied, “Get it from Lucknow, bhai; what’s the urgency to take on big work right now?"

Shri Prakash scolded, “You always talk such stupid things. Whoever we speak to about money puts us at risk because we don’t know if they are in touch with the police. I already told you that the police are sniffing around like sniffer dogs; they will find out where we are immediately.”

After one day, Anand said to Shri Prakash, “I’m also going to the PCO. Let me check on the well-being of the family; it’s been a long time. They must be getting worried by now. Bhai, which PCO is safe?”

Shri Prakash said, “Go past the fruit market. On the road behind it, there are three or four PCOs along the other road that leads to the fruit market. No one will be able to get there quickly, so you can speak with them in peace."

Anand left the hotel without taking a car and reached Baansmandi by taxi. He kept asking the taxi driver for directions to the area behind Baansmandi, but the driver couldn't understand him. After wandering around for a while, Anand still couldn't locate the exact spot where three or four PCOs were close together. The market was very crowded, and the taxi struggled to navigate through it. Anand decided to leave the taxi there and began searching for the place on foot. After about half an hour of looking without success, he spotted a PCO a little way down the road leading to the fruit market. He glanced around, bought a kilo of apples from the fruit shop next to the PCO, and asked the shopkeeper if there were three or four PCOs together nearby.

The shopkeeper said, “This is the PCO next to it. Talk here! What will we do with three or four PCOs?”

Anand Pandey also believed he was right; there was a nearby market, no danger, and we could talk from there. A Nepali boy was sitting inside the PCO.

Anand told him, “I want to talk to India.”

The Nepali boy struggled to understand Hindi, so he extended a piece of paper to Anand Pandey and gestured for him to write the number on it. "I'll get the number from here and pick it up in the cabin." Anand quickly wrote the number on the paper, and the boy picked up the nearby register and started to look through it. Pointing to the register, he indicated that a call had been made to this number yesterday as well. Anand Pandey was shocked to see the number from his home in Gorakhpur. He immediately stepped out of the PCO and scanned the area, then asked the Nepali boy at the PCO,

“Who called this number yesterday?”

The bill amount that the boy had written next to that number was about five hundred rupees, indicating that the call lasted for more than half an hour.

Anand asked, "Do you remember who called this number?"

The boy flipped through the pages of his records and showed that the call had been made to this number. Seeing this, Anand became even more surprised. He tried to find out what the caller looked like. From the description provided by the Nepali boy, it seemed that a young male was calling to speak, and he always called between twelve and one. Anand was uncertain, wondering how he had been unaware of who had been calling his house for so many days; it could be that the police had set a trap. Anand gave the boy the Lucknow number belonging to Pawan Pandey and said, "No one has called this number."

The boy looked at the register and shook his head; this number was not in it. Anand asked to dial the number for Lucknow, but Pawan Pandey was unavailable; someone else answered the phone. Anand inquired about Pawan Pandey and then hung up.

After this, Anand said, "When Pawan bhai arrives, tell him it was a call from younger brother in Gorakhpur." Anand Pandey exited the PCO and took a taxi to the hotel. As soon as he entered the room, Shri Prakash asked, "Is everyone okay at home?"

Anand replied, "I couldn't talk; neither Amma nor Babu ji was at home. I'll talk some other time."

Shri Prakash asked, "From which PCO did you make the call?"

Anand said, "Bhai, I called from the same place you mentioned."

After that, Shri Prakash remained silent, and a hush fell over the room. Anand Pandey intentionally withheld the truth because, according to the Nepali boy at the PCO, the caller could only have been Shri Prakash. He then recalled that due to other commitments, he usually left the hotel around noon after lunch and returned only an hour later.

Anand thought he should first confirm this, so he kept waiting for the next day. He was unable to concentrate on any work and felt worried because he had a sister at home. Knowing Shri Prakash's habits, he repeatedly doubted that Shri Prakash would engage in such long conversations with anyone else.

After lunch, like every day, Shri Prakash said again, "I will come back after a walk in a while." He then left the room. As soon as he came out, Anand told Sudhir and Rajan Tiwari, "I am going downstairs. I'm feeling some stomach issues. I will bring a Baralgan tablet."

Sudhir said, "There is a pharmacy in front of the hotel."

Anand quickly went downstairs and saw Shri Prakash leaving in his car. Anand immediately booked a taxi and instructed the driver to head to the fruit market. He arrived there before the crowd began to gather and got out of the taxi. As he walked slowly toward the PCO he had visited yesterday, his gaze fell on the car parked in the lot of Siddharth Hotel, from which Shri Prakash had just exited. It didn't take long for Anand to realize his suspicion was correct. After a moment, he passed by the PCO again and noticed Shri Prakash standing in the booth, talking, facing the wall. He paused for a moment to scrutinize the scene, ensuring no doubt remained in his mind. Checking his watch, he saw it was 12:20. Quickly, Anand left and went to a shop selling Indian film song cassettes, located quite far from the PCO, where he began browsing through cassettes of Manoj Tiwari's Bhojpuri songs. His attention remained fixed on the road leading out of the PCO and the car parked at the Siddharth Hotel. After about fifteen minutes, Shri Prakash emerged from the PCO and headed straight to his car. As soon as he drove off and started toward the hotel, Anand returned to the same PCO. This time, the boy he had seen yesterday was not there; instead, a middle-aged man, around forty-five to fifty years old, occupied the booth.

Anand Pandey asked him, "Yesterday evening, a small boy was sitting in your spot. I gave him a number from Lucknow, but today I forgot the diary with that number. Please check the register and let me know." The list was directly in front of the old man. As soon as he opened the register, Anand said, "Hand it to me; I'll take a look." With that, Anand took the register, and the number written in it was his house number. The bill read three hundred fifty-four rupees. Anand burnt with anger and told the man, "Your son didn't write the number down. I'll go get the diary." Saying this, he immediately left the PCO.

After stepping out, his gaze landed on the PCO in front of Siddharth Hotel. He walked straight into that PCO and dialed his home number, and the call was answered on the first ring; his sister was on the other end. Without waiting for a greeting, she said, “Everything’s okay, right? You just left for the hotel. Are you still at the PCO?”

Anand shouted angrily, “This is Munna. Who are you talking to?”

As soon as she heard her brother’s voice, she became nervous and hung up the phone. Anand understood everything. He paid the PCO man and went directly to the hotel.

Sudhir asked- “What happened? Did you get the medicine?”

Anand said, “Yes, I found it.”

Sudhir asked, “Then why did it take so long? The shop was just downstairs.”

Anand said, “I didn't find it here, so I walked to the Viratnagar market. I bought the medicine there and I had it, on my way back, with tea.”

Shri Prakash was also sitting quietly. He kept looking at something in Casio’s electronic telephone directory. Anand did not want to stay there even for a minute; the only thing going on in his mind was that either he should kill Shri Prakash or he should kill his sister after reaching Gorakhpur. He could not say anything at night. The very next day, again at about twelve o’clock, Shri Prakash left, saying that he would come back after finalizing the work today. Otherwise, he would go to Lucknow and finalize it there.

He went to the PCO and called Anand’s sister. Only after Shri Prakash said hello several times did she respond, “I was almost dead yesterday. As soon as your call got disconnected, Bhaiya called, and I thought you were calling again. Before I could even hear Bhaiya's call, I told him you were leaving for the hotel and that you were still at the PCO. Then she said, 'I am Munna speaking.' I got nervous and hung up the phone." Shri Prakash asked, "Amma ji, Babu ji, did he spoke to anyone?" She replied, "Where does Babu ji stay at this hour, and when is Amma's sleeping time?" Shri Prakash said, "Yes, he mentioned that Amma and Babu ji were not there. I couldn't talk to anyone." Shri Prakash then asked, "Did you talk yesterday or the day before?" Anand's sister replied, "It was yesterday." Shri Prakash said, "It's possible he left to make a call yesterday, but he didn't tell me. He was referring to the call the day before." Shri Prakash didn’t say much today; he mentioned he was going somewhere.

He disconnected the call with an excuse, and after arriving at the hotel, he mentioned that he had a significant job in Lucknow. Let's take the money there, and after completing the work, we will return. It was getting very cold; it was December, and the cold wave was forcing people to wear warm clothes. On the road dividers, very poor people were struggling to survive in old, dusty quilts or blankets. Rajan Tiwari had to get off in Patna only.

When Patna was fifty kilometers away, Anand said, "Bhai, should I also get down at Patna with Rajan?"

Shri Prakash said, "Why? Only I and Sudhir will go? The distance is so long that one more person is necessary."

Anand said, "Dhirendra will be in Surajbhan Dada's office. Take Dhirendra with you."

Shri Prakash said, "What kind of work has come up?"

Anand said, "There’s no work; Rajan bhai will do some shopping. He knows someone there. Next month is my niece's wedding, so we’ll buy something from here. The weather in Lucknow is very hot, and it will be difficult to buy the clothes we want in Lucknow so leisurely."

Rajan sat in the back seat next to Anand. Anand squeezed Rajan's hand and gestured for him to agree. This gesture was very subtle.

Rajan also said, “I’ll get your shopping done by tomorrow or the day after, and you will be free after that. I’ll buy the clothes here.”

After arriving in Patna, Rajan and Anand got off at Surajbhan's office. Surajbhan was in the office; he called everyone in and served them breakfast.

Rajan Tiwari said, “Anand and I will get off here; these people will go to Lucknow.”

Surajbhan looked at Anand and asked, “Anand, is everything all right?”

Anand didn't say anything. Surajbhan remarked, “It's never happened that you stay alone while leaving Shri Prakash. If you have any issues, tell me." Anand couldn't hold back and responded, "Now I will never work with him again, Dada. I'm telling you right now, I don't know when he'll cheat you also." Then Anand narrated the entire story and added, "Dada, you're aware of the cheapness he does for girls. He doesn't understand the difference between himself and others. He's been calling my sister for the past ten days. How can you trust this guy? He isn't related to anyone. I'll stay here with you; otherwise, he'll kill me too, just like he did the three of them. Just get us our weapons."

Surajbhan looked at Shri Prakash and asked, “Is what Anand is saying correct?”

Shri Prakash replied, “Yes, it’s correct, but it’s not my fault.”

Anand shouted, “Dada, if he says even one word, I will either kill him or die myself.” Surajbhan quickly intervened and told Shri Prakash, “You should take Dheerendra with you; if necessary, bring one or two more men along, and he will stay with us.”

Surajbhan asked Shri Prakash, “Where are the 9mm and .45?” Shri Prakash replied, “Dada, all the weapons are in the same bag; I’ve adjusted them under the seat.”

Surajbhan said, “Give two 9mm and one .45 to Anand, and take the rest of the weapons with you.”

He told Dheerendra, “You go with Ashok Singh.”

“When Shri Prakash tried to say something, Surajbhan replied, “To me, you both are equal; you both have worked for me. If you weren’t together, Shahiya would never have been killed. They both took revenge for Chutkun and Bhutkun together, so giving him his weapons is just a deal.”

Shri Prakash fell silent. As he moved toward the car, Surajbhan said, "You stay here. Sudhir and Devendra will bring their three weapons. They know what to do, and they'll also give him the magazines and cartridges."

Dhirendra and Sudhir went to retrieve the weapons from the car parked in the office lot. Surajbhan then looked at Shri Prakash and said, "Ashok Singh, I know that girls are your weakness, but if you betray your own people, then one day, they will turn against you. Never engage in such deceitful actions in your life. Whatever goods you desire, there's a whole market for it; you have the money, and you'll get whatever you want. You waste so much time on all this. Oh, and one more thing! From today onward, you will not look at Anand. Anand will do his work, and you will do yours, and neither of you will interfere in each other's tasks in any way. The three people you killed were also our men. They worked for me, and you shouldn't have done this in my home without consulting me. You all have helped me greatly in my tough times, which is why I forgave you, but the images of those guys continue to haunt me. Please do not repeat such a mistake again, even unintentionally."

After this, looking at Anand, he said, "Now you should also go home, but don't scold your sister. Ashok will never call again. From today on, you both need to go your separate ways because I know that whatever Ashok Singh has done to you, neither you nor anyone else can ever forgive him, and the two of you can never unite. Even if you did unite, one of you would be killed. Therefore, it's better for both of you to go your separate ways, and there should be no interference in each other's matters." Shri Prakash continued to listen to the whole thing with his head down.

Surajbhan asked loudly, "If either of you has any doubts, please let me know, or if I have said something wrong, tell me that as well."

Shri Prakash raised his head slowly and, looked at Surajbhan, and said, "Okay, Dada, I will accept what you are saying."

After this, Anand said, "Okay, Dada, what you're saying is correct."

In the meantime, Dheerendra and Sudhir returned with two 9mm guns, one .45, six magazines, and about 100 cartridges packed in polythene.

Surajbhan asked, “Anand where is your bag?”

Sudhir said, “I’ll bring it from the car.” Within five minutes, Sudhir returned with his bag. Surajbhan said, “Anand, put your things in the bag. Come with me to Mokama today; tomorrow, wherever you want to go, I’ll send you in my vehicle.”

He told Shri Prakash, “It will be late at night now, so if you want, you can also stay. I can make arrangements for you wherever you’d like.”

Shri Prakash said, “Dada, it is only 10 o’clock; I will cross Bihar in three hours, and then I will see whether I will go to Gorakhpur or Lucknow.” From there, Shri Prakash left directly for Lucknow.

Sudhir said, “Bhai, this was wrong?” Shri Prakash scolded Sudhir and said, “Don’t dig into small things, don’t find faults, nothing is wrong in the battle for supremacy, everything is right.” Muttering on the way, he went straight to Lucknow without stopping anywhere and started living in his house.

WHAT REGRET !

The next day, Shri Prakash wore a tracksuit early in the morning, kept an AK-47 in a bag with tennis rackets, and had a pistol on his back. He drove around the stadium with Anuj and Sudhir in his Maruti 800, parked the car in front of the children's school, and kept staring at women. He visited the nearby PCO to talk. Checking his behavior, it was hard to believe that his closest friend, Anand Pandey, had left him just a day earlier. There was no hint of regret in his conversation about losing his most trusted friend due to his bad behavior, which surprised Sudhir. While having dinner that night, Sudhir asked, "Why did Suraj Dada favor Anand so much, bhai?"

Shri Prakash said, "From now on, if you or anyone else even mentions Anand's name, no one will be more offended than I will. You know we are fighting for supremacy, and I have told you ten times that there is nothing wrong in the fight for supremacy. Remember to never mention Anand's name, even by mistake." Shri Prakash was furious hearing Anand's name. His presence was so dominating that Sudir and Anuj dared not ask any questions.

Three to four days later, one evening during a meeting, the new SSP of Lucknow, Arun Kumar, received information that Shri Prakash had been spotted again in Lucknow with his gang. Hearing the news of his presence in Lucknow after almost four months tensed everyone's brows. It was hard to comprehend that only a little time had passed since the martyrdom of RK Singh in Janpath, and he had reappeared. SSP Lucknow gauged the officers' expressions as if someone were reading Ellen Watts' timeless book, 'The Wisdom of Insecurity,' trying to make sense of a time of unrest. That day, the sky had been clear, and the stars had been visible the previous night, but this night felt different. The daytime was telling a different story.

SSP Lucknow said to boost everyone's morale, "When a jackal is about to die, it runs towards the city. Now, the time has come. Activate your sources again so this story ends forever."

Turning to Inspector Tewatia and Avinash Mishra, the SSP said, "Call the people from the west and have them start working as well. This time, there should be no mistakes. I will check with my sources where the activity is exceeding expectations. Everyone, keep your morale high; we will end this story for good this time." This statement boosted everyone's morale at SSP Lucknow, and they headed to their respective locations. The next day, around 11 am, the SSP sent a message instructing everyone to report to the orderly room of the police line within half an hour. Upon receiving the news, everyone hurried toward the police line, as it seemed a location had definitely been found. Everyone had gathered there when Arun Kumar arrived shortly after, and the conversation began.

Arun Kumar stated, "My source has confirmed that he was present in front of Montport School at around seven in the morning. After that, he was seen in front of Karamat Girls College at around eight in an Ambassador car with his two companions. Upon learning that he had visited these two schools, information from another source was already being confirmed. For some reason, he tends to go in front of schools for young children during school opening hours when parents drop off their kids. He parks his car somewhere near the schools and gathers basic information about someone. From the information received from SSP Lucknow, it is understood that a child from a prominent businessman or a respected individual is at risk of being kidnapped."

The kidnapping motive was communicated to the SSP, highlighting the gravity of the situation. Arun Kumar responded immediately, stating, "If a kidnapping occurs, there will be significant uproar this time. The government and DGP are already under substantial pressure. If a kidnapping happens, the public reaction will be very negative, and responding will be challenging. We need to work diligently to prevent such kidnappings at all costs, and this time, we must ensure a resolution under any circumstances. After all, how long can we keep tracking his location and inspecting the crime scene after the crime? The time has come to take action, especially since it seems this is occurring near the schools in the Trans-Gomti area."

A team member suggested, "A sub-inspector should be stationed at each of these schools to identify which children of influential businessmen or respected individuals are studying there. Compile a list and ensure their safety while they are going to and from school."

Arun Kumar immediately said, "Do not do this at all. If you do this, this matter will come out somehow, leading to chaos and panic in the schools. Parents will stop sending their children to school, and the police will be defamed for supposedly spreading this rumor to make their work easier. The responsible officer should visit three or four good schools in Trans-Gomti, where children of respectable families attend, and be present there with his team for one hour in the morning. Everyone has photographs. Except for one or two schools, the gates of the other schools lack sufficient space to park many vehicles, making it difficult to identify the person sitting in the vehicle. It is also essential that someone who goes should stay close to the school in a spot where all the people coming and going can be monitored. If it is very important, contact the concerned principal. Anyone entering or leaving the building inside the school should be monitored." For the police, this was a delicate and sensitive situation. They had to stop Shri Parakash and prevent any high profile kidnapping, and all these things were to be done without leaking any of the apprehensions; otherwise, the public panicky and media outcry would have made the police's life miserable.

Satyendra Veer Singh, Rajesh Kumar Pandey, Avinash Mishra, and Tewatia were instructed to go to different schools. Teams were assigned to monitor CMS (City Montessori School), Gomti Nagar, Saint Fundaris, Mont Fort, and Karamat Girls College, and everyone was asked to arrive in the morning before school began. There was a significant issue with space at Mont Fort and Karamat School, where it was challenging to observe all the visitors from a single location in the parking area. The biggest problem was that the school had a high boundary wall surrounding it, and the main crossing in Nishatganj was extremely crowded. Rajesh Pandey and his team made numerous attempts, but no suitable location was found.

We waited for the school to open, and when the Principal arrived, she was informed by the peon standing outside that CO Kaiserbagh requested to meet her. The Principal instructed her to come inside immediately. Rajesh Pandey entered the Principal's office and spoke with her; initially, she assumed that someone had come to discuss admissions. Once he was free to speak, he informed her that admission forms would be available after February. He clarified that he had not come for admission but for something very important. He said, “Tell me!”

Rajesh Pandey asked, “Madam, is there any place in your school, either in the front or on the roof, where a direct view can be maintained of the vehicles parked outside your gate and the people coming and going?”

The Principal replied, “What’s the big deal? You can keep an eye on everything from outside the gate, too.”

He was informed, “There are some plainclothes policemen outside as well, but no single officer can keep an eye on all the people coming and going. No such place has been found here; we’ve been checking for about half an hour."

The Principal said, “This is a girls’ school, and people will object to any police officer or employee staying inside. I will have to consult the management.” She immediately called a responsible officer from her management, spoke with him for a while, and then told me, "All the classrooms are upstairs, and there’s no room on the top roof from which you can sit and watch. I’ve been informed that aside from my room, there’s no place from which anything outside can be seen.” She even opened the outside windows to demonstrate that all surveillance can be done from this room. The Principal appeared a bit nervous.

She asked, “Whoever has to stay here, how long will they stay?”

Rajesh Pandey replied, “From the time the children start arriving until your main gate is closed.”

The Principal said, “Then it will take about three-quarters of an hour.”

It occurred to me that when a person is denied the chance to live the life they believe in and have faith in, they are compelled to go against the law. Everyone makes mistakes, but a truly great person achieves everything even after acknowledging and understanding that their actions are wrong. At this point, crime ceases to be merely a crime; it becomes an attempt. We were searching for a loophole in the vessel of secrecy, yet it must be stated that crime and fraud do not have a specific location—they simply happen. This was our way of uncovering the secrets on the literary landscape of crime, as we struggled with our policing techniques. Anyway!

In the meantime, the main gate of the school opened, and children began to arrive. Very young kids came in with their mothers or fathers. A significant number of two-wheelers were parked outside, and small cars were being parked along the side of the road as parents entered with their little ones while older children arrived independently children.

Most of the girls arrived on their bicycles. Everything was clearly visible from the principal's office. Rajesh Pandey was contacting outside teams through the wireless device in his hand. As soon as the gate closed, Rajesh Pandey began to leave after thanking the principal. The principal then asked, "Sir, is there anything to be afraid of, and who are you? What are you doing in Kaiserbagh?" Rajesh Pandey replied, “There is nothing to fear; I am the Deputy SP of the Kaiserbagh area."

The principal asked again, “Sir, the sounds coming from your wireless made it seem like you were waiting for someone, but maybe they didn't come?" Rajesh Pandey responded to the concerned principal with a suppressed laugh, “Madam, were you focused on your work or just on the wireless?" The principal replied, “Sir, this is the first time in my life that a police officer is constantly present in my office with his wireless on. I couldn't focus on anything else, and I don’t know why I'm feeling scared! If you could tell me whether this involves my school, I need to communicate with my management; it’s very important for them to know." Rajesh Pandey said, “Tell your management that if they have any questions, they should contact SSP Lucknow; there's no need to panic." With that, Rajesh Pandey left.

Almost all the officers who were sent to the schools had left after school hours. By eleven o'clock, everyone gathered again in the police line. There, they shared the information they had collected, but Shri Prakash or someone resembling him had not appeared at any of these places.

Rajesh Pandey recounted his story, saying, "The principal was asking a lot of questions and seemed a bit nervous; we will have to talk to her management team." Arun Kumar added, "We got a call from their manager that the principal and other teachers are nervous, not knowing what the issue is." The school manager stated, "Their principal, Saima Khalik, has an objection and insists that no police officer should be allowed to remain in the principal's room in this manner, even for half an hour."

Arun Kumar stated, "Their manager has been informed that there is no need to worry. We will be there for only half an hour or three-quarters of an hour when the school opens, and as responsible officers, she need not be concerned. I have also informed her that if the principal wishes, she can speak to me directly. All officers should carry out their duties; if there are any issues from the school, they should contact me directly." It was also discussed in the meeting that it is possible he may have gone to some other schools in addition to these four. Arun Kumar remarked, "Last time, when the information came, it was regarding these schools in Trans-Gomti, but it is surprising that he has been spotted at different schools each time. If he is seen near schools with the intent to kidnap a child, then he should only be seen near one school. It is also possible he has multiple targets in different schools at the same time, so he can locate his target in various places. We have no other way to act on this information except this. There are no law and order issues in the morning. There is no harm in conducting this surveillance for half an hour."

This sequence of surveillance near schools continued for four to five days. There were no issues anywhere except at Karamat school. The principal of Karamat would ask various questions daily, trying to understand why police officers come for half an hour in the morning and then leave. Rajesh Pandey also suggested that someone else should be assigned to Karamat, as there is no place other than the principal's room, making it impossible to monitor from one spot. The principal is likely frightened, and it appears that due to her fear, she has informed the other teachers that some incident is about to occur in the school, which is why the police officers come here daily.

On the third day, she also asked, "If there is any issue related to the school, then please inform SSP sir and close the school for a few days." Upon hearing this, SSP Arun Kumar responded, "If that's the case, then this matter will definitely come to light. I had already informed their manager about this. He called the manager and explained everything, then said, 'Please give me the Principal's number; I would like to speak with her directly.' The manager provided the Principal's office number, and Arun Kumar called her directly. Before making the call, he remarked, "Saima Khalik seems to be an elderly woman by name."

Rajesh Pandey said, "No, she is not elderly. She must be around forty-five years of age. She is educated and speaks mostly in English."

Arun Kumar said, "I will threaten her right now to not talk about this and that. I thought that if she was an elderly woman, then she would have to be explained. The Principal came on the phone; Arun Kumar expressed his displeasure to her and said "You are getting so worried without any reason. The officers are doing their job. It is very important to maintain the secrecy of the operation; you will also be informed when the time comes. If you are facing any problems, then tell me. There is no need to ask too many questions from the officers."

Arun Kumar said, "Now she won't ask so many questions, so everyone focuses on your work." Everyone went to their office.

JUNIOR GANG

Meanwhile, Anuj and Rajan Tiwari left Mokama the next day and reached Gorakhpur directly. Surajbhan got them out of Gorakhpur in his car with his men. On the way, Anuj called Satyavrat Rai. Satyavrat Rai lived in Hydel Colony, Gorakhpur, and was Anuj's close friend. He had known Shri Prakash since 1993, when Shri Prakash murdered Rakesh Tiwari of the locality. In 1993, Shri Prakash's friend Bablu Tiwari arranged the meeting of Satyavrat and Anand Pandey with Shri Prakash Shukla for the first time. Satyavrat and Anand studied together at MP Inter College, Gorakhpur. Satyavrat Rai did not have much money, Anand Pandey was a bit rich from home, and both started the dish antenna business in 1994.

During that time, the dish antenna business was operated solely based on intimidation and threat. Providing dish antenna connections across different areas, laying the lines, and collecting monthly rent from the connection holders could only be accomplished by someone with financial resources and muscle. Following Rakesh Tiwari's murder, Shri Prakash began to gain recognition as an emerging criminal, making him highly valuable in the dish antenna business. Since Anand Pandey had invested money, collecting payments from connection holders became a daily routine—sometimes resorting to beating and intimidation if payments were not made. In this environment, Anand Pandey and Satyavrat Rai strengthened their ties with Shri Prakash.

Collecting money for dish connections in various neighborhoods was the responsibility of different individuals. A significant amount of money was saved through this process, but gradually, tension developed among the collectors and local criminals. The efforts of Anand Pandey and Satyavrat Rai were progressing well, but they had a dispute with Raja Gupta, who was already involved in the dish business in the area. One day, two LMVs were stolen from Satyavrat Rai and Anand Pandey's location, and suddenly all the connections were cut off. Anand Pandey and Satyavrat suspected that Raja Gupta's men were responsible for this theft. They were searching for him when they spotted him at a tea stall. Anand Gupta fired at him, but he survived.

The police arrested Anand Pandey, who was sent to jail under section 307. Neeraj Singh, Sona Tiwari, Deepak Agarwal, and Hriday Chand were involved in the cable business, collecting money from their respective areas. Meanwhile, Neeraj Singh shot Hriday Chand, and later, Hriday Chand's friends—Anand, Sona Tiwari, and Deepak Agarwal—together shot Neeraj Singh with a pistol. Neeraj Singh was a friend of Shri Prakash, but after Neeraj Singh's murder, Anand and Shri Prakash had a falling out. While sitting with the other cable contractors, he reconciled Shri Prakash and Anand Pandey, stating that now that all the others in the cable contract are gone, it's not right to fight among ourselves. If we work together, all the cable operators in Gorakhpur will listen to us, and we will start earning good money.

In 1996, a new government emerged... with a new attitude... heralding a new dawn. During this period, Shri Prakash began visiting Anand's home. The first decision they made was that if they wanted to gain total control of the cable, they needed good weapons. Meanwhile, Shri Prakash and Anand together shot Anshuman Singh, and later, they also killed Dubey and seized his carbine. Throughout this time, Shri Prakash and Anand committed many murders to assert dominance, but Satyavrat Rai always remained loyal to Anand Pandey. Satyavrat Rai spoke with Anand Pandey several times during their journey from Surajbhan's house to Gorakhpur, and on one occasion, Anand Pandey broke down in tears while they were talking.

Anand Pandey said, "Satyavrat bhai, I never thought that Shri Prakash Shukla was such a dirty man. I did so many things for him, and when he started talking nonsense to you, too, I should have separated from him then. You did a good thing that you separated from him; he has left me completely naked. Thanks to Dada Surajbhan, he got our weapons back. Otherwise, he would have killed me and thrown me in the Ganga there, just like he did with the other people. Now we have to make new preparations, arrange for weapons, and then close Shri Prakash's ransom shop. First, we have to arrange for a vehicle, and then I am reaching Gorakhpur with an AK 47; meet me there and help me." Satyavrat said, “Bhai, you reach Gorakhpur. Devendra MLA of Bihar has arranged a car parked at Vipin's house in Mohaddipur. I will tell Vipin to take the car and meet you at Golghar. You leave Surajbhan Dada's car near Golghar, and you and Rajan Tiwari come straight to Lucknow by car. I will fill the fuel in it till Lucknow; come here, and we will sit and talk. I was already saying that the man was not good when he killed Dubey for the carbine; Dubey was his 24-hour companion. On our request, he would shoot anyone in the head without delay, without thinking, but you did not listen; well, what happened? Don't you remember that when money was needed for your brother-in-law - Sanjay Pathak's bail, the same man got your brother-in-law bailed after paying money through Sona Tiwari in Allahabad?”

While talking, Anand Pandey arrived at Golghar market, where he found the car that Satyavrat Rai had parked. After saying goodbye to the two people from Surajbhan who had come to drop him off, he took the same car to Lucknow to meet Satyavrat Rai, who was living in Indira Nagar, Lucknow.

Satyavrat Rai informed Anand, "Devendra Singh, the MLA, called about some work and provided the car for that purpose. He also wants a murder committed, and we'll be getting an AK-47 for it." Anand replied, "We are in desperate need of money and an AK-47. We'll take on this job, but I need to speak with Devendra MLA first." The following day, Satyavrat arranged for a phone conversation with Devendra MLA in Bihar.

Devendra said, “You all come here, do our work. You'll get an AK-47 and two pistols there. Take five lakhs from me before the work; if you want, you can take it after the work.” Anand, Rajan Tiwari, and Bablu Tiwari left from there.

On the way, Anand said, “Neeraj killed Hriday Chand on the orders of Shri Prakash Shukla. At that time, Hriday Chand was very upset. A man named Sengar from Banaras had taken money from Hriday Chand to get him a job. Hriday Chand, in his greed for money, had borrowed from many people and given it to Sengar in the hope of getting a job. But Sengar neither secured a job for him nor returned the money. Since Sengar was connected to big liquor businessmen in Banaras, he began to threaten him when I asked for the money back. Hriday Chand had told me many times that, at that time, he didn't get a chance because of Shri Prakash. Shri Prakash was annoyed with Hriday Chand and had him killed by Neeraj Singh. We need to stop in Banaras; first, we will go and ask Sengar for his money back. If he gives it, we will hand it over to Hriday Chand's children; otherwise, we will kill Sengar. Hriday Chand had noted down Sengar's name, address, and phone number, which I have."

Rajan Tiwari said, "Anand Bhai has embarked on an important task. Let's complete this work, and then we can take care of that on the way back."

Anand said, "No, first let's do a good deed, then we will set out for a bigger work, the work will be done in any case. Let's go to Sengar; whether he gives the money or not, we will kill him, and then Hriday Chand will get peace."

At night, everyone stayed in a hotel in front of the station and reached Sengar's house at 7:30 in the morning. Sengar opened the door, he recognized Anand as soon as he saw him.

Anand said, "Sengar, give Hriday Chand's money today; we will not go without taking the money; now it's enough." Sengar's wife made tea for the three of them.

Sengar said, "I don't have a single rupee to give; this year, I haven't got a single liquor shop in the liquor contract. Where will I get the money to give you?"

Anand took out his nine mm pistol, placed it on the table, and said that now the pistol is out of the waist, it will go inside the waist only when either you give me the money or all the bullets will go into your skull.

Seeing the pistol, his wife and three children started crying. Sengar silenced them and said, "He is our bhaiya, he will not shoot. I have never refused to return the money; give me a month's time, and then come, I will pay the full amount." On hearing this, Anand Pandey picked up the pistol, which was already loaded, opened the lock with his thumb, and fired all the bullets into Sengar's skull. Before Rajan Tiwari and Bablu Tiwari, Sengar's wife and three children, could understand anything, Anand Pandey put the pistol back in his waist and said, 'Let's go!' He locked the house from outside and, boarded the Maruti Esteem car and left for Patna. before reaching Patna, he called MLA Devendra Singh and informed him that they would arrive in an hour, asking where to meet. Devendra Singh replied, "Head to Kankarbagh; our man will contact you there." Anand was contacted again from a PCO before entering Patna. The MLA provided the details: the car would be parked in front of the Income Tax Office, and a man in a white kurta pajama would approach you. He will take you to your accommodation. "I will come by later tonight," he added. Anand Pandey went directly to Kankarbagh. At the designated location, three or four people were in a white Zen. A man dressed in a kurta pajama stepped out. Anand got out, introduced himself, and then followed the Zen passengers to a nearby house. It was a large, vacant property. The car was parked inside the garage, and everyone was informed that a man would stay in the outer room. Whatever food you need, he would bring from outside, heat it up in the kitchen, and wash the dishes. You won't need to go anywhere.

Around 10 o'clock in the night, the man sitting outside said, "MLA ji has come."

After praying, the MLA began his speech plainly, saying, "Please assist me with this task. I have brought the funds with me. You can take it now if you'd like, or come back and collect it after the work is finished. Please stay here until the work is complete. All arrangements for your food and beverages have been made."

Anand said, "We need one or two days to get his Kundali."

The MLA said, "I did not understand the meaning of Kundali?"

Anand said, “One Kundali is the birth Kundali, which is made by the Pandits, in which the entire story from birth to death is written, and we make another kundali. The Kundali, which we make, describes the place of death of the person, time, presence of weapons, family members, way to escape, way to avoid identification, and the way to prevent the police from reaching us after his death. Pandit ji makes the birth Kundali, we make the death Kundali."

The MLA said, "Okay, I understood, I understood. You need time to do reiki."

Anand said, "You understood it perfectly. Just give us one person from your side who is your confidant, someone who doesn't gossip and is strong-hearted."

The MLA replied, "I will definitely provide him, but he will only identify the person; that individual won't be present when the work is done."

Anand Pandey responded, "That is absolutely correct."

Meanwhile, as the MLA was about to leave, Anand Pandey interrupted him and said, "Devendra ji, we take the money after the work is done, but we need to receive it honestly afterward." The MLA replied, "Don't worry, the money will reach wherever you say within two to four hours after the work is completed, and yes, someone will come to meet you here at seven in the morning."

After the MLA left, Rajan Tiwari remarked, "Anand bhai, when he brought the money, he should have taken it. The MLAs of Bihar are bastards. After the work is done, they won't answer our phones or hand over the money?"

Anand said, "Not every MLA is the same, Rajan; if this was a rogue MLA, he would never have brought the advance money. Is it not possible that he gives the money and go, and then we will run away with the money? Now, we have started trusting him, and he has started trusting us. When the work is done, he will run and deliver the money."

Rajan Tiwari said, "Anand bhai, if you are saying so, I believe it, but it is not like that."

After having dinner at night, everyone went to sleep. Everyone was tired after the long journey. The next day, when I woke up at 8 am, the first thing that was asked from the man sitting outside was, “Has anyone come?”

He said, “Sir, he had come at 7 am.”

Rajan Tiwari, Bablu Tiwari, and Anand all got ready, and at 9:30 am, Rajan went to the garage, changed the car's number plate, and put on a Bihar plate. They then took the man and left. They spent three days doing reconnaissance. On the third day, the MLA arrived again around 10 pm. Anand and his companions returned immediately.

The MLA said, a little disappointed, “What will happen, Bhaiya? Is the Kundali ready?”

Anand said, “Don’t worry, when your work is done, the message will reach you automatically. Now the kundali is ready. Even Rahu and Ketu don’t have much power.”

The MLA was surprised, “What is this Rahu and Ketu?”

Anand said, “Rahu Ketu, those who carry toys with long rods, those with short rods have no power, don’t worry!”

Three days later, the three men parked their car at a turn near the railway crossing and stood there. After an hour, the target was seen sitting beside the driver's seat of the Tata Sumo. Bablu Tiwari had started the car and was holding the steering wheel. As soon as the car slowed down slightly at the turn, Anand fired four shots from a .45 pistol, hitting him directly in the head. The driver stopped the car, opened the door, and ran away. Rajan Tiwari fired four or five shots at the people sitting in the back. The man by the window fell down right there while the others opened the door of the Tata Sumo and fled. Anand opened the door and searched for weapons, pulling out an AK-47, two homemade pistols, and a revolver, while Rajan Tiwari retrieved three rifles. He got into his car with these weapons and left for Patna. After traveling 5-7 kilometers, Bablu Tiwari turned the car left, and Anand said to Rajan, “The road is deserted; throw the .315 bore rifles one by one at some distance.”

Rajan threw all three rifles one by one over a distance of 2 kilometers and then backed the car to reach Kankarbagh.

Rajan Tiwari asked, “Anand bhai, I consider the .315 caliber weapon to be the best weapon. Why did you have it thrown away?”

Anand replied, “This is the height of stupidity. The rifles were thrown there because the police will search at least six hours in that area and won't go any further. We'll collect brass from the spot and enjoy seeing the rifles in the field, then we'll harass the villagers for hours. Every house will be searched, and by then, we'll have reached Lucknow.”

Rajan Tiwari said, “Yes, you are saying the right thing, bhai.”

After reaching Kankarbagh, the car was parked in the garage, and the three started resting there. By six in the evening, the MLA also arrived, and he said to Anand, “Anand Bhai, you have got all the weapons; I have brought the money. I thank you. I am giving you six lakh rupees instead of five. I have made all the arrangements in the hospital, and I have already been admitted at six in the morning; I had got all the papers ready in the hospital. I have come to thank you, as soon as I go back, I will go to the hospital and get glucose water injected in my hands and feet. Because in the night or by midnight, an FIR will be lodged and these bastards will also name me. Please let me know if you need any other service from me.” Anand said, “Send the car in which you have come with one of your men to Lucknow and I am leaving my car and keys here. After four to six days, someone will come and take it.” The MLA readily agreed and said, “I have three cars with me; right now, I will get you, people, to Lucknow in one car, and in two to three days, I will get your car also delivered with Satyavrat.” Saying this, the MLA left one of his cars and went straight to the hospital in the remaining cars and lay down in the ICU. Anand, Rajan, and Bablu Tiwari were already ready and immediately left for Lucknow in the MLA's car. By 5 am, they got down near Lekhraj Market, one kilometer before Satyavrat's house in Indira Nagar, and asked the driver to go back. All three of them went to Satyavrat's house on foot and slept comfortably in Satyavrat's house.

In the evening, Satyavrat Rai's relative Bhunwar Rai, who lived in Marutipuram, also arrived. Anand Pandey, Bablu, and Rajan had woken up exhausted after many days and had not even eaten.

In the evening, Bhunwar Rai said, "Everyone should go home and have dinner there."

Rajan said, "Let's take a look at the AK-47 and the pistol we found, and tomorrow, we'll go somewhere to test them out."

Rajan Tiwari visited Satyavrat Rai's kitchen store, took down the bag from the upper shelf, opened it in front of everyone, and pulled out the AK-47. He checked the barrel for any stuck bullets and removed the magazine, which was full. He tested the trigger and bolt of the AK-47 and declared it to be in perfect condition. "Tomorrow, we will go somewhere across the Indra Canal to test it in the jungle," he said. He also examined the pistol and revolver. Both pistols were of the Munger brand and suitable for use. The oil and lubricants appeared to have been applied correctly, and the sliding slot wasn't stuck at all. The revolver seemed to be licensed and in perfect shape.

Anand said, "Bhai, now the firepower has improved; let's go after having food. Then we will have to look for a new target immediately. Money will be needed everywhere; without money, even relatives won't entertain us. We will have to bring down Shri Prakash at any cost and establish our supremacy in Uttar Pradesh and Bihar. We all did the work, and the businessmen gave the money to him."

Everyone left the house, took a tempo, and arrived at Bhunwar Rai's house in Marutipuram. Bhunwar Rai had already prepared food. Everyone drank alcohol and ate on the roof. At that moment, he had the entire six lakh rupees given by Devendra MLA. After eating, Bhunwar Rai said, "Anand bhaiya, if you had given me this Munger pistol, I could've made a killing. There's a new ATM just outside the Rajajipuram market, and a vehicle comes at 11 am to fill it with cash. A guard arrives with a double-barreled shotgun, and an employee goes to the ATM with the money bag to fill it up and then returns. If the gamble goes right, I'll get twenty-five lakhs, and whatever you ask, I'll give it to you along with returning this pistol."

Anand said, “No, you wait a little. Ajay Shahi has brought many Munger pistols; I will get them for you. You can give the money later; Ajay Shahi does not take Bihari weapons without testing them. This pistol is a reward for our first work; it is not right to give it away. It will remain with us. Rajan bhai will have two weapons, and Bablu will carry two. If you do this work, we will keep you with us and do something bigger.”

After having food, everyone came out together. Bhunvar Rai said, “Come on, bhai, I will drop you all till Indira Nagar.”

Everyone hired a tempo, sat in it, and arrived at Satyavrat Rai's house. There, Anand said, "Bhuvar Bhai, you’ve been living here for a long time; please tell me who the people are from whom we can easily get one crore rupees."

Bhuvar said, "Shri Prakash had many Kundalis done; we also got two Kundalis done for him. One is Lekhraj Dollar, a prominent figure, who will give two crores, and the second is Sushil and Vivek Ladhani, who owns the largest bottling plant for Coca-Cola. We had located Lekhraj Dollar's office but hadn’t reached his house yet, though we had seen both Ladhani's office and house."

Anand responded, "Also, find Lekhraj Dollar's house and get a complete Kundali done. We need money as soon as possible. First, we have to move the entire family from Gorakhpur to Ghaziabad or Delhi. Second, we need to buy a new Zen car immediately. I won't settle for a second-hand car; this time, I’ll purchase a new one and a license plate from Uttar Pradesh, Bihar, Rajasthan, Haryana, and Delhi. Once I secure sufficient funds, I’ll evaluate and test how much influence Shri Prakash has!"

Rajan Tiwari asked, “Anand bhai, what is the need to shift the family now? They are comfortably in Gorakhpur, and they will not agree to move out of Gorakhpur so soon.”

Anand said, “This Shri Prakash is a very dirty and degraded person; you don’t know. I don’t want him to cheat me now with his family. Without a car, we won’t be able to get any work done. Zen is the best car for traveling at a good speed over long distances. At least, whatever vehicles the UP police have, none of them can catch up to a Zen."

Rajan said, "You're right, brother. Police stations have Mahindra jeeps and rickety Peugeots, while circle officers have Gypsies in some areas. These two vehicles won't be able to chase down a Zen. Senior officers have Ambassadors, and they won't be able to drive faster than seventy." Bhunwar Rai replied, "Alright, brother. We'll meet tomorrow. Let's try to find the Dollar man's house."

On November 5, 1997, at ten in the morning, Bhunwar came to Satyavrat's house again and told Anand, "Anand bhai, we have deployed some boys, but Lekhraj, the Dollar man, has gone to Delhi. I'm coming after visiting his office. The office staff said the Sahib will only return in four or five days. We are considering that Bablu bhai and I should do the Ladhani work on our motorcycle."

Anand said, "Okay. You both go."

At the same time, Bablu and Bhunwar rode a Suzuki motorcycle to visit Vivek Ladhani's office and house. Coca-Cola was being unloaded at Ladhani's office. Five or six large vehicles and about fifteen to twenty workers were present there. The supervisor, who was standing nearby, was asked, "Is the boss inside?"

The supervisor replied, "Which boss, the big one or the small one?"

Bhunwar asked, "The small boss who is fair and thin?"

The supervisor said, "Okay, we're talking about Vivek bhaiya. He hasn't come yet; the season is over. Empty bottles are being collected from everywhere and brought here. This work has been ongoing all day, and in November, we'll gather bottles from all the dealers. Then, when the season starts, these vehicles will be filled from the plant. At that time, both the big boss and the small boss meet in the office day and night." After wandering around there, Bablu and Bhuvar returned at two o'clock.

Upon returning, they informed Anand, "Bhai, there was a huge crowd, and he didn't come to the office. We couldn't even find the vehicle number; we'll start heading to his house tomorrow morning." Bhunwar replied, “Bhai, I know him. As soon as he comes out, we’ll check the route, and then you can go. Also, call for your car from Bihar.”

Satyavrat said, “I’ll call him right now. The MLA will send the car.”

Anand said, “How are you going to contact the MLA on the phone? He left us at that moment and was admitted directly to the hospital.”

Satyavrat said, “Anand bhai, don’t worry. I have a lot of influence there. I can call anyone from his family. The MLA will come out of the ICU and talk to him. Now, such a big job has been done for him. If possible, he will send the car himself.”

Anand said, “Yes, he seems to be a capable man. Otherwise, who brings an advance for this kind of work, which no one is willing to do? When the MLA came to meet me on the first day, he brought the entire advance and was giving it to me. I refused it myself.” Satyavrat said, “Just wait five minutes; I’ll call from the PCO near Mazar Tiraha and come back.”

Anand said, “Okay.”

Satyavrat grabbed his motorcycle and left right away. Anand told Bhunwar, “I’ll also go tomorrow; if he comes out, introduce me to him.”

The next day, on November 6, 1997, Bhunwar and Satyavrat left without informing Anand and stayed at Vivek’s house, but Vivek did not come out. When they returned at lunchtime, Anand expressed his displeasure, asking, "If I had invited you, why did you go alone?" Satyavrat replied, “Bhunwar has to go to Gorakhpur tomorrow for some work, so I thought I should also see him. I need to gather information about the route and other details; even today, he didn’t come out of the house.”

Anand said, “Then it’s okay; if Bhunwar has to go for some important work, that’s fine. Otherwise, we’ll take him along tomorrow. We’ll see everything and then come back.”

Rajan Tiwari said, “The car will come at night; the MLA has sent it. In the morning, we will go fully prepared, and if we get a chance, we will take it.” Anand replied, “Okay.” Late at night, at 2:15, the person at the PCO next door knocked on Satyavrat's door and said, "You have a call." Satyavrat immediately went to the PCO, where the driver informed him, "I have brought the car; I am on the main road in Lekhraj Market."

Satyavrat said, "You stay there; I am coming myself."

Satyavrat left from there. Two men were standing there with a Maruti Esteem car,

They gave the keys to Satyavrat. Satyavrat asked, "How are you getting back?" They replied, "We will take the train." Satyavrat inquired, "Do you have money for the fare? Should I cover it?" They responded, "No, we'll manage." Satyavrat drove home and parked the car inside. Everyone woke up only after he went out. They were eager to find out what was happening. Satyavrat explained, "The MLA sent the car, but it's really dirty. Everyone needs to go back to sleep; we'll get up at six in the morning to clean it properly. You don't see such dirty cars on the streets of Lucknow, and if the work isn't done and someone notices it, the car will be recognizable from afar." Everyone went back to sleep. Early in the morning, at seven o'clock, Bhunwar and Satyavrat got up to wash and clean the car thoroughly. By nine in the morning, everyone was ready. On November 7, Satyavrat, Bhunwar, Anand, and Bablu waited outside Ladhani's house with the steam car. Vivek left his house and drove off in the opposite direction. Before Bablu could turn the steam car around and follow him, it was already out of sight. They headed straight to the office, but Vivek hadn't arrived yet, and everyone returned feeling disappointed. The next day, on November 8, Vivek left home around noon. They followed him, but his car didn't slow down or stop along the way. Due to the traffic, they couldn't overtake or halt the car, and by the time they decided to do so, Vivek had already entered the office.

Everyone parked their cars on the road outside the office all day long. When he got hungry in the afternoon, Bhunwar Rai bought some gram, ate it, drank water, and sat in his car. In the evening, as soon as Vivek arrived at the gate with his car at seven o'clock, Bablu parked in front of Vivek's car and started insisting that Vivek get in his car.

Hearing the commotion, some employees came outside, and Anand fired a shot before fleeing the scene.

These individuals arrived at the home of a relative of Bhunvar Rai, located two kilometers from Vivek's office. They retrieved the car cover from the trunk outside and placed it over the car. Anand emerged with his AK-47 and got into the vehicle with Vivek. The others—Satyavrat, Bhunvar Rai, and Rajan—went inside the house, where they drank alcohol and ate. Around 2:30 in the morning, everyone came out, removed the car cover, and fled with the car toward Delhi via Sitapur Road. An hour later, there was a commotion as news broke of another kidnapping, prompting all the officers to arrive at Ladhani's office.

Two shells from a nine mm pistol were found at the scene, and everyone understood a bit. All eyes turned to Shri Prakash. Vivek Ladhani had returned from abroad after completing his MBA, and his father was the largest Coca-Cola dealer and bottler in North India. His automatic bottling plants were located in Lucknow, Faizabad, and several other cities in the state. Once again, pressure was bound to mount on the police. Again, the same instructions came through on the wireless: all roads were to be closed, checks were to be performed, and the vehicle was dark-colored, with its number unknown. According to the wireless report, the entire city had been sealed. However, when Anand left for Delhi at 2 a.m. in a steam car with Vivek Ladhani, the vehicle was neither stopped nor checked anywhere. Anand dropped off Satyavrat and Bhunwar at the Ghaziabad border before taking Vivek to the newly built flat, D-106, in Dilshad Garden, Delhi. Arvind Singh Chauhan and Manish were already renting a place there for work. Vivek Ladhani was taken to a room there. After a few days, Ajay Shahi, the son of JE Vijay Narayan Shahi from Hydel and an old friend of Anand, was called from Gorakhpur. Anand would come there with an AK-47 in a duffel bag and talk to Vivek. He would jot down phone numbers and then call Vivek Ladhani from a distant PCO family.

The deal was finalized for Rs. 70 lakhs. All the phones in Vivek Ladhani's house were tapped, confirming that Vivek had been taken to Delhi. Vivek's father was very suspicious of him, so he was not cooperating much with the police. The police found the Delhi numbers from his house's telephone records and noted down his address. All the numbers turned out to be from different PCOs located in the market, about two kilometers from Dilshad Garden.

Vivek's father sent seventy lakh rupees to the designated location. A few days later, Anand Pandey, Bablu, Rajan Tiwari, and Manish picked up Ladhani from there at 11 pm and left him near the railway station. Vivek Ladhani's father was informed over the phone that his son had been left safely near the station. He was also given some money, and he would call you so you could come and pick him up. The first thing Anand Pandey did was buy a flat in Delhi with that money and invited his entire family from Gorakhpur to stay there.

The next day, he purchased a Zen car through a Sardar broker and registered it in the name of Rajeshwar Pradhan. In addition, he bought a Bullet in the name of Arvind. He also gave ten thousand rupees each to Satyavrat and Bhunwar, even though they were asking for twenty thousand rupees apiece. Anand said, "You all should go back to Lucknow and rest for a few days. Right now, there's a lot of pressure from the police, so let me make the family a little more settled. We need to arrange for cooking supplies, rations, and clothes for everyone. Only after that will we plan for the next target. Once everything is settled here, we'll come to Lucknow in a week or two, and from there, everyone will head to Gorakhpur." Shahi Arvind Singh Chauhan, Bablu Tiwari, Manish, Satyavrat Rai, and Bhunwar all left for Lucknow in different vehicles.

Ladhani arrived home. The police faced a lot of criticism in the newspapers. The SSP of Lucknow asked the entire team to meet with Ladhani and try to extract some information from him that would reveal the truth. The police suspected that this kidnapping was also orchestrated by Shri Prakash Shukla. The numbers that contacted Vivek Ladhani's father during the kidnapping were traced, revealing that two of those numbers were mobile numbers registered in Delhi. Satyendra Veer Singh and Tewatia were residents of Ghaziabad.

They had strong connections in Delhi and were well-informed about the city.

The SSP said, "The entire team should go to Delhi and camp there and at least find out the place where Vivek Ladhani stayed and all the people involved in the kidnapping."

All the teams reached Delhi. Inspector PP Singh, who was acquainted with Satyendra Veer Singh, was assigned to a police station there. He provided significant assistance, and the PCOs from which the calls were made were identified. The PCO owners were spoken to separately, and efforts were made to inquire about the appearance of the caller. How many people visited, and what language did they speak? After three to four days, with the help of the PCO owner, the house in Dilshad Garden where Vivek Ladhani was held was discovered. Neighbors revealed that this place had been locked for a few days, but occasionally a boy from Zen would arrive in the evening. Sometimes he would stay overnight, while other times he would leave immediately. Occasionally, three people would come to meet him.

All the team members sat together and speculated that this place might be used solely as a meeting spot. Do Shri Prakash and Anand Pandey live elsewhere? Meanwhile, after considerable effort, the little conversation I had with Vivek Ladhani led to the conclusion that none of the individuals who kidnapped Vivek and kept him in a flat in Delhi's Dilshad Garden for an extended period resembled Shri Prakash. Vivek was shown an AK-47, a 9mm pistol, and other weapons, and whatever he identified was confirmed to indicate that those individuals must have had an AK-47, a .45 pistol, and a revolver. Someone who knew PP Singh informed the nearby residents that as soon as any person arrived at this flat, they would notify them. Satyendravir Singh, Tewatia, Avinash Mishra, and Rajesh Pandey were active in three to four vehicles on both roads leading out of that colony every day since morning. On December 14, 1997, around 11 o'clock, Satyendra Veer Singh received a message on his mobile that a boy from Zen had arrived at the flat alone. He provided Zen's number, color, and location, prompting everyone to be alerted. It was 11 a.m. There was a lot of commotion in the colony, and everyone communicated via mobile phones, deciding that it wasn't right to harass him in the neighborhood. There are three exits from the colony, and separate teams should be deployed at all three. They needed to chase him and intercept him wherever it was slightly quiet and bring him down. Satyendra Veer Singh and Tewatia were in one team with their car, while Rajesh Pandey, Parashar, and a new sub-inspector formed the second team. After a while, the person stationed near the flat informed that the boy from Zen had arrived and was starting his car to leave.

After merging onto the main road, he turned the car from the lane heading towards Delhi to the one leading towards Ghaziabad. Pandey was promptly informed that the car had gone in that direction. At the same time, a car approached from the opposite direction, and Rajesh Pandey began to pursue it. The lone driver of the car was driving at a slow speed while talking on a mobile phone. After traveling about a kilometer, in a somewhat deserted area, the Zen was overtaken, and the car was halted. Before the driver could react, the door was opened, and he was pulled out. As soon as he was made to sit in the car, his pistol was seized and tossed into the back of the Tata Sumo. The car was searched, but nothing was found inside it.

Satyendra Veer Singh was informed that he had been located, but this is not Shri Prakash. It is likely he is Anand Pandey, though he is using a different name. Shortly after, all the teams arrived, and he was questioned in the car. He stated that he was Anand Pandey and that he had a quarrel with Shri Prakash Shukla, and they had been separated for a long time. The interrogation took place in the evening. He did not provide any further information during the questioning. When the questioning turned a bit stricter in the car, he confessed to kidnapping Vivek Ladhani. He was asked about the AK-47 and each time, he provided different locations where it was supposedly kept. He was also questioned about the money received from the kidnapping. He responded, "I gave the kidnapping money to Satyavrat. He took it to Lucknow, from which he took out only ten lakhs, with which he bought a small house and a Zen car."

His words were not believable. The clock was not going to stop! It was nine o'clock by then, and after being questioned more strictly, he said,

"Come, I will take you to the place where I have kept the AK 47. After taking him about twenty kilometers ahead, Narula took him to a small hut at the turn and pointed out, "If you knock on the door of the house in front, a woman will come out. There is a bag under the plank in front, and an AK 47 is in it." Tewatia and Satyendra Veer Singh went there and found the bag under the plank. They brought it back, searched it, and found an AK 47 and a magazine, and cartridges tied in a polythene bag. In the hope that perhaps the ransom money is also kept in this house, the entire house was searched but no money was found. After searching the room, as soon as they came to the car, they opened the door of the Tata Sumo and kept asking him where the money was kept, tell me, otherwise you will be killed. Suddenly Anand Pandey jumped from the seat with all his might and tried to run away. Making a path between Tewatia and Satyendra Veer Singh. It was pitch dark, and there was a fear that if he went ten steps away, then the STF might lose his sight, and there would be a big problem.

Rajesh Pandey and Parashar jumped in pursuit of him. While running, he stumbled over something and fell. Everyone tried to catch him, but in the darkness, he attempted to grab the weapons. At the same moment, as he tried to run again, he was shot. When he was shot, Anand collapsed. In the dark, it was unclear where the bullet had struck. Immediately after the shooting, the Delhi Police Control Room was notified.

The Delhi Police also arrived. Afterward, when he was shaken and examined, he was found dead. An AK-47 and a pistol were recovered from him. The Delhi Police gathered all the information and searched Dilshad Garden. Some diaries and papers belonging to the Delhi Police were found there. With their help, the police located Anand Pandey's house, where his family lived. Later, some ransom money was recovered from that location. Anand's family members were brought in, and he was identified. The next day, the Lucknow police felt some relief after reading this information in the newspapers, but still, all the newspapers reported that Shri Prakash had not been caught. When the Delhi police circulated the serial number from the AK-47 in the morning, and that number appeared in Delhi newspapers, CBI DGP Loknath Behera immediately came to the police station and began gathering information about Anand Pandey and his gang.

Rajesh Pandey asked Shri Behera, "Sir, is he wanted in any CBI case?"

"Behera ji said, no, the AK-47 recovered from him is one of the weapons dropped from a foreign plane in Purulia. I am the one investigating the incident of weapon drops from the plane in Purulia." It is crucial to know how this weapon from the Purulia drop ended up with him. The entire team returned to Lucknow that evening with information collected by the Delhi Police throughout the day. The next day, the whole team met again and felt satisfied that Shri Prakash's most trusted criminal had been killed, but everyone was surprised to learn that after the Janpath incident, Anand and Shri Prakash had begun to have differences. When Anand Pandey found out in Viratnagar that Shri Prakash had developed ill intentions toward his sister, Anand Pandey completely distanced himself from Shri Prakash and formed his own gang.

Murders were committed in Bihar to enhance the gang's firepower. The gang obtained an AK-47 and a pistol, then kidnapped Vivek Ladhani, a prominent businessman from Lucknow, and secured the ransom money. However, the police had no inkling that Anand had separated from Shri Prakash and formed his own gang.

This was a very thought-provoking point: everyone was unaware of such a significant incident within the gang. All the officers had their own sources but still could not uncover the truth. It was widely believed that the old sources of information now needed to be renewed. The informants were no longer effective enough to reveal such serious matters within the gang. Informants who used to make bold claims were even discussed by name, as they suggested they had personal connections with the gang and may have even shared meals with them several times. It was decided that everyone should find new sources and demonstrate more seriousness in gathering information.

WHITE AMBASSADOR

Satyendra Veer Singh and Rajesh Pandey had offices in the same building in Kaiserbagh. They were sitting together, discussing the processions in old Lucknow. Tension increases significantly during the Muharram procession in the old city, requiring a large police presence. This discussion was ongoing when suddenly the wireless set on the table to the left of Satyendra Veer Singh's chair in the SP City office began receiving reports of indiscriminate firing on people sitting in an Ambassador car with a red beacon near the Shiv Narayan Petrol Pump in the Thana Cantt area. Upon hearing this information, Rajesh Pandey shouted, "Sir, let's go! Has that bastard killed someone again? There's a red beacon on the car—some big shot has been killed!" Both of them were traveling in the same car to reach the Shiv Narayan Petrol Pump via Hazratganj. Just before Loreto Convent, many officers' cars were leaving Raj Bhavan Colony, suggesting that the incident had not occurred there. They stopped the car and asked some policemen standing nearby.

"Has any incident taken place?" The reply was, "Senior IPS officer CD Kanth has committed suicide by shooting himself with his own revolver in his house. All the officers are gathered there. Some have arrived, and some are leaving."

On hearing this, the driver was asked to reach the spot quickly. The intersection of Shiv Narayan Petrol Pump came at a distance of five minutes. An Ambassador car was parked on the road going from Lucknow to Kanpur and Allahabad at the turn of Shiv Narayan Petrol Pump intersection, and a large amount of blood was coming out from under the Ambassador car and flowing down the slope towards the drain on the side of the railway line. The place where the car was parked was at a very high altitude. After crossing the entire road, there is a small drain between the track and the railway gate, in which blood is flowing.

As soon as police crossed the railway crossing and saw a red light on a white Ambassador car and a large amount of blood flowing from under the Ambassador car, crossing the entire road and coming out on the other side, it did not take long for the police to understand that Shri Prakash had really done something big. On the front of the car, it was written on a red board "Vice President, Uttar Pradesh Co-operative Bank". On going closer, I saw that sitting next to the driver was a gunner in uniform, and sitting on the back seat were two strong men wearing white kurta pajamas, whose faces were now unrecognizable. A large amount of blood was flowing from the head and face and flowing down in the car.

The incident seemed to have taken place twenty-twenty-five minutes ago. A large crowd was gathering. The place where CD Kanth Sahab committed suicide was not very far from his residence, and many vehicles of police officers were either going towards his residence or coming out. In a short while, it was known that the deceased was Vice President of Uttar Pradesh Cooperative Bank Upendra Vikram Singh, and his driver and gunner. The other person sitting with Upendra Vikram Singh was a big contractor from Allahabad whose name people were saying was Shukla.

The policemen in the vehicles of SP City and Rajesh Pandey were collecting shells and bringing them back to display. The shells discovered at the crime scene indicated that an AK-47, a .45 caliber pistol, and a 9 mm pistol were used in the murder. The presence of the .45 caliber pistol provided a clear indication.

Satyendra Veer asked Rajesh Pandey, “Any doubt?”

Rajesh Pandey said, “No doubt.”

There were two or three beetle leaf and cigarette shops at the corner of Shiv Narayan Petrol Pump and a few tea shops across the crossing. After enquiring with the shopkeepers separately, we got to know that a white Maruti car was already parked right at the corner, facing the railway gate. As soon as this Ambassador car and the Tata Sumo following it turned towards the Allahabad Kanpur road, their speed slowed down considerably. When the people sitting in the

Maruti saw the car coming down in front of Somnath gate, two people got out of the car. When the Ambassador slowed down considerably and turned to its left, the person sitting in the driving seat put his hands in the open windows of the Maruti and took out an AK 47, and the person sitting right behind him took out two pistols. The person with the AK-47 fired indiscriminately; the car stopped at its place. As soon as the car stopped, the person with the pistol fired at the two people sitting in the back, and the person with the AK 47 broke the broken glass further, inserted the AK 47 inside, and shot the driver and the gunner in the head. Meanwhile, the person firing from the back seat shot the two people at close range on their heads. There were four to five people sitting in the Tata Sumo, which was following the Ambassador, who was also seen carrying guns, but as soon as the person with the AK 47 ran towards the Tata Sumo with the AK, the Tata Sumo turned sharply and ran back towards Loreto crossing via Katai bridge. While these two people were firing at the people sitting in the car, the person sitting in the back seat of the Maruti came and sat on the driving seat and both of them sat comfortably in the Maruti and went towards Sultanpur Road.

In a short while, a crowd gathered there. A large number of police officers and journalists reached there. These four were murdered in a very gruesome manner. Eyewitnesses said that after first hitting them with AK 47, the four persons in the car went close and shot two bullets each on their faces. The face was so disfigured that the eyes, ears, and nose could not be seen. The forensic team was asked which bore weapon could have caused such serious wounds, then they told that if the bullets had been fired from a distance, then a 315-bore rifle would have blown off such a large part of the face, but the bullets were fired from close range. From the 0.45 cartridges found at the spot, it appeared that there is no doubt that the bullets were fired from close range on the 0.45 face, due to which the entire face was blown off. The members of the forensic team also said that point four five bore is an American weapon, and it is said that this small weapon was used in the British era for hunting animals. Upendra Vikram Singh's family members also reached there. All the bodies were taken out of the Ambassador and sent for postmortem.

Upendra Vikram's brother and other family members went to register a case in Lucknow's Cantt police station. While registering the case, these people had also named some people citing old family rivalry. As usual, then a checking campaign was carried out in the whole city. Information was received about the arrival of miscreants at the big government dairy farm near Gosainganj, but despite all efforts, nothing could be found. The next day, in the core team meeting, the SSP said, "Despite having the information that Shri Prakash has come to the city, we could not stop this incident!"

From Upendra Vikram Singh's daily routine, it seemed that he stayed in the guest house located in the Cooperative Bank building, next to the District Magistrate's residence in Lucknow, or near the stadium in front of the Hindi Institute. There was only one route for vehicle movement, which allowed monitoring of Upendra Vikram Singh's activities. Everyone was now aware of the ongoing situation regarding Shri Prakash being repeatedly spotted near the stadium in the morning and in front of Trans-Gomti in the evening. Upendra Singh would often visit a close friend's house in Trans-Gomti in the morning, and on some occasions, he would take his friend along for a morning walk in the stadium as well. Perhaps for this reason, Shri Prakash would go to these areas early in the morning to wait for his target.

After this serious incident, when the Lucknow Police faced criticism and Lucknow's security was ridiculed in several evening newspapers published on the same evening, the pressure on the Lucknow Police intensified once again. It seemed that Shri Prakash and his gang were becoming more powerful than the police and the government. This raised concerns everywhere. It was decided that, for the time being, barriers should be set up on all roads going in and out of Lucknow, and vehicles entering would be checked 24 hours a day. This time, it was also ordered that if young men were seen in vehicles with red and blue lights, they should be checked as well. If any VIP or police officer was in those vehicles, they should be informed why this checking is necessary, and there is no reason to take offense. After the incident, Shri Prakash returned to Gorakhpur.

Anuj and Sudhir told Shri Prakash, "Mokama is safer. The police are harassing us in Gorakhpur; why don't we go to Mokama and stay there? After all, a policeman has been killed again, so the police will be more aggressive." Shri Prakash replied, "It's not a good idea to go to Mokama right away. I don't know what's going through Dada's mind. Since I killed those three people in Dada's house, I've noticed a slight change in Dada's behavior. Who's going to check on us or raid our homes in Gorakhpur? We should only go there."

One day, Pawan Pandey called from Gorakhpur, saying, "Ashok Bhai, the police have raided both our office and home in Faizabad. If you plan to come here, please let us know in advance, and we will make arrangements elsewhere."

Shri Prakash said, "Right now, we don't have any plans to go there; all your work is done. You have secured all the contracts and liquor business in Faizabad and Sultanpur. There are no obstacles in the way. If you ever need money, just let me know, and I'll send it." Pawan Pandey replied, "Ashok Bhai, I've been to Lucknow two or three times, but each time the police stopped the vehicle and checked it. There's a lot of strictness in Lucknow right now. Until things cool down, it's not worth coming here." Shri Prakash responded, "We know everything, Pawan bhai; don't worry. I'll come when I need to."

Sudhir, sitting nearby, said, "Bhai, don't be stubborn like this. Let's stay in Nepal for a few days. Pawan bhai is right; we will come back when the situation calms down."

Shri Prakash said, "Absolutely not; this time, if any policeman stops the vehicle by putting up a barrier, I will shoot all the bullets of AK 47 in his head. After that, you will see that the police will remove all its barriers, and no matter how hard these officers try, the police will never stop the vehicle at the barrier."

After a while, he called Manju in Kanpur and said to her, "Take any train from Kanpur to Gorakhpur. I'm giving you the number of a PCO. When you get to the PCO, just tell whoever you meet your name, the train number, and which train you're on. I will pick you up at Gorakhpur station."

Manju must have said something from there, prompting Shri Prakash to lash out at her and say, "I don't need the coach number or berth number. We'll find you at the station, and the person who comes to pick you up will bring you to me; don't worry about that." After the call ended, Sudhir remarked again, "Bhai, it's possible that the police reached Manju, and then they'll track us down through her."

Shri Prakash said, "You know dogs never enter the lion's den; no policeman will come here. We know all the ways; I will tell everything to the person who goes to take Manju." Sudhir asked again, "What is the need to call Manju here? Is there a shortage of girls here? Should I call those Muhaddipur girls here!"

Shri Prakash growled, "Don't act too smart, don't you know, Inspector Cantt. has already called the Muhaddipur girl along with her father and interrogated them. When you don't know the whole story, then why do you take it lightly? I will tell you why I am calling Manju here."

One day, Shri Prakash said to Sudhir and Anuj, "Surajbhan Dada is in trouble; a minister from Bihar has sent him to jail. This task is significant, but if we succeed, Bihar will also be ours. No one has the audacity to refuse any work in Bihar. Uttar Pradesh is nearly under our control. We just need to handle Harishankar Tiwari a bit more; if he doesn't agree, I'll set up a copper and brass bullet store in his head as well. However, before meeting with Surajbhan Dada, it's crucial to secure a lot of money because the task he mentioned is somewhat risky. The entire government will be on our tails there, but if the job is completed, there won't be any issues."

Anuj said, "Get the remaining money from Moolraj Arora, then we will go to Mokama."

Shri Prakash said, "That bastard starts crying and the police have got all his phones disconnected." Sudhir said again, "Bhai, he had noted down the names of six or seven people from Lucknow. If they're caught, we could easily get ten or twenty crores. Then, everyone can head to Thailand for a few days. We can have fun there and then return; by then, the police will also have cooled down."

Shri Prakash said, "You are absolutely right. I will get the diary now. He wrote down the numbers, but it's not right to speak first; we should first examine their kundali. If they each contribute fifty lakh rupees like this, then we won't need to catch them. After completing Surajbhan Dada's work, we'll leave for Nepal from there, and then we'll return after traveling around Thailand for a bit." days."

Shri Prakash took out his diary and called three or four boys in Lucknow. One boy was informed about Sanjay Seth, another about Sarna Marble, another about Ladhani Coca-Cola, another about the Raymond showroom in Hazratganj, and another about Lucknow's top heart specialist, Dr. Mishra. Everyone was directed to gather the complete Kundali. First, determine their address; next, find out when they leave home, where they go, what time they return, how many people live in the house, how many vehicles are there, and which schools the children attend. Record the numbers of all the cars, the driver's name, and a description of their appearance. No detail should be omitted in the kundalini, and if there is any Rahu Ketu in the kundalini, then obtain their kundalini.

Sudhir said, "Bhai, tell the boys right away to gather information about the gunner and the security guards too. They are new kids; who knows what they might think?"

Shri Prakash told Sudhir, "Now, these boys are no longer just boys. He has more brains than both of us; he will uncover even those things that haven't been asked. After sharing the horoscope, these guys don't want anything less than ten thousand dollars." Sudhir asked, "No one has ever received a better horoscope than Suresh; why didn't you tell him?"

Shri Prakash said, "Now I won't get the horoscope read by Suresh; his greed has increased. Secondly, once, while getting Moolraj's horoscope done, he made too much noise. Moolraj became suspicious of him. He had been doing this continuously for four or five days. When Moolraj informed the police, they caught him and took him to the Sultanpur police station. Fortunately, all the paperwork for his car was in order. He had no luggage or weapons, and his university ID was also valid. Therefore, the police thought he must have been hanging around there for many days because of some girl from the apartment. Suresh is very clever; he even told me that a girl from this apartment goes to university, and he keeps standing here because of her."

Sudhir said, "This is a good job; if we find any one of them, our trip to Singapore will be confirmed."

Shri Prakash told the boys, "As soon as the kundali is complete and the target goes inside the house, tell us the complete kundali immediately." The first number was the number of Raymond showroom owner; the boy had told the complete Kundali.

Shri Prakash asked how many Rahu and Ketu there were. The boy replied, "Bhaiya, in the Hazratganj showroom, two people sit in chairs outside the door. One has a double-barrel gun, and the other has a single-barrel gun." Shri Prakash then asked, "Who is sitting in the car?"

The boy said, "While coming, his father sits in the car. Both come together but the father goes back during the day itself. After closing the shop, Lala comes alone with the servant, and the servant sits on the front seat with a bunch of shop keys in a black leather bag, and Lala sits behind."

After listening to the entire story, Shri Prakash Shukla called Lala. Shri Prakash called him at night and said, "Lala, I have called you twice. Didn't you see how Vivek Srivastava and Virendra Shahi were killed? Today, I would have killed you, but I thought that maybe you will come to your senses and you will deliver the money. Today the minister's family had come to your shop to buy clothes, with all the pomp and show. Today you left in a white Tata Safari at quarter to eleven in the morning. Your father was sitting behind you, wearing a white shirt and black pants, and you were wearing a pink checked shirt and black pants. Your old driver was wearing blue pants and a shirt. You arrived at Mehrotra's paan shop near the stadium in the morning. There you met two more men, one of whom was a short and fat man. He took you alone towards the State Bank and was talking to you about something; after that, you had made him buy paan. When you were talking to him alone, I passed by you. For a moment, I felt like shooting four bullets in your head; then, I thought I would talk to you for the last time today. If you come to your senses, then it is fine; otherwise, any day, I will fill your head with copper, and then your family will give you double the money. During the day when the minister's family had come for shopping when you had come to drop them outside, and after they had left, you were climbing the stairs of the shop; even then, I could have killed you. In the afternoon, you also went to Aminabad Bhasin's shop. After leaving the shop and returning from there, three people also ate Prakash's kulfi at Prakash Kulfi Wala's shop. I could have easily killed you there and escaped in the crowd; no one would have even known. Just now, when you got out of the car and your servant gave you the black bag containing the keys, no one was there then. If I wanted to kill you, you would not have even uttered a word. The driver had taken the car and gone to park it in the garage; even the family members would have come to know about it after hours. People would have just noticed that your lifeless body lying face down in front of your own house."

Lala's face turned pale. Lala started pleading calling him bhaiya, Ashok bhaiya, business is going very slow. I don't even have fifty lakhs in my bank account, from where will I give it. Shri Prakash said, "Where will you get it from? You know that. I am telling you only because today I was following you the whole day to kill you. You must have guessed that if I wanted, I could have killed you today very easily." Shri Prakash said that I will call you again tomorrow morning. There is only the whole night, you think comfortably; you will have to pay the money; if you don't pay, then after my death, your wife and children will give it." Lala's face turned pale; as soon as the phone was disconnected, his wife asked, "What's the matter? Who was it?" Lala said, "It was the same Ashok Singh who killed Virendra Shahi Vivek Srivastava and kidnapped Mulraj Arora and extorted money from him. His real name is Shri Prakash Shukla." Lala's wife became very serious on hearing the name Shri Prakash Shukla and said, "He is a big goon; his name has been appearing in the newspaper for a long time. He was the one who shot the police inspector in Janpath." Lala said, "Yes."

Lala's wife asked, "What is he asking for?"

Lala said, "He is asking for fifty lakh rupees."

The wife asked, "For what?"

Lala said, "Without any reason, the goon is asking for tax. Where will I get so much money? He has asked me to call again tomorrow morning. He was around me from when I left my house to when I returned home. He has told me every small thing one by one, who had come to meet me? What color clothes was I wearing? I had left the shop for a while; I had gone to Bhasin Bhai's shop to settle some old accounts with him, and he was also telling me about that place. As he is saying, I had no idea that someone was following me all day, and his statement is absolutely correct. He can kill me anytime, very easily. My mind is not working as to what should I do? The amount is very big. If I give it to one person, ten more will come up, I will keep giving it to whom. If I don't pay, he will kill me." Lala's wife said, "Talk to Mulraj bhai; he will tell me a way." Lala immediately called Mulraj Arora. After talking for a while, Lala hung up. His wife asked, "Did you find a way out?" Lala said, "Moolraj is saying that when he was kidnapped, he too got himself released by giving a little money and promised to send the rest of the money soon, but he has not been able to send the money. Ashok Singh is also harassing him repeatedly for money. Moolraj says that he is upset and is going out of Lucknow for a few days. He also said that he was a very dangerous man. The place where he had kept Moolraj is some place in Bihar.

His gang possesses various types of guns. There, he displayed an AK-47 for the first time, of which he has not just one, but three or four. Moolraj further explained that there is no option other than paying money to save his life.

Lala's wife said, "Then tell the police, how will they be able to kill if the police are with them?" Lala replied, "Moolraj was explaining what the police did. He was taken from his office in Hazratganj in broad daylight and driven to Bihar. Even if the police were seen anywhere along the way, they were seen saluting him. It seems he has connections in the police from top to bottom. I also tried for three or four days, hoping the police would show up, and both the money and my life could be saved, but no one came, and I had to pay the money. Lala's wife said, "It doesn't seem right to give money without a reason. You should go and talk to the SSP tomorrow." Lala said, "You're not understanding. The way he followed me today—I was eating kulfi at Prakash Kulfi Wala's place, and he was standing there too. And yes, he even told me which school and which class both our children are in." Lala's wife exclaimed, "Oh my God! Then it's not right to take risks. Tomorrow, discuss giving a little less or more; how can so much money be given all at once?" Lala replied, okay.

It was almost nine o'clock the next day, and Lala's breath was coming in fast and slow. Lala called his wife and said, "I don't have the courage to answer his call. He will definitely call, so you pick up the phone and tell him that I've gone to take a bath. If he pushes the matter further, tell him we are really troubled and have no money. If it gets settled, then give me a signal, and I will come and talk on the phone."

He was explaining this to his wife when the phone rang. Lala's wife immediately answered, but it was a call from Lala's younger brother. Lala stood behind, listening. Both he and his wife felt relieved that it wasn't his call. A sense of relief spread through them. The phone rang again as soon as the call ended, and a voice came from the other end.

"I am Ashok Singh. Where is Lala?"

The wife said, "He has gone to take a bath." Then a voice came from the other side asking how long ago he had gone to take a bath. Lala's wife replied, "He was waiting for someone's call; he just went to bathe. I couldn't hear who is speaking, but I will let you know when he returns."

A voice came from the other side "Who are you?"

Lala's wife said, "I am his wife."

She said, "Tell them that Ashok Singh called and he shouldn't have left the phone and gone when the time was mentioned. I will call in a little while." Lala's wife said, "Okay, Bhaiya, I understand; maybe he was waiting for your call. Bhaiya, please have some mercy on us; our children are still very young."

Shri Prakash said, "Why should I show you mercy? You attended a birthday party the day before yesterday, carrying at least three kilos of gold and diamonds. You looted all of Lucknow; what am I even supposed to say to you now? I'll call you in half an hour. By the way, what's your name?"

Lala's wife said, "My name is Bhagyashri."

Shri Prakash said, "If your height were a little more, there wouldn't be a more beautiful woman than you in Lucknow; your voice is very nice."

Upon hearing this, Lala's wife dropped the phone. Lala, standing behind her, grew nervous and quickly picked up the phone, placed it back in the cradle. Lala's wife was drenched in sweat. Lala asked, "What happened? Did you settle for anything?"

The wife said, "He seems to be a very dangerous man. If you talk, you'll have to pay. He knows everything about everyone; he mentioned the birthday party at Atul Agarwal's place the day before yesterday."

Shri Prakash called again after half an hour; this time, Lala answered the phone.

Shri Prakash said, "Lala ji, what have you decided? Do you want to live or die? I don't have time, and you must tell me today itself." Lala got nervous and replied, "I won't be able to arrange as much as you are asking for, bhaiya. I can give you a small amount if you insist."

Shri Prakash said, "How much can you give?"

Lala said, "I can give you five lakh rupees."

On hearing this, Shri Prakash became terribly angry and said, "You motherfucker baniya....Do you think I am a beggar, you baniya dog? Now, will you give the full fifty lakhs, or will you will be liberated from your body, your family members will perform last rites in the buffalo pond tomorrow ?" After saying this, Shri Prakash disconnected the phone; Lala's wife was standing nearby, and she asked, "What did he say?"

Lala said, "As soon as he heard five lakhs, he started abusing."

Lala's wife said, "Give him what he's asking for. Nothing is more important than life; we can earn money again."

Lala said, "Where are we going to get so much cash from? Income tax officials are already making rounds every day, we will have to answer to so many people?"

Lala's wife said, "Give me the money or the entire family will be ruined."

Lala said, "It was different back then when only Bhasin and I were in Hazratganj. These three new showrooms have opened; it will take ten years to earn that much money again." His wife said, "Tell him that I will pay the full amount, but please get their showrooms closed."

Lala said, "What nonsense are you talking about? If this matter ever comes to light, you'll go to jail, and I'll go to jail too. If the call comes again, I'll talk about ten instead of five. For the rest, I'll say that I will pay ten every three months and complete fifty in a year."

Lala's wife said, "You're thinking the right way." The husband and wife were chatting when the phone rang. Lala answered the phone, and a voice came from the other end.

"You bastard baniya... this means you've decided that you don't want to live in this world," Shri Prakash shouted from other side.

Lala pleaded, "Bhaiya, don't do such injustice. My children are very young. Until a year ago, our situation was very good. There were only two clothing stores in the entire market. These three new showrooms have opened up, slowing our business."

Shri Prakash said, “Who are these three?”

Lala counted the names of all three in one breath and mentioned that two of them are Sindhis and one is a Baniya. Shri Prakash said, “The Sindhi is the one who is small and fair. The one who has opened only a saree showroom speaks very sweetly.”

Lala said yes.

Shri Prakash said, “Only if you provide the full amount will you be the one to rule in Hazratganj. When you help me so much, it will be my duty to make you shine in the market.”

Lala said, “Yes bhaiya”.

Shri Prakash said, “If you send the entire money tomorrow, then these three shops will be closed in a week.” Lala said- “Oh no, Bhaiya, don’t do this. Though all three are big bastards, but they have children too, but I will pay you in full in a year.”

Shri Prakash said, “What did you say? A year? You’re crazy! I need the money tomorrow.”

Lala said, “For such a large amount, Bhaiya, if you don’t give me some time, where will I get it? I know I have to pay the money, and if I don’t, you could kill me whenever you want.”

Shri Prakash said, “How much money can you give me tomorrow?”

Lala said, “Bhaiya, tomorrow I will send you ten lakhs. For the rest, I will pay in three-month installments. Exactly three months later, I will give you ten more and send every penny I owe."

Shri Prakash said, “Okay, have ten lakh rupees ready on the counter tomorrow. Yes, remember not to be clever at all. It shouldn't happen that you see policemen in plain clothes at the shop. My guy will go to collect the money, and if he even gets a scratch, I won’t kill you alone; first, I’ll have both your children killed, then your wife, and finally, I will kill you. Do you understand or not?”

Lala said, “Yes bhaiya, I understood.”

The next day, Nipendra Pandey, a counselor from Hazratganj, arrived outside the Raymond showroom to collect the money. He noticed many people standing around who recognized him. Nipendra left immediately. He then went to the Hanuman temple in Hazratganj, parked his motorcycle, and took darshan of Hanuman ji. Afterward, he walked on foot, entered the front gate of the coffee house, and called a boy from the PCO, instructing him to go to the Hanuman temple.

He called him to the temple. He waited for him, standing by the motorcycle near the Hanuman temple, and kept talking to the people he met. After a while, the boy arrived.

Taking the boy alone, he said in front of Khadi Ashram, "Go straight to Raymond's showroom. Lala is sitting there in a blue shirt. When he is completely alone, tell him softly that Ashok Singh sent you. He will give you a bag. Take the bag and come straight to me. It will only take three to four minutes to complete the work. Finish the work quickly."

The boy replied, "Yes, brother, I'll do it right away."

The boy went straight inside and came out after two minutes with Raymond's plastic bag. Nipendra quickly took the bag. He handed the boy a hundred rupees, immediately wrapped the plastic bag from Raymond, placed it in the motorcycle trunk, and headed straight home. That night, Nipendra received another call from Shri Prakash.

Shri Prakash asked, "What happened? Did the bastard give the money?"

Nipendra replied, "Yes, bhaiya, I have got the money."

Shri Prakash asked, is the money complete or not?"

Nipendra replied, "Bhaiya, the money is complete, its ten lakhs."

Shri Prakash said, "Nipendra bhaiya, you take out one lakh rupees from this. Tomorrow, someone will come to you; give the rest to him, and he will deliver it to us." Nipendra was very happy. He had got one lakh rupees with little effort; he immediately said, "Bhaiya, if you have any other work for me, please let me know."

Shri Prakash said, "Yes, Nipendra bhai, I will definitely tell you."

After this, Shri Prakash called the Kundali boy Rakesh Mani and said, "You had done a very good Kundali of Lala. You had not made any mistake; all the arrows hit the target, and the work was done; tell me, what do you want? What should I get for you?"

Rakesh Mani said, "Bhaiya, please get me a weapon."

Shri Prakash said, "Are you crazy? If I get you a weapon, will you ever be able to do kundali in your life? If the person whose Kundali is to be made gets suspicious about you or the police catches you during checking, they will also attach two kilos of marijuana along with the pistol and implicate you in false case. All your studies will be wasted, and even your family members will abuse you a lot. You study, do a good kundali, and then I will give you a job. For now, go to the shop of Calcutta & Style in Hazratganj; its owner is Sindhi. Just tell him what Ashok Singh has sent you. He will give you ten thousand rupees; it is winter, so buy warm clothes." Rakesh Mani said, "Yes, Bhaiya." Rakesh Mani could not sleep the whole night after hearing about ten thousand rupees. As soon as it was eleven in the morning, he reached Hazratganj, went to the shop owner, and told him only this much that Ashok Singh had sent him. The shop owner took out ten thousand rupees wrapped in a newspaper from the drawer and gave it to the boy. When Shri Prakash was talking to Rakesh Mani, Sudhir Tripathi was listening to the entire conversation. After the conversation was over, Sudhir said, "Bhai, don't spoil the mind of these guys. You gave ten thousand rupees for a work worth two thousand rupees."

Shri Prakash immediately said, "Look, Sureshva had got it in his mind that no one does the work of making horoscopes better than him. Rakesh had extracted such information in every minute that when I was talking to Lala and telling him the story of the day, Lala was shocked. He started gasping for breath on the phone itself. Lala is a very scoundrel, he handed over the phone to his wife. Lala's wife was also stunned to hear the horoscope that Rakesh Mani had made for

Lala's children. She did not even utter a word; Lala immediately gave the money. Now Lala will give the entire money in a year. Even if there is an emergency, we will ask for money from him." Shri Prakash again said, "Sudhir, the question is not about one Lala. He is a big businessman in the Hazratganj market. Hazratganj and Aminabad are the only two areas of big businessmen in Lucknow. Aminabad has already come under control by doing the work of Ghanshyam Pathak. Hazratganj also has to be taken over. All the money these traders give here and there has to be stopped. We will take all the money and then we will dominate the whole of Lucknow. Do you understand the meaning of domination over Lucknow?"

Sudhir said, "I did not understand."

Shri Prakash said, "Look, these traders from the entire city give whatever amounts they ask for to the councilors in their areas, their MLAs, members of the trade board, leaders, and the police at the police station. These thieves take a significant portion of their earnings. These bastards don't take any money from their own pockets; they sell goods worth ten paise for one rupee, draining the public's resources and distributing it among these people. Whichever trader you talk to pleads that a lot of money is spent every month, yet these bastards manage to get a new car every two months, a new house every two years, and a new shop every ten years. All the people to whom they distribute money need to be stopped. We have to gather all the money and reclaim it from them so that our work can continue and our future plans can be fulfilled."

Sudhir asked, "Bhaiya, did you not understand the point about the future planning?"

Shri Prakash said, "First of all, note one thing: whoever comes in the way of the fight for supremacy should be removed ruthlessly. Be it a leader, police, goons, brokers. If they do not listen after being told once or twice, then they should be shot in the throat. As soon as this system comes under our control, whoever is in the government will listen to us. Sudhir, the fight for supremacy does not end here. Once this source of money for the leaders and policemen is closed, they will be desperate. They will start pressuring the traders for money, and whoever pressurizes the traders for money will have to be killed. Be it the police or the leader. After we fight the elections, our government will be formed."

Sudhir said, "Bhai, a lot of money and a lot of people are needed to fight the elections."

Shri Prakash said, "You are foolish; these traders will gather this money and crowd of people for us. They will organize the rally. The public is a daily wage laborer; give us one day's wages, and make us stand wherever you want for the whole day. There will be a crowd, there will be a rally, there will be fuel for vehicles, there will be flags, and we will win the election as well."

Sudhir said, "Bhai, you have thought ahead of time, then it will be fun."

Shri Prakash said, "With Anand Pandey running away, there was always tension in the mind that he knows us very closely. If he informs us, it will take time for us to achieve our goal. That motherfucker was killed like a dog. We will also deal with MLA Devendra Singh; because of him, Anand got an AK 47 and three pistols. He was killed at the right time, otherwise he would have created problems for us."

Sudhir immediately said, "Bhaiya ji, he left your side, and that's why he was killed. If he had done this work with you, he would have never been killed. By arresting him and keeping him in Delhi, he made a grave mistake, as it's written in the newspapers that the police killed him after tracking him from where he was arrested. If Anand had stayed with you, he would have never gone to Delhi. He would have comfortably stayed in Bihar, he would have received money, and his life would have been saved."

Shri Prakash said, "What the old people have said is correct. When a jackal is about to die, it runs towards the city. This bastard ran towards Delhi and was killed. Now we are completely safe. We must finish our work quickly and establish our supremacy in the entire state. Elections are just after two or three years. Remember that we will contest the next elections and win them. The government will not be formed without us even if fifteen people win. As soon as we win the elections, the police will stand in a line and salute and the same police will travel in vehicles in front and behind us for our security. We have to work a little harder, and first, to win this battle for supremacy, only one-fourth of the work is done."

Sudhir said, "Bhaiya, how will we deal with the police?"

Shri Prakash said, "If the police come in between our fight, we must deal with them. Be it a sub-inspector or a senior police officer. Ever since RK Singh was killed, whichever sub-inspector or constable you talk to, he greets you only by saying, Jai Hind."

Sudhir said, "Yes, bhai, but how will we fight the government?"

Shri Prakash said, "Hey, you fool... will you ask about the entire five-year plan now? Now wait and see what happens in the future."

Just two days later, the money Lala had given reached Shri Prakash. Every day, after talking to Mulraj Arora and Lala at night, Shri Prakash started taking the numbers of big businessmen of Lucknow and started using boys from Lucknow to get their kundali. Every day, he used to call one or two people, and according to the kundali told by the boys, he used to say those businessmen about their daily routine. The businessman felt that he was following me like a shadow, and he would kill me whenever he wanted. The businessmen were so afraid of his words that they had no choice but to give him the money he was asking for.

Shri Prakash started with fifty lakh rupees from these businessmen but would close the deal for two and a half lakh rupees. Sudhir and Anuj also interrupted Shri Prakash, saying there is more risk in taking less money from more people; the situation could escalate, and then the police would become involved.

Shri Prakash replied, "It's good that the situation comes to light; we'll see who steps forward. Then there will be a face-off, and that's when it will get exciting."

Sudhir responded, "Yes, bhai, what you say makes sense."

BUSINESS SECURITY

On the other hand, about ten traders of Hazratganj, the most beautiful market of the capital Lucknow and the Janpath market built inside it, had been victims of Shri Prakash until now. Meanwhile, a trader from Hazratganj was murdered in Alambagh, so a meeting of the Vyapar Mandal was called. Banwari Lal Kanchal and the prominent traders' leaders were already angry with the police, but they also got a chance. They came to Janpath and held a meeting, and it was decided that traders were being murdered. The businessman is the one who feeds everyone, whether it is a leader or the police, and the businessman will get shot. All this will not work; we must come out on the road. The next day, it was decided that the market should be closed, and all the traders would sit at the Hazratganj intersection and block the road. This protest should be held until the murderers of the traders are caught and the police do not assure the safety of the traders. When the meeting was over, Suri of Calcutta & Style and three prominent businessmen who had given money to Shri Prakash out of fear told Kanchal, "President Ji, we want to talk to you in a separate room."

Kanchal said, "Okay." Immediately, everyone went to Suri's underground floor showroom, where a crowd of other business leaders gathered with Kanchal.

Suri told Kanchal, "We need to speak privately. Keep those people out there." Kanchal and six or seven businessmen sat in the inner cabin of Suri's showroom. Suri instructed his staff that no one should approach the cabin, and the door was closed from the inside. They began their conversation, stating, "President Ji, we are very concerned. Every day, we receive calls from Ashok Singh, and we have all given him two hundred to four hundred thousand rupees. Please find a solution, or we must shut down the business."

Kanchal was speechless. He thought to himself that if he were asked to donate five or five thousand rupees to the Vyapar Mandal, he wouldn't contribute. Instead, he suggests taking two thousand now and three thousand later. However, he is giving someone five lakh rupees.

Kanchal immediately said, "You people did not register a case."

Upon hearing Kanchal's words, the crowd turned against him, declaring, "You haven't dealt with him yet; he is the same scoundrel who killed Virendra Shahi in Indira Nagar and Inspector RK Singh here on Janpath in broad daylight. He kidnapped Moolraj, who was freed only after a ransom of crores was paid." Stunned by their words, Kanchal responded, "It doesn't matter how powerful the scoundrel is or whose government it is; it is the government's duty to support the traders. We will bring this to the Chief Minister's attention and will work to get him arrested as soon as possible."

The traders said, "Mr. President, we want to apologize. Right now, we cannot provide any donations to the Vyapar Mandal. We also ask you to keep this matter between us confidential. He will demand the same amount if he finds out about this." Kanchal replied, "Don't worry, no thug can extort money from the traders. The Vyapar Mandal belongs to you; you people form it. If you don't give donations, this organization will cease to exist. Who will advocate for you then? All the traders will be exploited like this, and no one will protect us."

The traders said, "We are being looted. Who can save us? You are our president, and we thought it best to tell you. However, we must reiterate that this matter should not go public. Tomorrow, we will block the roads at Hazratganj and close the entire market. All the traders will be there, but the issue of law and order will be discussed, emphasizing that the police are challenging the shops three times a day. Yet, a police inspector was murdered in the middle of the market. The police have not been able to find the killers or arrest anyone to this day. None of us will share our story, and we also request that you do not mention this to anyone. Ashok Singh has committed many murders, but the police have done nothing to stop him so far. If you share our story anywhere, the matter will be exposed, and we will be killed."

Kanchal said, "Okay."

Kanchal was shocked to hear about these traders and started to think that if this criminal was the same one who murdered Shahi and Sub-Inspector, RK Singh, shot dozens of bullets at the most prominent lottery businessman in the city, Vivek Srivastava, and fired hundreds of rounds from an AK-47 at Dilip Hotel, just ten steps away from the Vidhan Sabha, then this criminal is very dangerous. It's not right to talk about him more tomorrow.

The next day, at the designated time, the people of the Vyapar Mandal began gathering at the Gandhi statue in Hazratganj. All the traders who had fallen victim to Shri Prakash urged more and more traders to join them, but no one mentioned Shri Prakash's name or acknowledged that he was extorting money from them through threats. They insisted that the greater the number present, the more pressure could be applied to the government. Traders are being murdered, and police, sales tax, and municipal corporation officials are harassing them.

Traders began arriving in large numbers. Many of them had paid extortion money to Shri Prakash. At his request, small traders ensured that as many people as possible attended the meeting. By 12:30, the area of the park in front of the Gandhi statue was filled, and more people gradually gathered on the road across the railing. The officials of the Vyapar Mandal were passionately speaking into the microphone. There were concerns about the safety of the traders.

They were taking bribes. They were abusing the government, government departments, and the police. Banwari Lal Kanchal was in touch with his small-time leaders on the spot and repeatedly asked how much the crowd was. When his small-time leaders called and said, President Ji, please come now, the crowd was complete, and the park was packed. People were standing on the road outside the park as well. Hearing this, Kanchal Ji started feeling proud in his heart; he started seeing the future that the bigger the crowd, the more effective the pressure to make him an MLC would be.

After a while, Kanchal was seen coming to Hazratganj crossing in four to five vehicles. The slogans of Vyapar Mandal Zindabad and Banwari Lal Kanchal Zindabad started gaining more momentum. Without wasting time, Kanchal climbed the stairs and stood on the stage built at Bapu's feet. Like the other leaders, he started looking around to estimate the size of the crowd gathered. Seeing the vast crowd, Kanchal's face automatically showed signs of happiness. Seeing the crowd, Kanchal grabbed the mike and started speaking, "We are being killed, we are being looted, we are being beaten. The government is not being affected; the government is not paying any heed. We are standing here, and all the vehicles with red and blue lights are coming and going to their places, blowing horns. When the horn sounds at the crossroads, it feels like a vehicle passing through our chest. We have to show this government that no government has ever run and will never run without our support. Friends! There is no use in standing here; no one will listen to us. Everyone should go to Hazratganj's crossroads, and we will sit there until some responsible person from the government comes and listens to us."

On hearing this, all the traders ran towards the intersection. There was a sudden stampede at the intersection, and shutters of shops started falling one after another in Hazratganj. People were not able to understand what had happened. In a short while, Kanchal also reached there and stood at a high place on the corner towards Allahabad Bank. In the meantime, the overzealous workers of the Vyapar Mandal started forcefully stopping the vehicles from coming and going. Kanchal was feeling happy seeing this scene in his mind and was thinking that if the car of some minister or officer had come in the meantime and the workers had tried to stop it, I would have intervened and increased my number.

Kanchal repeatedly called the traders, saying, “Everyone should sit down peacefully; traders have never believed in violence. We have done big movements. We always reach our voice to the government in a peaceful manner. The crowd seen at the Hazratganj intersection is also historic. The traders seem to have much pain in their hearts, so everyone has gathered here, leaving their work.” Whenever Kanchal said we would break every brick, we would not let you rest, or you should mend your ways. Otherwise, we will pull you down from your chair, the traders started clapping. Kanchal was overwhelmed by the loud clapping. While talking, Kanchal came to the incidents that happened with the traders. He also mentioned the recent incidents with traders in Gorakhpur, Ghazipur, Kanpur, and Lucknow. Kanchal said emotionally, "A criminal committed big crimes right here under the nose of the government; the government could not do anything to him. If the government cannot do anything, then leave it to us. Organized traders have much power. We also know how to deal with goons and criminals."

From the tone of the conversation, it seemed that Kanchal suddenly realized that he had spoken too much, and then he said, "But we never take the law in our own hands; it is the job of the police. The police should protect the traders and the markets. If any incident happens with the traders, we will launch a state-wide movement, block the roads, and close the market."

As soon as the Hazratganj crossing was jammed, long queues of vehicles were seen everywhere. There was jam everywhere from Hazratganj to Begum Hazrat Mahal Park, Nishatganj, Hussainganj crossing, and Bandariya Bagh crossing. All the government offices are located in this area. The Vidhan Sabha and Raj Bhavan are also in this vicinity. In a short while, there was chaos. The top officials and leaders of the government were stuck in this jam. The SSP and DM were told to clear the Hazratganj crossing immediately, send officials there, and clear the area after convincing them. Otherwise, it would be removed by force. How can someone block the entire city like this?"

The ADM City and SP City reached there within ten to fifteen minutes with their entourage. Many PAC personnel from nearby police stations and police lines reached the spot. Seeing many police coming, the traders understood that something would go wrong now. The weak-hearted people started slipping away from there slowly. Kanchal also noticed many police officers and people secretly slipping away from the meeting. Kanchal shouted from his hand-held loudspeaker, "I hope our voice has reached the ears of the government; please see which officers have come." On hearing this, SP City and ADM City started going through the crowd to where Kanchal was giving his speech. People sitting on the road and standing on the side began giving way to those officers. Banwari Lal Kanchal roared again, "Look, the government has sent two officers to us. We will tell them our whole story, and after telling them our story, we will all return to our shops and open the market. Our closing the market distraught the public; we must care for the public." The crowd understood that this entire ruckus would be over in the next ten minutes; by then, ADM City and SP City had reached near Kanchal. Kanchal shouted again, "The government representatives have arrived. Now, we will read the memorandum to them."

Kanchal read the entire memorandum but left out one point: ' Strict action should be taken against the criminals who extort money from traders by threatening them.' After reading the rest of the memorandum, he gave his memorandum to ADM City. While providing the memorandum, Kanchal did not leave until the last photographer took his photo. When Kanchal noticed that the intersection had become empty while he was about to leave and traffic had started, he too quietly sat in his car and left.

The next day, this news was published on the first page of the newspapers that trader leader Kanchal opened a front against Shri Prakash. Whenever Kanchal used to hold a protest or a meeting, he had instructed his driver to bring all the newspapers from the market the next day, Kanchal enjoyed reading about his media coverage. The driver went to all the newspaper shops early in the morning and bought all the prominent newspapers. The driver was happy to see Kanchal's photo. Almost all the newspapers had Kanchal's photo blocking the Hazratganj crossing and speaking to him or giving a memorandum to the ADM. He bought all the newspapers, brought them home early in the morning, and asked the servant who looked after the inside work of the house to take them to Kanchal's bedroom. The servant said, "Saheb has not woken up yet." The driver said, "Keep all the newspapers in the room itself. I know the President; as soon as he wakes up, he will ask for the newspapers." The servant did the same and returned and said, "I have kept all the newspapers on the small table near the master's bedside."

Hey, sir. I will read all the newspapers as soon as he wakes up."

This is what happened. Kanchal called out as soon as he woke up in the morning, but when he saw that all the newspapers were kept there, he got up and started reading. Seeing on the front page of many newspapers that the business leader had opened a front against Shri Prakash Shukla, Kanchal began to sweat in the extreme cold of the AC of his room, which was running at eighteen degrees Celsius. He could not understand how something he had not said got printed in the newspaper. Kanchal picked up his phone; first, he called Dainik Jagran reporter Hemant Tiwari and said, "Tiwari ji, you have written on the front page that I have opened a front against Shri Prakash Shukla. I did not say this?"

Hemant Tiwari said, "I have not written anything wrong. You only said that strict action should be taken against those who are extorting money and goonda tax from the traders. The city knows who is extorting money and from whom the money has been collected." Kanchal's face turned pale, and he said, "Tiwari ji, I had told you in general that I do not know the full details. Please tell me."

Hemant Tiwari said, "Kanchal ji, don't talk nonsense. You know everything; the traders told you this in a separate meeting. First, tell me whether you got a call from Shri Prakash. Why are you so worried so early in the morning?" Kanchal said, "Oh no, bhaiya, don't say that; why would he call me? What enmity do I have?" Saying this, Kanchal greeted and disconnected the phone.

Even in the coolness of the AC, Kanchal could not stop sweating; Kanchal called Suri of Suri Garments. As soon as the phone was picked up from the other side, Suri said, "President Ji, will you get us killed? I had requested you so many times that this matter should not go out anywhere and his name should not be mentioned anywhere; what was the need to mention his name? Now we will have to leave Lucknow and run away." Kanchal was unprepared for such a question; he said, "I did not take anyone's name in yesterday's meeting, and neither did I take Shri Prakash Shukla's name. I am shocked to see the name in all the newspapers. I also spoke to one or two newspaper people. One newspaper person also referred to the meeting held at your place the day before yesterday evening. Now tell me, who told the people in the newspaper about our secret meeting? I did not mention it to anyone; this matter has come out from among you people, and I am worried. One by one, all the newspaper people have written the same thing. All the office bearers of the Vyapar Mandal, all the showroom owners of Hazratganj, and all the small and big shopkeepers of Aminabad, Hazratganj market were also present there. You can ask anyone; I did not take anyone's name, and neither did I take his name, nor did I take your name. Rather, I was surprised you were the most worried, and none of you was present in the meeting."

Suri said, "President ji, are you talking like children? If we had been present there and our photo had been published in the newspaper, we would have been in Bhainsakund by now. The family members would have been crying, and the people of Bhainsakund would have been preparing the funeral pyre. You don't know; he keeps minute-by-minute news from waking up in the morning to reaching the bedroom. He tells us the timing of when Mehrotra got down at the paan vendor's place and at what time he ate paan. Was the train on the right track or the left? Now listen to one thing from us, too. We talked to everyone this morning, and now we will not donate a single penny to the Vyapar Mandal. Now, we will protect ourselves." Saying this, Suri disconnected the phone.

AGAIN SAME PROCESS

All the teams gathered at SSP Arun Kumar's place at 11 am. The SSP first asked, "What is the development? I hope you people have found good sources and informers afresh. After Anand Pandey's death, there is a need to focus only on Shri Prakash Shukla. One more thing: Shri Prakash is very clever; someone must have joined his group after Anand Pandey's death. This information has not reached us yet. Although we gather every evening, there was a need to gather in the morning today because the news of tomorrow's big demonstration of the Vyapar Mandal is printed on the front page of the newspapers today. The DGP has expressed a lot of displeasure. He called everyone to his office at noon. Satyendra Veer Singh and Rajesh Pandey will accompany me to the DG's place; the rest of the people should go to the field, contact their sources, and collect the location and other information. I am going to DG's office with Satyendra Veer Singh and Rajesh Pandey." Sitting in the car, the SSP and the other two officers reached DGP's office. After waiting in DG's room, all three officers were called inside. On seeing the three, DGP asked, "Where are the others?" Arun Kumar said, "I have sent the others to verify some information. I will bring them along if you give me time in the evening." DGP said, "Let me hear your stories. Otherwise, you should have brought all the people along." Addressing Arun Kumar, DGP said, "SSP sahab, now the public has come out on the streets, and all the traders have come on the road and blocked Hazratganj crossing for two hours. You have no idea how much resentment was expressed at the top. Whenever you are asked about progress, you tell one story or another. The SSP also got angry and said, Sir, you must be thinking that we are sitting idle; if we were telling stories, then Anand Pandey would not have been killed in Delhi. By recovering his AK 47 and two pistols, Shri Prakash's firepower has also been reduced. He is continuously running away due to police pressure; after 17 January 1998, no incident occurred in Lucknow. We have done big raids at all his possible places. According to our information, he fled to Nepal. Sir, if we talk like this, then how will we be able to work? We have also brought those officers with us who hardly get two to three hours of sleep. Mobile phones have become very popular; information has started coming directly from mobile phones. Satyendra Veer and Rajesh Pandey do not miss any information; the information is verified in every situation. If you think we cannot do it or are telling stories, remove us." Satyendra Veer Singh and Rajesh were stunned. Arun Kumar stood up from his place.

The DG said, "Hey, there is no need to be so emotional. After all, we are also asked. Whatever you people tell me, I pass it on to the higher authorities, and the political person always says that he is not interested in stories. Why was no action taken? Tell me this. The government is furious about the traders' protest yesterday. The incident on which these people staged such a big protest and jam does not seem to be the reason. It appears that Shri Prakash has started threatening the traders. The traders of Lucknow are closely connected to the political persons, irrespective of the political party they belong to. It is slowly being heard that Shri Prakash is threatening prominent business people and extorting vast amounts from them. This is the same anger that was visible in Hazratganj yesterday. The way this anger of the traders has come out on the streets is not a typical incident. If no action is taken soon and some other incident happens, the traders will go on a state-wide strike, and the government always has to bear the brunt of the traders' anger, no matter whose government it is.

I have called you only so that you can understand the seriousness of this. Put your men among the traders and try to discover why the traders have become so angry. The murder of the trader in Alambagh was purely due to personal reasons. The traders of Alambagh neither blocked the road nor staged any protest. Everyone knows that the incident happened due to personal enmity, so how did such a big protest and jam occur at the Hazratganj crossing below the Vidhan Sabha? Go and explain this to every team member, and in two to three days, it should be known at any cost what the reason for this anger of the traders is?" Saying this, the DGP signaled everyone to get up, and all three people came out of the DGP's room. As soon as he came out, Rajesh asked Arun Kumar,

"Sir, why were you so angry?"

Arun Kumar said, "This is the first time you have come in front of the DG; I am tired of hearing such things every day. I had thought he would praise you guys for Anand Pandey's encounter and encourage the team, but then the same thing started, which I said to myself every day. Whatever I said in anger, I should not have said." While talking, SSP Sahab reached his office. He dropped Satyendra Veer and Rajesh Pandey there and said, "Call the entire team and explain to everyone properly what the DG has said, but I will say one more thing: the DG has a point, and there is some point. Otherwise, Baniya will take action against one of his men.

I cannot even afford to lose a single penny. If the big traders have come out on the road after closing their shops for four hours, there must be some issue. We will meet in the evening."

Rakesh Mani Tripathi tried to call the number from which Shri Prakash had called at 8 pm to get Lala's Kundali done, but the phone was switched off. Rakesh Mani sent an SMS saying, "Bhaiya, I had to talk about something important." Shri Prakash's call came within fifteen minutes. Shri Prakash said, "Tell me." Rakesh Mani said, "Bhaiya, today the news has been printed on the front page of the newspapers that the state president of the Vyapar Mandal, Banwari Kanchal, has opened a front against Shri Prakash Shukla. This is in all the Hindi newspapers. Yesterday, these traders blocked the Hazratganj crossing, closing all the city's markets. Kanchal's statement has been published that action should be taken against those who extort money from traders. Shri Prakash said to let them write whatever they want. We will only benefit from it being published in the newspapers; now they will give the money easily."

Rakesh said, "Yes, Bhaiya, you are right. I want to tell you that I think Lala must have told me somewhere about giving money; otherwise, how would this matter have come to that? The dharna was done to protest against the murder of a trader of Alambagh. Then where did this talk of extortion come from? Kanchal has also threatened that if action is not taken against the criminals, he will close the market of the entire state."

Shri Prakash said, "Let them do it; it is good for us." Rakesh said, "Okay, bhaiya." Shri Prakash disconnected the phone.

The next day newspapers again printed on the front page about the meeting of the SSP and the two officers at the DG's place that the DG tightened the screws on SP City and CO Kaiserbagh. A statement from the DG also mentioned that if strict action is not taken against the criminals soon, he will take action against the police officers. The news of the DG's displeasure was printed in all the newspapers. Rajesh Pandey asked the SSP, "Sir, how did this news reach the newspaper people?" Arun Kumar said, "I also found out in the morning. Maybe DG Sahab mentioned it to some press person, and these people spiced it up and published it."

On the same day, at around 7:30, Shri Prakash's phone came to Rakesh Mani. Shri Prakash asked, "What is printed in the newspapers today?" Rakesh Mani said, "Today, it is printed in all the newspapers that the DG has threatened Arun Kumar, Satyendra Veer Singh, and Rajesh Pandey a lot. If not taken, strict action will be taken against these people. Bhaiya, since yesterday evening, there has been a lot of strict checking in the entire district. At every intersection, the police are stopping even pedestrians and searching them. I don't know why; I am terrified. Bhaiya, you are sitting very far away; this Lala is a filthy person; he may tell us about those persons to whom I gave money after collecting it from Lala, and then the police will reach us. The family members will be outraged.

Shri Prakash said, "Hey, you were asking for arms, and I did not know that you were such a coward. The police can never reach you. Yes, the police can reach Nripendra Pandey because many know him in Hazratganj. I had sent him to the wrong place. I sent him in a hurry because I could not find any person. He does not know anything about you. Do not worry. Let us wait two to three days to finish Kanchal's Kundali. I will fix her first and then fix the rest."

Shri Prakash called Rakesh Mani the next day and said, "You do not go anywhere right now; stay in the room. If any Kundali needs to be done, I will tell you." Immediately, he called Virendra Shukla and said, "Shall I tell you one thing? Will you not be afraid?"

Virendra said, "Bhaiya ji, what is there to be afraid of in this? I will do whatever you tell me. There will be no unnecessary talk."

Shri Prakash said, "There is a business leader from Lucknow, Banwari Lal Kanchal, who needs his Kundali prepared."

Virendra said, "Yes bhaiya. It has been published in the newspapers for two days, and your name also appears."

Shri Prakash said, "Get the Kundali prepared properly. It may take four or six days. I will call and ask once the day after tomorrow."

Shri Prakash called Virendra again a day later and asked him, "What happened? Has his Kundali been prepared, or is it still left?" Virendra said, "Bhaiya, everything is done; just a little is left. Call me tomorrow evening, and I will tell you the complete Kundali."

Meanwhile, Shri Prakash asked for information about other people, among them the Kundali of K.K. Rastogi, the owner of Solomon & Solomon Medical Agency. Shri Prakash listened to all the information Rastogi gave and noted it in a newspaper before him. He tore out the portion written in the newspaper and put it in his purse. The next day evening, he called Virendra Shukla, "What happened? Did you get Kanchal's Kundali?"

Virendra said, "Yes bhaiya. I have been waiting for your call since evening; I have got his complete Kundali."

Virendra started telling Shri Prakash about his daily routine from morning. Where did he go, which car he used, how many people were there in the car, what kind of clothes he was wearing, which offices he visited, which market he visited, and how many meetings he attended. When he had told everything, Shri Prakash asked, "How many Rahu and Ketu are there with him?"

Virendra said, “Bhaiya, I did not see anyone carrying big weapons. I could not find out who was carrying small weapons.” Shri Prakash said, "Tomorrow, look more carefully; guess which of the people in his car has a small weapon and how many people sit in the car right behind, what weapons they have. From the way of walking, we can guess who has what on their waist." Virendra said, "Ok, bhaiya, I will tell you tomorrow."

When Shri Prakash called the next day again, Virendra said, "Bhaiya, today he also had a gunner with him who was carrying a stun gun. Two to four people were sitting behind in the Safari. At the back, one of them was a young boy who seemed to have a licensed weapon. Two people in the car behind also seemed to be carrying weapons."

Shri Prakash said, "These baniyas will all run away at the first shot; they will not even be able to lay their hands on the weapon. We will have to check the gunner. Well, you have done a good job, okay."

Virendra had said that Kanchal does not return home before 10 pm.

AMAZING BHAUKAAL

Shri Prakash called his family at around 10:30 p.m. The servant answered the phone. He said, "Sir is in the bathroom. I will inform him as soon as he comes. What name should I tell?"

Shri Prakash said, "Tell them that Suraj Gupta wants to talk to Vyapar Mandal President, Mau." The servant said, "Okay." Half an hour later, Shri Prakash called again, and the same servant answered. Shri Prakash asked, "What happened? President Ji has come."

The servant said, "Yes, sir, he has come. Are you Suraj Gupta speaking from Mau?" Shri Prakash said, "Yes, you recognized correctly." The servant said, "I will make you talk to him immediately." After a while, Kanchal came on the line. As soon as he came, he said, "Tell me, Gupta ji."

Shri Prakash said, "Bho#@%ke, I am not Suraj Gupta. I am Ashok Singh speaking. If you recognize me, then it is fine; otherwise, I will introduce myself."

Kanchal said, "No, no, I recognized you. Tell me, how did you call?"

After cursing him a lot, Shri Prakash said, "You are gathering the Baniyas and creating pressure. You don't know that I had come out to deal with you today. In the afternoon, I was standing there when you went to Alambagh and showed off your leadership in front of fifty-sixty people in the park in front of the market. You drank a glass of water in the middle of your speech, and from there, you came out of the park and sat down to drink tea in the clothes shop in front. If I wanted, there would have been a lot of holes in your head. I should tell you once that you are taking on the wrong person. You did not take his name in the meeting, but how did it get printed in the newspaper that you started a front against Shri Prakash Shukla? I am telling you clearly that if you close down the state, then I will shoot so many bullets with AK 47 in the market itself that your front eye will stick to the back. Your family will refuse to accept the body, saying that this cannot be Banwari Kanchal. Did you understand or not?"

Kanchal said, "But what is my fault?"

Shri Prakash said, "I have been saying this for so long, and I cannot understand. If you create drama again by holding a meeting of the traders or by closing the market, I will deal with you in 24 hours. Listen to one more thing carefully: if you trouble any businessman for donation, then imagine what I will do." Kanchal said, "Bhaiya, I have been in the Vyapar Mandal for a long time; I will have to go on the call of the businessmen." Shri Prakash said, "Absolutely go, but if you put even a little pressure on the government or the police, I will do the same to you as I did to Inspector RK Singh." Shri Prakash asked, "You are the president of the Vyapar Mandal; how much donation do you get in a month?"

Kanchal said, "Bhaiya, there is no monthly system. We take membership fees from people, which are deposited in the bank account. Apart from this, sometimes, when there is a function of the Vyapar Mandal, the traders are requested to deposit money in the Vyapar Mandal's account. Apart from this, no collection is made from the traders, and there are many factions in the Vyapar Mandal. Some people give money; some people do not. All the city traders know about Vyapar Mandal's account. We cannot withdraw even a single penny from it ourselves."

Shri Prakash said, "Ma@#%cho% are you lecturing me? You always carry four or five vehicles and fifteen to twenty people. Does your father get the vehicles filled with fuel?" Kanchal said, "Bhaiya, all of them are officers of the Vyapar Mandal. They bring their vehicles and get the fuel filled themselves." Shri Prakash said, "Let us find out about that too; if you pressure anyone for a donation, no one will be worse off than me. I have heard that you take a lot of money in exchange for getting the work of traders done from the officers and ministers?" Kanchal said, "This is wrong, Bhaiya; if we do this, our opponents will raise this issue and remove us."

Shri Prakash said, “Okay, keep in mind what I say. I will not call again. If anyone finds out anything, then you will be killed.”

After saying this, Shri Prakash disconnected the call. When Kanchal hung up, his face turned pale. He did not notice when his son came and stood next to him. Kanchal's son asked, "Papa, whose call was it that you got so worried about?"

Kanchal said, "Oh, it's no one; it's people from the organization. A problem has come up, and it has to be solved. It's very late; you go and sleep." The son left from there. Kanchal dialed Suri and asked, "Bhaiya, tell me how Ashok Singh's voice is; he speaks in a somewhat Purbia accent." Suri said, "Yes, President. Nothing, he speaks in a completely Purbia accent. He seems to be from the east or Bihar." Kanchal asked again, "Does he abuse a lot at every opportunity?" Suri said, "Yes, he abuses very badly."

Suri further asked, "What happened, President Ji? Did you also get a call from him?" Kanchal said, “Oh no! He had called someone, and they wanted to hear from me. First, I thought to give your number directly, but then it came to my mind that if I gave it, the matter would come out. Okay, go to sleep.”

Kanchal took out all the newspapers in his room, sat on the bed, and started reading. He read all the newspapers about the Vyapar Mandal and the protest and started reading his statement repeatedly that a state bandh would be called if the criminals were not caught.... Then he kept the newspaper, lay down, and could sleep after a long time. As soon as he woke up in the morning, he first called Urban Development Minister Lalji Tandon and said, “Babuji, I have to talk very urgently; please give me time.”

Lalji Tandon said, “There is a cabinet meeting right now; come to the office at two o'clock.” Kanchal said, “Babuji, give me time from home; I have to talk about something significant.”

Tandon said, “Come to the office. We will talk in the resting room; no one will be there. There is no certainty at home as to what time I can reach.”

Kanchal reached Lalji Tandon's office at 1:30 and waited for him. Tandon Ji arrived after a while. Lalji Tandon ignored Kanchal. Many other business leaders were sitting there. He met one or two of them, shook hands, and asked about their well-being. Kanchal did not like this. When Tandon sat in his office, Kanchal requested his PA outside several times to tell Babuji that Babuji had called him. After a while, a call came on the intercom from inside. The PA said the names of many people and, last of all, told Kanchal's name.

Tandon Ji said, "Send Kanchal."

The PA signaled that Kanchal went straight to Tandon ji, touched his feet, and said, "Babuji, I am very worried; I cannot understand anything." Lalji Tandon said, "Tell me, what is the matter? What is the problem? Last week, you challenged the government by blocking the entire city; what problem can you have? Now you have become a big leader."

Kanchal took a pitiable posture and said, "Babuji, please save my life."

Tandon Ji said, "Who will kill you?"

Kanchal said, "Babuji, Shri Prakash Shukla will kill me."

Tandon said, "Who is Shri Prakash Shukla?"

Kanchal said, "Babuji, he is a big criminal. He killed Virendra Shahi, Vivek Srivastava, and the inspector in Janpath." Tandon also got confused and said, "Yes, you are talking about the name that appears in the newspapers?" Kanchal said, "Yes, Babuji."

Kanchal said, "Babuji, he has started extorting money from the traders of Lucknow by threatening them and has forbidden everyone to donate money to anyone, neither to any party nor to the Vyapar Mandal nor the police. Whatever work needs to be done by these people, I will get it done; it is my responsibility. The whole city is terrorized. The worst happened, Babuji, when he called me at night yesterday and followed me the whole day. He told me every detail of the day, where we were, Babuji. He can kill me at any time. You talk to the DG. He has taken over the entire Vyapar Mandal."

Lalji Tandon said smilingly, “If the Vyapar Mandal was in his control, how would you have staged such a big protest? You have even announced that you will close the entire state market.” Kanchal bowed down and touched the feet of Lalji Tandon and said, “I will not shut down any market and will never mention dharna; he will kill me.”

Lalji Tandon said, “Okay, go, I will talk to the police, DG.”

Kanchal left from there, and immediately after him, officials from the Vyapar Mandal group opposing Kanchal reached Lalji Tandon. While talking, Tandon said, “Kanchal was jumping a lot. Now, he will not shut down any market; he is on the line.” After these traders left, Lalji Tandon got the DG on the phone.

Lalji Tandon asked, “Is this Shri Prakash Shukla a rogue?”

Tandon Ji's face also started to pale after listening to what the DG was saying from the other side. Finally, Tandon ji said, “Then we will have to talk to the honorable Chief Minister Kalyan Singh ji. How can a rogue challenge the entire government? Kalyan Singh ji is strictly against miscreants; he will take some action.”

Lalji Tandon called the Chief Minister's office that day and asked for his time, but he did not get it. Even after trying hard for two or three days, Lalji Tandon did not get time to meet him, so he thought that the cabinet meeting would start soon and he would discuss everything with the Chief Minister in the cabinet meeting itself.

Three days later, in the cabinet meeting, Lalji Tandon said, “Chief Minister, please give us two minutes; we have to discuss something significant.”

Chief Minister Kalyan Singh said, “Is it a personal matter?”

Lalji Tandon said, “It is not a personal matter.”

Kalyan Singh said, “If it is not a personal matter, then tell us here; the problem will be solved in front of everyone.”

Lalji Tandon said, “A big criminal has made life difficult for us. Right here under your nose, he is collecting extortion money from the big business people of the city. There is a lot of anger among the business people. Without anger, such a big crowd would not have gathered in Hazratganj on the call of people like Kanchal. I know the business people of Lucknow very well. Now, he has committed big crimes in Lucknow. He had killed Shahi. He had gunned down Vivek Srivastava here on Latouch Road. When the assembly was in session, he had fired AK 47 in Dilip Hotel." Kalyan Singh said, "All the ministers are present here. Has this criminal committed any crime in any other district, or have all the incidents happened in Lucknow only?"

Sood Prakash Shahi said, "Yes, Chief Minister, he is a dreaded criminal. He is a resident of Gorakhpur and has committed many big murders in Gorakhpur."

Kalyan Singh listened to him seriously and said, "Okay, we will do something."

After the cabinet meeting, the Chief Minister said to his secretary, "Call the Principal Secretary, Home, DG, and SSP Lucknow in the evening." Everyone arrived in the evening. Principal Secretary Rajiv Ratan Shah, DG Police KL Gupta, and Arun Kumar SSP also reached the meeting.

Chief Minister Kalyan Singh said, "Today, a lot of concern has been expressed at the cabinet meeting. There is no control over the criminals, and serious incidents have happened in the state capital. Shah ji, you will have to see more closely where the shortcomings are and why crime is not being controlled."

Principal Secretary, Home said, "Sir, we have already discussed this. We will review it again, and our teams will be engaged. Our team in Delhi has killed his most important associate; we will soon take action against him as well." The Chief Minister said, "Why has this action not been taken till now? Tell us clearly if you lack resources or need any officer." The DG said, "Then we will review it once again; if there is any need, we will tell you."

The next day, it was published in the newspapers that Cabinet Minister Lalji Tandon raised the issue of the security of business people in the cabinet to end the terror of Shri Prakash Shukla and said that Shri Prakash Shukla had created terror in the city. The businessmen are scared, and the police are not doing anything. It was also published in the newspapers that Lalji Tandon wanted to tell the Chief Minister privately, but the Chief Minister said that the entire cabinet is present here. So, let's talk here. When Kanchal read this news in the newspapers in the morning, he panicked and went to Tandon Ji's place again. This time, Tandon Ji called him immediately. Kanchal said, "Babuji, how did the cabinet matter come out? Now, he will kill us. You are a minister; there are hundreds of security personnel around you. We have to move around alone among the businessmen." Tandon said, "That is why I asked for time to talk to the Chief Minister separately. Perhaps the Chief Minister also could not understand the seriousness of this. He had less time, so he only asked to talk to the cabinet. Once the Chief Minister said it, it was not right for me to back out. Some traitors among our people have told the press about this. I also have doubts about one or two of my colleagues. I will talk to the Chief Minister separately."

Kanchal said, "Babuji, what will happen to us? He has threatened me so much yesterday that I cannot tell you. I will go out today but will not return until this matter is settled."

Kanchal left for Mumbai the next day evening. That night, Virendra Shukla, who had made Kanchal's Kundali, left a message on the PCO number Shri Prakash gave that he wanted to talk. Half an hour later, Shri Prakash called.

Shri Prakash said, "Tell me, Virendra, I am pleased with you. You calculated the correct Kundali. Kanchal was shocked. He ran to Lalji Tandon." Virendra said, "Yes, bhaiya, today it is on the front page of all the newspapers that Lalji Tandon has raised this issue in the cabinet."

Shri Prakash said, "Yes, I know. I have employed a boy who reads all the news at 8 in the morning." Shri Prakash asked, "Tell me, do you read English newspapers?" Virendra said, "Yes, Bhaiya, I am doing an MA in English."

Shri Prakash said, "Which English newspapers are published from Lucknow?" Virendra said, "Bhaiya, they mostly write about Pioneer and Times of India. There is a Deepak Sharma in Pioneer; he writes a lot about you. Is Vishwadeep Ghosh in the Times of India; he also writes sometimes. But Deepak Sharma writes very strongly, tearing apart both the government and the police."

Shri Prakash said, "You will read both the newspapers in the morning and tell us in Hindi. When it is published in the English newspaper, it creates a buzz because the top officials of the government read only English newspapers, and the news of English newspapers spreads all over the country." Virendra said, "Yes, Bhaiya, you are right. Whatever news you say is published here in the local Times of India and 'Pioneer,' and the next day, it is published in some form or another in Indian Express and Delhi.

It appears in the Times of India. Both of these are the most prominent newspapers in the capital. People of the capital read them, people from different parts of the country live there, and an authentic atmosphere is created there."

Shri Prakash said, "Get all the English newspapers of Delhi also."

Virendra said, "Bhaiya, there is no need to order. All the newspapers of Delhi come to our department library." Shri Prakash said, "Okay, you also tell us daily what comes out in the newspapers of Delhi. To get published in the newspapers of Delhi, you will have to do some other work."

Shri Prakash said, "Tell me why you sent the message. Is there anything special?" Virendra said, "Yes, bhaiya, Kanchalva has gone to Bombay by Pushpak this evening. I have seen in the chart that his name is on berth number twenty-one of the second AC, and there are four other persons with him. It is the eighth compartment from the engine."

Shri Prakash said, "This train will reach tomorrow evening." Virendra said, "Yes bhaiya." Shri Prakash said, "Keep dialing the railway inquiry number and keep asking. When the time of the train's arrival comes, inform us half an hour in advance." Shri Prakash asked, "Did the bastard have a mobile in his hand?" "Yes, bhaiya, he had a mobile with Ericsson's thick antenna in his hand." Shri Prakash said, "Okay." The next day in the evening, when Virendra sent a message again, Shri Prakash understood. Shri Prakash immediately called him and asked, "Where has the train reached?"

Virendra said, "Bhaiya, we are here at Charbagh Junction; we are constantly checking the train from here. It will reach Bombay VT in ten minutes." Shri Prakash said, "Okay."

Ten minutes later, Shri Prakash dialed Kanchal's mobile.

Kanchal immediately picked up the phone, and as soon as he picked it up, he said, "Banwari Lal Kanchal."

A voice came from the other side, "Ashok Singh speaking. How far will you run? You have just landed on the platform; come out of the VT, and I will see you. I have just landed from the coach behind you." Saying this, Shri Prakash disconnected the phone. Kanchal suddenly stopped. With a suitcase in his hand and a water bottle in one hand, he started running on the platform. The four people accompanying him could not understand what had happened suddenly. After running ten steps, he saw an RPF constable coming. Kanchal hugged him.

He said, "Save me." He was also surprised as to what had happened. He said, "Where is the GRP police station? Take us there."

Seeing his gestures and attire, the constable understood he was responsible citizen. He quickly took Kanchal towards the RPF police station. The four people who had accompanied him also started running behind Kanchal. Kanchal looked back every half a minute, and as soon as the RPF police station came, he went inside. He stood in the shelter inside the police station. Inspector RPF was present; he quickly got up and said, "Bhai sahab, what is the matter?"

Kanchal said, “First, close the door; he will kill me.” The inspector said, “Don’t worry, no one can enter the police station, no matter how big a criminal is; this is Bombay’s VT station.”

He made Kanchal sit, and the four people followed him. Kanchal was still scared, and he repeatedly looked towards the gate. The inspector asked, “Bhai sahab, tell me the whole story; what is the matter? Tell me fearlessly. No one can harm you here.”

Kanchal told his full details and said, “As soon as I stepped on the platform, I got his call. Inspector Sahab, you tell me, how did he know? Because he told me that I was in the compartment behind. It means he got down behind me. He was following me even when I was in Lucknow.” Kanchal started saying, “He is a big criminal. He killed Uttar Pradesh's biggest mafia, Virendra Shahi, in Lucknow. He commits all murders with AK 47. He has taken over the whole of Lucknow." On hearing this, the inspector's expression changed. The inspector immediately took out his diary and started noting everything in it. The inspector asked, "Tell me his appearance."

Kanchal said, "I have not seen him. I only know that he calls people by Ashok Singh, while his real name is Shri Prakash Shukla. One of his photographs was published in the newspaper, which I will send you through someone, or else you tell your commissioner to get it from Uttar Pradesh DG Police." The inspector said, "But, AK 47 is a huge weapon; how can anyone carry it openly in Bombay?"

Kanchal said, "He killed a sub-inspector, who was a reader of SP City, openly in Janpath, and his AK 47 was recovered from his companion in a sports bag. Lucknow police killed his partner there, but he again got another AK 47. Just this January, he had killed UP Co-operative Bank Vice Chairman Upendra Vikram Singh and his three companions with the same AK 47.”

The RPF Inspector racked his brain and said, “Yes, I saw this news on TV. Four people were killed. Well, so he is this same criminal.” The Inspector immediately picked up the wireless set. He gave an order to all the police officers posted at the railway station that he should be stopped and checked immediately if any passenger had a sports bag.

The inspector also instructed the other people deployed for security outside the VT station, stating that the sports bag must be checked.

After this, the inspector gave Kanchal tea and sent him out with his two constables. He said, "Arrange a taxi for them and take them to a safe place where they want to go." Kanchal heaved a sigh of relief. He thought that even if he were following him, he would either run away or get caught after seeing the checking of the bag. Kanchal quietly went out with the police officers, sat in a taxi, and left for his relative's house near Bandra.

Kanchal was not able to get rid of Shri Prakash's ghost. He asked the taxi driver, "Tell me, where do you live?"

The driver said, "Sir, I am from Gorakhpur. Many drivers from our side drive taxis here. Fifty percent of the drivers here are from eastern Uttar Pradesh."

Kanchal got scared once again. Several times, he talked to several people and told the driver, "bhaiya, drop me here; my relatives are coming here in a car to pick me up." The taxi driver immediately stopped the car at the stand ahead, turned the meter, and told the fare; he took the money and moved ahead. The people with Kanchal asked, "Bhaiya, is anyone coming here?"

Kanchal said, "No, we will go by some other taxi; we will not go by his taxi. He lives there in Gorakhpur, you will not understand. Just look around and see if there is any Marathi-speaking driver in the other taxis parked here; then, we will go by that driver's taxi." After some time, the man accompanying him came with a taxi. By talking to him, Kanchal tried to find out whether he was from Uttar Pradesh or Marathi. When satisfied that he was a local person, he sat in his taxi and left. On the way, Kanchal asked the driver, "Where are the good hotels here?"

The driver told Kanchal the names of three or four big famous hotels. Kanchal said, "The best hotel is probably the Taj Hotel; you take us there." The people sitting with Kanchal were speechless; they could not understand why the president suddenly thought of staying in the Taj, a costly hotel. He could not afford anything less than five thousand rupees per day, yet he kept quiet and quietly reached the Taj Hotel.

Kanchal reached his room and asked the room attendant many questions, “Can a person go to a room without asking the reception?” The attendant said, “No sir, he is not allowed to go until he tells whom he wants to meet and which room he wants to go to. Whoever comes to meet you, first the receptionist will call your room and tell his name, only then an attendant will take him to your room.”

Kanchal immediately told the boy accompanying him, “Whoever is in whichever room, write their name at the reception.” He asked, “Bhaiya, who will come to meet us? No one even knows where we are staying.” Kanchal said, “Still go and write it down.” After some time, Kanchal also checked himself. Calling the reception, Kanchal asked, “Have you written the correct number of the people staying in the rooms with me?” When he got the answer he wanted, Kanchal heaved a sigh of relief and turned on his switched-off mobile. Turning on the phone, he immediately called home and told his family, “If anyone asks, tell them I have gone to Calcutta. Do not tell them that I am in Bombay, but tell them that I am switching off my mobile. I noted down the mobile number of the person accompanying me and told them that if they wanted to talk to me, they could call that number. Do not call in front of anyone; call only when alone. Talk only if it is essential.” Only after giving so many instructions was Kanchal able to go somewhere, eat food, and sleep.

STF – SPECIAL TASK FORCE

Meanwhile, Anuj and Sudhir told Shri Prakash in the hotel room in Viratnagar, "Bhaiya JP Singh again took the contract of ballast supply in Gorakhpur the day before yesterday."

Shri Prakash got furious and said, "How dare JP? His father was shot 150 times; come on, everybody, get ready. If he is not killed today, then he will stand up with his head raised. If anyone other than us or Surajbhan Dada takes even a penny's contract of the railways, then it will be a shame for us."

Everyone agreed, "It is fine, bhaiya, we are leaving." Everyone left from Viratnagar. They reached Gorakhpur by night. Shri Prakash was furious. He said, "We have to finish him off today itself. As soon as he reached Gorakhpur, he contacted many boys and put them all on this work. At eight in the morning, he got information that JP Singh was coming to meet with some of his people in Gorakhpur Cantonment in connection with the tender. Shri Prakash immediately reached the cantonment with Anuj and Sudhir. After waiting for half an hour, JP Singh was seen coming in his car. Shri Prakash fired a burst fire from AK 47 at JP Singh. JP Singh had fallen before the people sitting with him could understand. Shri Prakash shouted, "Jai Bajrang Bali," and left again.

Shri Prakash was driving the car himself, and from there, he started going straight towards Nepal. Anuj said, "Bhaiya, where are you here?" Shri Prakash said, "One should not interrupt while going. When the car stops, understand that we have come for her." Anuj became silent; after some time, Anuj said again, "Bhaiya, father was not feeling well; I was thinking of going to see him."

Shri Prakash roared, "JP is considered an ordinary man. His men will work day and night. The boys sitting with him know everyone; they also know everyone's whereabouts. If you want, you can find out. All of them must be sitting at the captain's bungalow. They must press the captain that we will be found if we conduct raids immediately. In such a situation, will you see Babuji? Everyone will be killed. Amid a battle for supremacy, one should never forget the family members. I will send a boy right now; he will meet Babuji. If there is any shortage, he will fill it out and tell us that Anuj Bhaiya is about to come; some incident has happened. Anuj bhaiya will come to meet you in a few days."

Anuj calmed down, and these people left from there. Shri Prakash did not go towards Viratnagar this time; he reached the Raxaul border directly. He went to Hotel Himalaya, about ten kilometers inside the Raxaul border towards Nepal, and parked the car in the back parking. Everyone came inside; the boy sitting at the reception touched Shri Prakash's feet and told everyone the room number. Everyone went to the room, sat together, and ate; after that, they slept. One day, Shri Prakash called Moolraj Arora from Raxaul and threatened him, saying, "Don't think that we have forgotten that you have given only half the money; if you back out this time, you will have to pay the full amount. The four people whose names you had told me they are not coming soon. I am in dire need of money. You think hard and tell me who else is there who will give one crore straight away."

Moolraj said, "Bhaiya, we have told you all their names. These people lie; they will not give the money until you tighten them properly." Shri Prakash said, "On tightening them, they give only five to ten lakhs; how will that work?" Moolraj said, "Bhaiya, why don't you tighten Rastogi of Solomon & Solomon? I had told you everything about him." Shri Prakash said, "The bastard is telling that his company has gone bankrupt." Moolraj said, "He has the most money."

Shri Prakash said, "Okay, I will see. But find two or four more names. Otherwise, you will get up again this time. If you get up this time, I will inform Surajbhan Dada. Your brother, who was DRM, has also been transferred now." Moolaraj said, "Such a situation will not arise."

After disconnecting Moolaraj's call, Shri Prakash dialed KK Rastogi, and as soon as he started talking, he abused him. KK Rastogi hung up. After disconnecting the call, Shri Prakash dialed four or five times, but KK Rastogi did not pick up. Shri Prakash was furious. After waiting half an hour, he dialed KK Rastogi from Sudhir Tripathi's phone. Rastogi picked up the phone immediately.

Shri Prakash said, “You will not pick up my call. I have called only to tell you that we will pick you up now.” Saying this, Shri Prakash disconnected the phone. KK Rastogi got a little worried and immediately called the Principal Secretary of the home, Rajiv Ratan Shah, and told him the whole thing. Rajiv Shah said, “Don’t worry, I will get you security by telling the SSP.” The Principal Secretary, Home, called the SSP and told him everything. He said, “Rastogi is our friend and should be given full security.”

Rastogi’s wife was a classmate of the Principal Secretary, Home, Shri Rajiv Ratan Shah, at L’Martinier Girls College. She also spoke to Mrs. Rajiv Ratan Sahib at night and expressed concern. Arun Kumar had been removed from the post of SSP by then, but Rajiv Ratan Shah respected him a lot. Rajiv Ratan Shah called Arun Kumar and told him to come to the office by noon. The Principal Secretary, Home, also called the DGP. At noon, everyone gathered in the Principal Secretary’s room, where the discussion started.

The Principal Secretary, Home said, “That day in the cabinet meeting, the Chief Minister was very upset that he had never told anyone about the son of a son.

There is no interference in the police work, yet why are the crimes in the capital not stopping?” The DG said, “I understand that the Chief Minister is worried after the traders jammed Lucknow that day, and the same thing is being said repeatedly about how to stop Shri Prakash Shukla.”

During the discussion in the cabinet, the Chief Minister had said, “If there is a lack of resources or men, then we will definitely provide them, and crime should be completely curbed. No matter how many resources you give to such a large police force in Uttar Pradesh, they all get consumed in this sea, and you do not even realize it. One thing comes to my mind: Why should a separate unit not be formed to finish off Shri Prakash Shukla and his gang? The people working on the

Shri Prakash Shukla gang should be removed from the districts and posted in some special unit. Arun Kumar has said this many times, what is the opinion of the rest of the people?"

The DGP said, "The suggestion is good. Where will this separate unit be opened? How many resources are needed? For this, it is necessary to have a government order. If these things are considered, then it will make a difference." Arun Kumar said, "Sir, half the time in the district is spent on protocol and law and order; some days, the whole day is spent in this. Working on the information received about Shri Prakash's gang is difficult. If there is only one task, then we will do this work by working hard day and night."

The Principal Secretary said, "If everyone agrees, then I will get its approval from the Chief Minister right now." The Principal Secretary immediately called the Chief Minister. Chief Minister Shri Kalyan Singh came on the telephone line in two minutes. Rajiv Ratan Shah said that today all the officers are sitting here, and everyone has agreed that a separate unit should be formed to finish off the Shri Prakash Shukla gang, which has no connection with the district police." The Chief Minister said, "What things will be required for this? The Principal Secretary of the Home said, "First of all, a government order should come that they should get a separate building. We will make some vehicles available immediately, and some vehicles bought for the Haridwar Kumbh will be given to them after the Kumbh is over. We will leave the selection of men to Arun Kumar."

The Chief Minister said, "It will not be possible to provide a separate building right now. For now, if there is a separate building in any police station or outpost, start working in it. Whatever else is required for vehicles and weapons, you bring it, and we will approve." The matter ended. Principal Secretary Home said to Arun Kumar, "You have to do two things: first, give the list of who will be in your team by tomorrow, and second, you also inform about which police station in Lucknow can have a separate building available. I will get the proposal passed in the next cabinet and get a government order for a separate unit."

Principal Secretary Home said, “What will this unit name be? Decide that too, and tell me.” Arun Kumar said, “I have a name in my mind; if you agree, then give that name. Since this unit is being created for only one work and that for a special work, it would be appropriate to name it ‘Special Task Force.’”

The Principal Secretary said, "Arun, you have suggested a good name, and it is correct. You people go and give us the names of the people and the building where the office can be found by tomorrow." Arun Kumar said, "Sir, I have one more request about the building; it should not be taken up on any police station campus. While following this gang for the last few days, it seems that Shri Prakash has made a good inroads in the police as well. In such a situation, an office should be opened in a building separate from the police station."

The Principal Secretary said, "Make it in the DG office." Arun Kumar said, "Sir, making it to the DG office will be wrong. All the senior officers are there; if anyone calls us, we cannot refuse. If you give permission, we will find a separate rented house. Many police officers are running in rented houses. It is only a few days, and we will operate the STF from a rented house." The principal secretary at Home said, "I will ask the chief minister, and I will get approval for this also." After this, everyone went to their respective places. Arun Kumar went straight to the SP City's office in Kaiserbagh. Satyendra Veer Singh and Rajesh Pandey were already sitting there, busy with the information about the Shri Prakash gang. Arun Kumar entered, soaked in sweat, and the officers stood up. Arun Kumar sat down and said, "It is good that everyone got together. The government has decided to form a separate team to eliminate the Shri Prakash gang. Who will be on this team? This task has been entrusted to me. No one has worked more on Shri Prakash than you two. If both of you agree, then I will also give my consent. Otherwise, it won't be easy to work with new people. There is a lot of pressure from the government. Resources will be less, and getting them will take a lot of time. You have been in Lucknow for a long time, so you will use your contacts to fulfill your small needs. You people also suggest names for the people below. I will also check the people with me. Remember that whoever comes will come on his own will; the work will not be done by applying pressure or forcibly calling someone."

Satyendra Veer and Rajesh Pandey said, "Sir, you should not doubt that we will work with you in different units, and if God wishes, we will succeed very soon."

Arun Kumar asked for a paper and wrote an application to the DG stating that he wanted to be in the unit being formed to eliminate this gang. Along with him, Additional Superintendent of Police Satyendra Veer Singh and Deputy Superintendent of Police Rajesh Pandey have also expressed their desire to work in this unit. Arun Kumar signed the paper below, extended it to Satyendra Veer Singh, and said, "You will also have to consent to this." Satyendra Veer immediately gave his consent and extended the application to Rajesh Pandey. The names of the Inspector and Sub Inspector were also discussed there. Arun Kumar said, "You people search for more names and people; we will get it approved later. First, the list of officers has to be issued with the government order." Arun Kumar went to the DG Police Office with this application.

A week later, Arun Kumar said, "The government order has been issued. This unit has been named 'STF,' i.e., 'Special Task Force,' and has been formed for only six months. For now, you people should leave your respective charges and join STF in the DGP office, and then we will look for a house together where this office is to be opened."

The next day, Satyendra Veer Singh, SP City, Lucknow, and Rajesh Pandey, Kaiserbagh, received the order that these people be attached to STF immediately. Until the rest of the arrangements are made, these people will continue to receive their salaries from the Lucknow district. After the order came, Satyendra Veer Singh and Rajesh Pandey handed over their charges from Lucknow district on the same day. Arun Kumar, Satyendra Veer Singh, and Rajesh Pandey visited the DG office and met ADG Law and Order Mr. Ajay Raj Sharma and DG KL Gupta. After giving necessary instructions, it was repeatedly said that they should quickly find an office and start working. Till now, all three officers had Lucknow Police vehicles, and they kept roaming in different areas every morning and evening to find a house on rent. The most significant difficulty was that whenever a house was liked for the STF office, the landlord used to ask which department you people work in. On hearing the police name, the landlord used to make some excuse or another.

It was written in the government order on which date the office would open and which areas of organized crime would be handled by the STF. The starting date was approaching, but the office had not opened yet. Meanwhile, Inspector OP Tripathi and Inspector Malviya also joined the STF. As the date was coming closer, the officers of the DG office were also putting pressure. ADG Law and Order called everyone to his office and said, “In three to four days, look for some office and start work. If it is not suitable, we will change it later.” Rajesh Pandey said, “Sir when I was CO Mahanagar, there was a dispute in a house in Vigyanpuri. Its owner, who was a retired Deputy Superintendent of Police, was found dead inside that house. His sons lived in Punjab but did not have good relations with their father, so no one came for the last rites. Some people from Mahanagar tried to occupy the house, then Shriram Arun, who lives next door, called and told about this incident that this is a police colony, it is a policeman's house, how did outsiders come, investigate it, and take action. I went to the spot. The papers found with the occupying people, based on which they wanted to occupy, was a will, which prima facie looked fake. A case was filed against the people who had occupied it, and they were sent to jail. That house is still lying in the same condition. Big grass has grown there.

Ajay Raj Sharma said, "I understand which house you are talking about. It is probably the house next to Suresh Pal Singh's. That place is perfect. Find out its current status, and if you can contact his sons, then take it on rent, though his sons have never come here. Police officers living nearby will surely have some number." The next day, Inspector OP Tripathi and Malviya went to the police station and discovered that the attachment process was not completed in this house. The inspectors went directly to Additional City Magistrate Zaidi and told him, "If its process is completed, then hand it over to the police for security reasons. Our office will open." Zaidi said, "To date, no one has come to plead. Since you people have come, I will give the order today itself; this has been pending for a long time." He asked for the file; all the proceedings were completed, and only the order was left to be given. Zaidi ordered its attachment and ordered the Mahanagar police station to take care of it and secure it from a security point of view. Taking this order, both the inspectors went to Mahanagar and told him, "The city magistrate has handed over this house to you. Please order the newly opened police STF to keep it safe."

The inspector immediately ordered both the inspectors of STF to protect it. Arun Kumar, Satyendra Veer Singh, and Rajesh Pandey went to the inspector the next day. This building had not been painted for many years; there was no electricity connection. The household goods of the deceased Deputy Superintendent of Police had gradually disappeared, bushes had grown all around, and there was a lock on the main door. Inspector Mahanagar was contacted, but the lock was broken in the presence of a sub-inspector. Everyone went inside, and everyone was disheartened to see the condition of the building.

Arun Kumar said, "How will it become usable in three days!" Inspector Malviya and Tripathi said, "Everything will be done in two to three days. Electricity connection has to be installed; cleaning has to be done by employing eight to ten laborers, and painting has to be done. If some money is arranged, all this work will be done." Arun Kumar said, "I will arrange the money right now, ADG Law and Order." Arun Kumar went straight to the ADG office and told him he needed money to get and start the house. ADG, Law and Order said, "I have some money to start it immediately, take it, and whatever money is spent on this, I will get it sanctioned from the DG."

Arun Kumar returned immediately and gave money to both the inspectors immediately. Cleaning work started on a war footing. It was to be inaugurated after two days. On the morning of the inauguration, Arun Kumar, Satyendra Veer Singh, and Rajesh Pandey went to see it. It was hard to believe that everyone had seen this same house two days ago. It was completely whitewashed from inside and outside.

The outer wall was yellow, and the outer gate was whitewashed. All the grass and weeds had been removed, and the area where the grass had grown had been leveled. The houses next to each other belonged to senior police officers. Everyone's eyes lit up on seeing the house. There were a total of six rooms in the house. There was a big courtyard and much space at the back, too.

Arun Kumar said, "When the government has set today as the deadline, let us inaugurate it today itself."

Satyendra Veer Singh said, "Sir, after the inauguration, we will have to sit for some time. There should be chairs and tables to sit on. Where will we get them? Funds have not been allotted for that; how will we work?" Arun Kumar said, "If the office has to start today, it will start today itself." Rajesh Pandey said, "Sir, where this road opens to the vegetable market, there are tent house shops. We can rent some chairs and tables for a few days. The electricity people will come by afternoon, the electricity connection will also be installed. We need a stenographer; you can get him from the DG office or elsewhere. Until there is a posting here, we should start our work."

There were four Godrej cupboards in the house, probably the thieves could not lift them, and there was one cupboard in each room, whose latch, etc., was fixed by both the inspectors. Four small locks were ordered. Arun Kumar said, "Let's go to ADG, Law and Order, and after taking time from him, we will inaugurate it." Everyone reached the DG office, met Ajay Raj Sharma in his room, and told him, "That house has been cleaned and whitewashed and repaired. If you give us some time in the evening, we can inaugurate it and start the work. After having a place to sit, we need a phone. There is a forensic science laboratory of the city right in front; if you arrange a telephone connection from there for two to four months, our work will start." Ajay Raj Sharma looked at the calendar and said, "I am free at four; I will come only at four o'clock." Arun Kumar said- "Sir, I will come to pick you up." I will leave Rajesh and Satyendra Veer Singh there. Till then, they should have prepared for the inauguration. Four tables, fifteen chairs, one sofa, and six planks from the tent house were immediately loaded on a trolley and taken to the new office. Painting was happening in both the rooms inside; all these chairs, tables, and sofas were arranged in the outer room. Mattresses, white sheets, etc., from the tent house, were placed in the verandah while entering the house, and the temple priest in front of the polytechnic was asked to perform the inauguration puja. The priest was given the necessary money to come with all the materials. Inspector OP Tripathi bought red tape and scissors from the market. Pandit Ji had reached there before and made all the arrangements for that day in the verandah. Pandit Ji asked, “Who is today's Jajman?” He was told that ADG, Law and Order, is today's jajman. In both the rooms in front, incense sticks were lit to remove the stench of fresh paint. At precisely 4 o'clock, Arun Kumar reached the office with Ajay Raj Sharma. Ajay Raj Sharma was pleased to see the office from outside and said, "There cannot be a better place for STF. The building in front across the road belongs to the police, and all the houses around this building belong to the police officers. No outsider can come here. There is no problem from the security point of view either." While talking about this, Ajay Raj Sharma moved towards the red ribbon; at that time, there was no plate to give him the scissors, so OP Tripathi took them from his pocket and gave them to him. Ajay Raj Sharma cut the ribbon. Pandit Ji recited some mantras, and everyone sat down to worship on the verandah. At the time of the inauguration of the STF office, there were only eight to ten people, out of which five police officers, employees, drivers, and gunners of the remaining three officers were present.

Arun Kumar said, “When the government has set today as the deadline, let us inaugurate it today itself.”

Satyendra Veer Singh said, “Sir, after the inauguration, we will have to sit for some time. There should be chairs and tables to sit on. Where will we get them? Funds have not been allotted for that; how will we work?” Arun Kumar said, “If the office has to start today, it will start today itself.” Rajesh Pandey said, “Sir, where this road opens to the vegetable market, there are tent house shops. We can rent some chairs and tables for a few days. The electricity people will come by afternoon; the electricity connection will also be installed. We need a stenographer; you can get him from the DG office or elsewhere. Until there is a posting here, we should start our work.”

There were four Godrej cupboards in the house, probably the thieves could not lift them, and there was one cupboard in each room, whose latch, etc., was fixed by both the inspectors. Four small locks were ordered. Arun Kumar said, "Let's go to ADG, Law and Order, and after taking time from him, we will inaugurate it." Everyone reached the DG office and met Ajay Raj Sharma in his room. He said, "That house has been cleaned, whitewashed, and repaired. If you give us some time in the evening, we can inaugurate it and start the work. After having a place to sit, we need a phone. There is a forensic science laboratory of the city right in front; if you arrange a telephone connection from there for two to four months, our work will start." Ajay Raj Sharma looked at the calendar and said, "I am free at four; I will come only at four o'clock." Arun Kumar said- "Sir, I will come to pick you up." I will leave Rajesh and Satyendra Veer Singh there. Till then, they should have prepared for the inauguration. Four tables, fifteen chairs, one sofa, and six planks from the tent house were immediately loaded on a trolley and taken to the new office. Painting was happening in both the rooms inside; all these chairs, tables, and sofas were arranged in the outer room. Mattresses, white sheets, etc., from the tent house, were placed in the verandah while entering the house, and the temple priest in front of the polytechnic was asked to perform the inauguration puja. The priest was given the necessary money to come with all the materials. Inspector OP Tripathi bought red tape and scissors from the market. Pandit Ji had reached there before and made all the arrangements for that day in the verandah. Pandit Ji asked, "Who is today's Jajman?" He was told that ADG, Law and Order, is today's jajman. In both the rooms in front, incense sticks were lit to remove the stench of fresh paint. At precisely 4 o'clock, Arun Kumar reached the office with Ajay Raj Sharma. Ajay Raj Sharma was pleased to see the office from outside and said, "There cannot be a better place for STF. The building in front across the road belongs to the police, and all the houses around this building belong to the police officers. No outsider can come here. There is no problem from the security point of view either." While talking about this, Ajay Raj Sharma moved towards the red ribbon; at that time, there was no plate to give him the scissors, so OP Tripathi took them from his pocket and gave them to him. Ajay Raj Sharma cut the ribbon. Pandit Ji recited some mantras, and everyone sat down to worship on the verandah. At the time of the inauguration of the STF office, there were only eight to ten people, out of which five police officers, employees, drivers, and gunners of the remaining three officers were present.

The inspectors informed the police station and the CO, but no one was interested. Ajay Raj Sharma was an outstanding cricket player. He was the UP IPS cricket team captain for ten consecutive years but was heavily built. Pandit Ji signaled him to sit down, but he had difficulty sitting due to his heavy body. OP Tripathi immediately brought a chair from inside. After placing the chair, Pandit Ji asked, “Is there any problem performing the puja while sitting on the chair?” Pandit Ji said, “There is no problem; the puja can be performed while standing.” After finishing the puja, a coconut broke, and everyone reached the room where the sofa was placed. After a while, Pandit Ji came in front of everyone with a box of sweets, and everyone took the prasad. Ajay Raj Sharma Sahab asked, “Arun, do you want to sit in this room?” Arun Kumar replied, “We all will sit in this room. Everything will be organized in a few days. It will be easier to work from here, and more results will come.”

MURDER IN HOSPITAL

Shri Prakash told Sudhir, "Now you go to Lucknow and read the advertisements for houses available for rent in the newspapers to see if houses are available for rent in posh localities." Sudhir asked, "What do you mean by posh?"

Shri Prakash said, "Ask the house number of the owner whose house is advertised in Gomti Nagar, Indiranagar, Vikas Nagar, or whose number is given, and go and see the house yourself. There are many advantages to buying a house in a posh locality. Even the people living next to each other do not know who came and who went. People in posh colonies do not have time to pay attention to such things. It will be easy to keep a hold from there. All are big people; if something goes wrong, neither will anyone tell nor be ready to testify. This will have to be done soon because it is necessary to keep a hold. All the big Lalas have come under control; now, no one can go astray in Lucknow. There are still two places left: one is the leader, and the other is the police. Let us test their strength, too. The grip should be such that the leader and the senior officials get scared; once the police and the leader are suppressed, we will dominate the entire state."

You know that once we dominate UP, no government can be formed in the state or the center without us. We will have a pistol on the leader's temple 24 hours a day, and we will get a ticket for whoever we want. We will get so many seats that no one can form a government in UP without us. Once we dominate the UP assembly, no government can be formed in Delhi without UP. Just think, people like Harishankar Tiwari and Mukhtar Ansari will ask for a meeting time."

Sudhir said, "Bhaiya, there is more risk in this; if we pick up such a person, the entire government and police will be after us. Then how

many days will we stay in Nepal?" Shri Prakash said, "Dominance is only of the one who has a strong weapon in his hand, and if he fires the first shot, there should be strength in the ass."

Sudhir left for Lucknow from there. After coming to Lucknow, he stayed at Satyavrat's house and bought all the Hindi newspapers from the newspaper shop at B Block crossing. He wrote down all the telephone numbers and addresses written on the house for rent advertisements in every newspaper in his diary. Then he started calling everyone one by one. Everyone told me about the features of their house and the rent charged. Sudhir would ask everyone in which area it was, how far the market was, and what kind of people lived nearby. After two to three days of hard work, Upadhyay, a landlord of Kanpur, told us about his house in the posh colony of Indira Nagar. Upadhyay said, "I do not live there; the old tenant has vacated, and no other tenant lives in that house. I will give the entire house on rent. All the necessary resources are available inside the house, food items will have to be brought from outside, and food will have to be cooked." The landlord said, "I will give the house only to family members." Sudhir said "We will also stay with our family. My brother and sister-in-law will come and stay here. Bhabhi will deliver next month; we will clean the house beforehand. After the delivery, brother and sister-in-law will come; they will stay." Upadhyay was asking for a very high rent. After much reluctance, Upadhyay agreed to reduce the rent a little.

He said, "Please reach the pond house; I am sending a servant with the keys. He will come and show you the house." The next day, Sudhir saw that house; the house was safe. Big cars were parked in front of all the houses nearby. Sudhir immediately thought that Shri Prakash had asked for such a house. Sudhir went to a PCO and told Shri Prakash the whole thing. Shri Prakash said, "Pay the rent in advance."

Sudhir paid the advance rent to Upadhyay's servant, locked the house, and kept the keys with himself. After this, Sudhir went straight to Satyavrat's house and told him I was leaving Lucknow, and our work was done. Saying this, he came straight to the new rented house in Indira Nagar and stayed there. At night, he also checked the nearby market for food, got the food packed, brought it to the new house, and ate there. After this, he called Shri Prakash and said, "Bhaiya, bring everyone here; the house is fit." Shri Prakash said, "Okay, fine, I will come in a day or two; till then, you stay there and do a recce of KK Rastogi on Gokhale Marg. Find out all the things about Rastogi: where the office is, which vehicle he comes and goes, who is there in the house, at what time he leaves, and at what time he reaches home." Sudhir said, "Okay bhaiya." Shri Prakash said, "Go to the university hostel; I will tell Hriday Narayan that he has one good vehicle; take it. All the papers are kept in the vehicle itself; it is a brand new Hero Honda." Sudhir said, "Okay." Sudhir went straight to the hostel, took the car from Hriday Narayan, and came to the house in Indiranagar. Coming out in the evening, he took several rounds around KK Rastogi's house. There was no kiosk or shop near KK Rastogi's house where he could stop and keep an eye for a while. He could only watch him when he came to the main Gokhale road. Sitting at the tea stall on the corner, he kept an eye on the number of cars coming and going for a long time. At around 7:30 in the evening, he saw KK Rastogi's car, which was turning into the lane and going towards his house. Sudhir followed him. He saw which was Rastogi's house and which car was parked there. The next day, during the morning walk, Shri Prakash told him that Rastogi was going to the Botanical Garden for a morning walk, so Sudhir stood at the gate of the Botanical Garden. A huge crowd came for a morning walk, and many tea and biscuit carts were set up there. In the morning, an entry pass was required for those visiting this Botanical Garden of NBRI. Sudhir saw that KK Rastogi came, parked his car in the parking, and went straight inside by showing the pass. Sudhir sat outside at the tea stall; after a while, people started coming out after a morning walk. After a long time, KK Rastogi came out and took out his car. Sudhir followed him to his house. Returning there, Sudhir came to his house, told Shri Prakash the whole thing, and said, "Bhaiya will wake up comfortably. He walks alone in the morning but takes his son with him while going to the office. This is his only son. His son returns from the shop in the afternoon, but the driver accompanies him."

Shri Prakash said, "We will reach it by tonight."

Sudhir said, “Okay.”

Shri Prakash, Anuj, and two more boys reached Lucknow by eight at night. Sudhir went to Bhootnath Market to pick them up and brought them to the house. Seeing the house, Shri Prakash said, Sudhir, you have found a perfect home; the car will also be parked inside, and there will be no problem. Sudhir said, “Yes bhaiya.” Shri Prakash said, “It is too late now; he must have returned by now; we will see tomorrow morning.”

Sudhir said, “Bhaiya, who has to pick up, the father or the son? The father is very heavy and tall, and several people must pull him out of the car. It will be easy to pull the boy. No need to put in much effort.” Shri Prakash said, “Then we will lift the boy; it is the same thing. If one gets up, the other will pay; let's figure it out in the morning. Everyone will go, and once we identify ourselves, we can work comfortably.”

May 26th, 1998, summer morning. Leaving one boy at home, everyone else sat in Shri Prakash's Maruti 800 and parked it in the street in front of Rastogi's house. The car had black glasses. Shri Prakash was driving the car himself and had kept the car started. After fifteen minutes, Sudhir said, “Bhaiya, the car is leaving now.” After two minutes, the car came out. The car was at a bit of height, and both Rastogi and son Kunal were sitting there. Sudhir said, “It's fun, bhaiya; both of them are going for a walk together; identify them both.”

Shri Prakash did not say anything but immediately started his car and parked behind his car at the signal. After driving a little further, Shri Prakash said, “I will overtake the car and park it, pull the boy quickly.”

Within a minute, Shri Prakash drove his car from behind, moved a little ahead, and stopped Rastogi's car while parking it on the front side. Sudhir and Anuj immediately got down, opened the car door towards Kunal, and said, “Get out, show the car papers!” Kunal had almost come out; by then, Shri Prakash also came out and, pointing a pistol at KK Rastogi, said, “You idiot, if you won't pick up my call. I had told you that I will kidnap you soon.”

On hearing this, KK Rastogi tried to pull Kunal towards himself by holding his hand, but Sudhir and Anuj pulled Kunal out and quickly made him sit in the middle of Maruti's rear seat. Shri Prakash told KK Rastogi, “Don’t try any tricks; I will kill the boy.”

As soon as Shri Prakash was sitting in the driver’s seat and was moving ahead, KK Rastogi started the car quickly and hit the Maruti. The collision was powerful, and Maruti's rear door was crushed. Shri Prakash got down from the driving seat very swiftly and shot KK Rastogi several times, and Rastogi died on the steering of the car. Then he started the car and went straight to his house in Indiranagar. As soon as the vehicle started, Sudhir said, “Bhaiya, we have narrowly escaped today.”

Shri Prakash said, “There is nothing to escape from this; if he had done more drama, I would have killed both of them. We have the horoscopes of many baniyas of Lucknow; we would have picked someone else.”

In the meantime, the car reached that house in Indiranagar. The car was taken inside, and Kunal's eyes were covered with a handkerchief. Sudhir and Shri Prakash put pistols on Kunal's back and waist, saying, “Don't try to be smart!” The boy who was already inside opened the door, and everyone went straight to the bedroom with Kunal. After taking Kunal to the bedroom, Sudhir came out, removed the cover from the car's trunk, and covered the car directly.

After coming inside, Sudhir said, “Bhaiya, the back door has been flattened too much. The door can be used to identify the person; we have covered the car, and it is still daytime. The car must be removed at night; we must arrange another car. We will take the car to Faizabad and get it repaired.” Shri Prakash said, “No need to worry; we will finish everything. A tremendous tender has been received.” After a while, Kunal's blindfold was removed.

Shri Prakash said, "Your father is courageous; if we had not killed him, we would have died."

Kunal asked, "How is Papa's?"

Shri Prakash said, "We did not wait to see whether he is alive or dead; we will find out from the newspaper tomorrow."

Kunal got nervous. Shri Prakash said, "Give him water to drink, give him tea; he will be normal in two to three days, and then we will talk."

Sudhir brought all the Hindi and English newspapers from B Block crossing the next day. This was the biggest news on the front page of all the newspapers. Shri Prakash read this news carefully in every newspaper and said, "The bastard was not picking up the phone; this was bound to happen. By the way, he seems to be a huge man, all the newspapers have written about him, he is very powerful too. It is also written in all the newspapers that this is the work of some big gang." Shri Prakash told Anuj, “Please read and tell me what is written in the English newspapers.” After a while, Anuj said, “It is written in all the newspapers, but in ‘Pioneer,’ Deepak Sharma has written very clearly that Shri Prakash did this murder and kidnapping. It is also written that the police and the government have surrendered before Shri Prakash. STF has been formed to deal with Shri Prakash, but it is also not powerful. Shri Prakash laughed, saying, “Find out Deepak Sharma’s number and tell me; I will talk to him; the man seems nice.”

It was also written in the newspapers that Shri Prakash had threatened earlier by calling, and KK Rastogi has family relations with the Principal Secretary, Home. It was also written in all the newspapers that the Chief Minister had expressed great displeasure to the DGP and the Principal Secretary, Home, that even after I said so much, the most reputed drug businessman of the city was murdered, and his son was kidnapped. Arun Kumar, Satyendra Veer Singh, Rajesh Pandey, and others also visited the spot. After reaching there, it did not take long to understand that this work could not have been done by anyone other than Shri Prakash Shukla. Once again, the entire police came under pressure.

Till now, the police were thinking that after the killing of Anand Pandey, this gang would remain quiet for a few days, but this did not happen. Everyone stayed inside the house for four to five days and kept talking to Kunal. They kept guessing which numbers the police might have tapped and whom to talk to so that the information reached Kunal's wife and his family. Only Sudhir was allowed to leave the house. He used to bring food in the morning and evening and collect newspapers. Kunal came to know the next day that his father had died. That is why he was not answering questions; he was sitting silently. On the fifth or sixth day, Shri Prakash received a phone call from Surajbhan of Mokama, "Ashok bhai, where are you?" Shri Prakash told him, "Dada, I have a big tender."

Surajbhan said, "Keep the tender safely there and come to Patna immediately; I have important work. This work is vital. I must deal with the biggest threat to my dominance in Bihar."

Shri Prakash said, "Dada, give me a week or ten days; it will take at least a week or ten days to finish the tender."

Surajbhan said, "When you have the tender, there is no problem. Keep it safe; the work will be done after a month, but I must finish it quickly; please come in two or three days." Shri Prakash said, "Okay, Dada." Shri Prakash was in a dilemma; he asked Sudhir, "When will your car be ready?" Sudhir said, "Bhaiya, the car is being made; it is ready after dent painting; it will come tomorrow morning."

Shri Prakash said, "I have to leave from here for Patna tomorrow evening." Sudhir said, "Bhaiya, how can we leave him and go?"

Shri Prakash said, "Dada never insists so much; there must be some issue, and that is why he insists so much. If we delay, he will also have doubts; it will be better if we reach him by tomorrow night." Sudhir said, "Okay, bhaiya, who will stay here!"

Shri Prakash said, "These two who came with us from Gorakhpur will stay here only. Give them some money and explain it to them properly. If anything goes wrong, I will kill both of them." Sudhir said, "Yes, bhaiya, I will explain it to them properly."

Meanwhile, Shri Prakash talked to Surajbhan many times. But Surajbhan only asked him to come to Patna quickly. By the next afternoon, Sudhir had come home from Chinhat in his car, and all three had made all the preparations. They cleaned all the weapons, arranged them in the bag, and kept their clothes; at seven in the evening, Sudhir brought the car after filling the petrol tank. Around 7:30, Shri Prakash, Anuj, and Sudhir left for Patna.

Before reaching Patna, Shri Prakash called Surajbhan and asked, "Dada, where do you want to come?" Surajbhan said, "Keep the car parked near the old location of the bank in Kankarbagh; someone will come and take you to the new place. Let me know when you reach; I will talk to you."

Shri Prakash reached Patna, and this time, Surajbhan's man took him to the new flat. It was a brand-new flat. There was one bedroom and a well-arranged kitchen; the other two had mattresses on the floor. A man had already cooked food there. All three had their food; they were exhausted and went to sleep. Surajbhan arrived the following day. This time, Surajbhan had parked all his vehicles well before the flat and reached the flat on foot from the back path.

Shri Prakash was waiting for Surajbhan. As soon as he arrived, Shri Prakash said, "Dada, it seems there is some vital work. Otherwise, you have never insisted so much."

Surajbhan said, "Yes, it is something like that."

Shri Prakash said, "Dada, I received a big tender, and I had to take the payment for that. No problem, I will return it after completing your work."

Surajbhan said, "How Braj Bihari Prasad is after Munna Shukla. He is in the government and is the most powerful minister in Lalu Yadav's cabinet. He was recently caught in CBI, so Lalu Yadav has removed him from the cabinet, but here in PGI, a full court is being held morning and evening, and the work is going on as before. He has started suspecting that Munna Shukla has trapped him in collusion with his enemies. He cannot get us killed, but he is preparing to send us to jail using government power. You know that once someone goes to jail, there is no way to get out quickly. That is why most people avoid going to jail in Bihar. It is unlike UP, where people immediately surrender to the court, go to jail, and return on bail after four to six months. That is why there is no custom of surrendering to the court in Bihar. There are more benefits to absconding, but I cannot abscond. It is with great difficulty that I got a hold in Bihar; everything will end soon after I go to jail. That is why Braj Bihari Prasad's work has to be done."

Shri Prakash said, "Dada, there are about thirty-forty people with him. Twenty-twenty-five people have rifles, but it doesn't matter; it is your order, and the work will be done. We will start working from tomorrow."

Surajbhan told him the number of the private room of PGI and other details. Shri Prakash went to PGI the same day. He saw that outside the floor on which Braj Bihari Prasad's private room was, five seven people were sitting on chairs with rifles, and three policemen were also with them. The way to the gallery of the floor was blocked. They also interrogated the attendants of other patients on the floor, and if they suspected anything, they searched for their belongings and clothes. Shri Prakash went to all the floors in the lift and saw them. At four in the evening, Braj Bihari Prasad came down to the lawn. Twelve chairs were placed, and gradually, fifteen people came and started telling their stories. Most of the people had come for some work, and Braj Bihari Prasad was also calling people for his work. Behind the chair, Braj Bihari Prasad was sitting on fifteen to twenty uniformed men; almost the same number of people stood with three hundred and fifteen bore rifles. In the evening, Shri Prakash returned and talked to Surajbhan on the way. "Dada, if you know any doctor in PGI, please tell me. I will have to get admitted there. Without getting admitted, it will be difficult to get this work done."

Surajbhan said, "I will come to you in a little while; it is not right to talk on the phone. People from UP are after you, and it is repeatedly coming in the newspapers that the UP police tap your phone. Shri Prakash said, "Okay, Dada." At around eight in the evening, Surajbhan met Shri Prakash.

Shri Prakash told him about PGI, saying, "Unless you enter there as a patient, the work will be delayed. It is essential to get admitted there; you will have to be admitted on the same floor. No one will admit you like this. You will have to get referred from somewhere, and there should also be a doctor in PGI who can arrange a private room on the same floor."

Surajbhan said, "There is a boy from Mokama who is a surgeon in PGI. I will ask for his name, address, and mobile number and tell you I will talk to him after you contact him. He is not very old; he has been in PGI for just two years. See how much he can help; if he cannot, then tell me. Till then, I will find someone else and tell you."

Surajbhan called many places while sitting there and got that doctor's number quickly. He spoke to the doctor on his number and said, "Tomorrow, Ashok Singh will go to meet him; he has come from outside, and his health is terrible. Get him some help. There are two more men with him, so try to get him a private ward so he can be treated properly. Get him the help, he says."

Surajbhan made Shri Prakash note down the name and number of the doctor. The next day, Shri Prakash, Anuj, and Sudhir reached PGI, and after asking around, they reached the same doctor they asked about the problem. Shri Prakash said, "I have been having a lot of pain in my chest for many days; I am unable to understand. I have consulted many people in Banaras. I have also got myself examined in BHU, but the pain has not gone away."

The doctor called the receptionist and said, "He is coming; please get his registration and file ready. Also, tell me whose patients were there in the OPD." After getting registered, Shri Prakash took his file, reached the doctor in Mokama, and showed him the registration papers and the rest of the file. He also told him the name of the doctor he had to consult in the OPD. The doctor in Mokama asked the patients sitting there to sit for a while and took Shri Prakash to the doctor. On reaching the doctor's place, the doctor in Mokama whispered something in the OPD doctor's ear, and he understood it. The OPD doctor asked him to get four or five health-related tests done and also wrote that he should be admitted. The doctor in Mokama took him to his chamber and asked over the telephone, "If any private room is vacant on the first floor, please tell me?" Perhaps the reply came from there, "It is not vacant today; it may be vacant tomorrow."

The doctor said, "Get it done by tomorrow. I am sending the admission papers. He is my patient, so get him admitted to the private ward there." The doctor from Mokama said to Shri Prakash, "Get all the tests that the doctor prescribed and move tomorrow to the private room on the floor where you wanted to stay."

Shri Prakash got all the medical tests done that were prescribed during the day. The next morning, he went to the doctor again in Mokama. The doctor sent a man with Shri Prakash to enquire about that private room from the cardiology department, and it was found that the formalities were being completed. The patient's family members were also coming; it would be vacated by two o'clock. The room would be cleaned and ready in an hour. You lie down there; then, the doctors would keep visiting. You will not face any problems; keep the admission slip with you.

Shri Prakash reached that floor at two o'clock with his complete file, papers, test reports, and admission slip. At the beginning of the gallery, many people were sitting on chairs; there were also policemen. Shri Prakash took out all his papers and told him the doctor had asked us to get admitted here; the room number was on the slip. The people sitting there said, "You are very young; what disease do you have?" Shri Prakash said, "Heart operation is required; there is a blockage in two of the heart tubes." On hearing this, the people sitting nearby started regretting that this boy had a heart problem at such a young age. One of those boys went to drop him off in his room.

Shri Prakash told the man who had gone to drop him off, "Our two brothers are downstairs too; they will bring our luggage in a little while. My family members have also left; they work in a cloth mill in Ahmedabad. They will reach out in two days if we get a reservation today."

After going to the room, Shri Prakash called Sudhir and told him, "Both of you bring a pillow, two sheets, one or two utensils, glass, patient kurta pajama, all this from outside. Tell the room number to the boys of Braj Bihari Prasad sitting outside; they will let us in." Sudhir went outside PGI and bought all these things, and in an hour, he reached the gallery to go to Shri Prakash's room. People stopped him; he immediately told them the room number. One of them asked, "Are you his brother?" Anuj and Sudhir said, "Yes." Those people let Anuj and Sudhir enter the gallery without asking anything else.

After going inside, Anuj said, "Bhaiya, we will not be able to do any work here and come out; we will be killed." Shri Prakash said, "I thought you were brilliant. You are educated and can speak English, but you are stupid. It is not right to kill him here. Now, the work you people have to do is that Braj Bihari Prasad holds court on the lawn downstairs in the morning and evening; he goes with ten-fifteen people. This Chintu, who is sitting with him, also goes with him. He stands with him there when he starts going, then goes down with him. See how many times he goes by stairs, how many times he goes by lift, where the people are standing, for how long he sits there, and what the ways to go out of the lawn if there is no way, then look closely at where to park the car after jumping over the railing and wall. Dada is distraught; this work has to be done quickly."

Anuj and Sudhir used to come out after two to four minutes of Braj Bihari Prasad joining the people in the gallery and going downstairs. Then, after roaming around for a while outside, they used to call to inform us about his arrival. In two to three days, they collected all the information. Shri Prakash called Surajbhan and said, "Talk to Sudhir and Anuj this evening; two good cars and two to three boys will be needed." Surajbhan said, "Okay."

Shri Prakash said, "When he holds court outside, other patients are also visible there."

Sudhir said, "Yes, many patients walk around with their family members with glucose bottles in their hands and then go back."

Shri Prakash said, "Okay, tomorrow you must bring two glucose bottles, hand tape, and a hospital blanket from the market." Sudhir said, "Bhaiya, how will you cover yourself with a hospital blanket in this extreme heat?" Shri Prakash said, "Doctors also say that you should not get exposed to the wind." Sudhir brought all the things from outside.

Shri Prakash said, "This time, I will leave before Braj Bihari Prasad reaches the lawn. Please remove the pipe from the bottle and stick it to the hand with tape, cover yourself with a hospital sheet or shawl, and tie a towel on the head. I will leave slowly and keep moving around the lawn; it is also important to see the paths that you people have seen for the exit. He will come and sit, so it is also important to see from where to enter." Anuj said, "Okay bhaiya."

In the evening, Shri Prakash tied his head with a towel and wrapped the hospital shawl around himself. Anuj held his hand, and Sudhir came out of the room holding the glucose bottle. On the way, the people sitting with Braj Bihari Prasad asked, "Has his health deteriorated?"

Anuj said, "Yes, bhaiya, he had to undergo a heart operation; he is also showing some effects of paralysis. The doctor said he has to walk for an hour in the morning and evening." The people sitting there said, "Bhaiya, he must walk until he is well; the heart operation cannot be done properly."

They took Shri Prakash to the same lawn where Braj Bihari Prasad used to hold his court. Shri Prakash started walking in circles around the yard. Sometimes, when Shri Prakash straightened up and started walking fast, Sudhir would say, "Bhaiya, everyone is watching; stroll." Meanwhile, Braj Bihari Prasad approached the lawn with his fifteen-twenty people, and chairs were arranged. Some people sat on the ground; some remained standing.

Shri Prakash said, "Let's move towards the back side and closer to him."

Anuj and Sudhir took him to the back and walked away. A few people outside asked who he was. The people sitting in the gallery, who were with them at that time, said, "The poor guy is worried and had a paralysis attack two days ago." Two to four other patients were also strolling there, so no one noticed much. After making two rounds of Braj Bihari Prasad, Shri Prakash signaled them to go back, and from there, they came to their room.

Shri Prakash was drenched in sweat. He scratched the bottle and tube, kept it outside, and said, "We have to finish the job in one go, and after finishing it, we have to leave quickly." He said, "Bring all the weapons in the bag. When I come down from upstairs, Sudhir, you bring the bag to the downstairs bathroom. Anuj will stay outside the bathroom; if someone comes, we will tell them that the patient's condition is terrible; he has been taken to the toilet and will come out in two minutes. Anuj will say this loudly so that we become alert inside. I will keep the AK 47 under the blanket for two minutes. You guys put your pistols. Dada's boys, sitting on the vehicles outside the railing, should also be ready with weapons. If someone comes running towards the car, we will cover for him there, and the job will be done. This work has to be done tomorrow, and we have to leave. It is not right to keep the tender for so many days. I will also check on him now.

Shri Prakash called the boy living in the Lucknow house and asked him, "Is Kunal alright?" He said, "Yes, bhaiya, he is fine. He is insisting on clothes. Since then, he has been wearing the same underwear and vest. If you scold him too much, he starts crying."

Shri Prakash said, "Ask him for the number of underwear and vests, get a towel from the market, and bring a tracksuit. If the clothes are filthy, make him wear the new tracksuit and wash the old ones. Remember that the clothes should not be dried outside on the balcony or on the roof. Put them under the fan in the other room. They will dry in four to five hours."

Shri Prakash asked, "Tell me, did he try to run away?" The boy said, "No, bhaiya, he did not try to run away. He cries all day long and eats with great difficulty." Shri Prakash said, "Okay, we will come soon."

The next day, on 10th July 1998, as decided, Anuj came down with Shri Prakash carrying a glucose bottle and a pipe in his hand. Shri Prakash had put on a red blanket. On the other hand, Sudhir reached the bathroom with an AK 47 and a 0.45 pistol, a 9mm pistol, and an extra magazine of AK in his sports bag. After a while, Sudhir came down with Shri Prakash. Sudhir took the bag and went to the bathroom, where Shri Prakash and Anuj stood outside. One or two people who came to use the toilet were told that there was a severe patient inside; he would come out in two minutes, and they should be ready then. In two to four minutes, Shri Prakash hid the AK in the blanket, and Sudhir put the 0.45 pistol on his waist. As soon as he came out, Sudhir signaled Anuj to take the bag and put the 9mm magazine inside.

From there, both of them reached the lawn with Shri Prakash. Reaching the railing, he threw the bag on the other side of the railing and signaled the people sitting in the car to take the bag and keep it in the car. After half an hour, Braj Bihari Prasad arrived with his people. When he entered the lawn, Shri Prakash, Anuj, and Sudhir passed before him. Before Braj Bihari Prasad could understand anything, Shri Prakash fired the burst of AK 47 on Bihari; he fell on the spot. Sudhir and Anuj also fired in the air with their pistols. Fifteen to twenty people accompanying Braj Bihari Prasad ran away from there to save their lives. Shri Prakash, Anuj, and Sudhir jumped over the railing and reached the car. They kept the weapon in the vehicle and ran from there towards Lucknow. After coming out, Shri Prakash called Surajbhan, and Surajbhan said, "Hold the phone. I will connect right now."

After a while, Shri Prakash received a call from Surajbhan from the PCO.

Surajbhan said, "Ashok bhai, how can I thank you? You have done a great job for me."

Shri Prakash said, "Dada, you know that I never refuse your orders. My car is parked there; I will send one of my two other cars. Nothing is in it so that I will send my car with the keys. I will stay here near the dhaba. My car will come in an hour or two; I will send your car."

Surajbhan said, "You can go in that car." Shri Prakash said, "No, the car has been used at the scene; it is wrong to go with it. Send my car, I will go in that." Surajbhan said, "Okay." Shri Prakash, Anuj, and Sudhir sat in the car and waited for their car and kept laughing while talking about how they killed Braj Bihari. Sudhir asked, "Bhaiya, where did you get this idea of blankets? It wasn't even that cold."

Shri Prakash said, "In my childhood when someone in our village got paralyzed, the villagers would say that the person should not be exposed to cold. People would go out wearing blankets and sheets. If someone asked, I would tell them the same thing." Shri Prakash said, “Look, I always say that the one who fires the first bullet hits the target; he is the king on the battlefield. His brother-in-law had at least twenty armed men, so there was no need to be afraid of the police officers; they ran away as soon as the bullet was fired. The problem is only with those who are family members and carry rifles. Sometimes, they even risk their lives.”

Shri Prakash added, “While running, I had seen that more than half the people had dropped their rifles there. After we left, we heard the sound of four to six rounds of firing. Find out that the police officers must have fired these rounds to protect themselves. When senior officers arrive at the scene, they will tell them that I had fired, but while running, I lost my balance, and the bullet missed him. Most police officers are not able to fire. Remember that the first bullet should hit the target whenever you have to work, even if it takes a little longer.”

Shri Prakash said, “Sudhir bhai, a new doctor, was sitting in the chamber of the doctor from Mokama. I went to her chamber three times, and she was sitting there all three times. The doctor from Mokama was busy for a while, so I asked her. She did not tell me her name but told me that she is a resident doctor and is junior to the doctor from Mokama.” Shri Prakash said, “Sudhir, somehow find out her name. If you cannot find out, I must come to Patna again.” Sudhir said, “Bhaiya, I have not seen her.” Shri Prakash said, “I am telling you.” Shri Prakash described her appearance and said he had not seen a better doctor than her in PGI. Sudhir said, “Bhaiya, I have not seen more beautiful girls than in Lucknow. Manju from Kanpur is no less than anyone.” Shri Prakash said, “You don’t know anything. Find out the name and number quickly. Otherwise, I will have to come to Patna.” Sudhir said, “Bhaiya, you had told me that Suraj Dada had introduced me to that doctor. That doctor knows that Surajbhan has sent you there. The police will not leave Surajbhan.”

Shri Prakash said, “Even if his neck gets chopped off, the doctor can never have enmity with Surajbhan. Dada had given his name after a lot of thought. If the people in the private room apartments are also asked how this room was allotted, everyone will tell the doctor's name because the doctor had taken us to that gallery to get a private room allotted. The doctor must have thought of his answer; you know, the police cannot beat up a doctor. They can only create pressure. If the police beat up the doctor, the doctors will immediately go on strike, and the PGI will be closed. If the doctors create more pressure, the police officers will also be suspended. So don't worry about this, but do find out the name and address of that lady doctor. Sudhir said, “Okay, bhaiya, I will try my best.” Anuj said, “Bhaiya, the acting of paralysis that you did is beyond comparison.” Saying this, all three burst out laughing. All three were laughing and talking about different things while waiting for the car, and in a short while, the car arrived. Giving the keys to Surajbhan's car to the boy who had brought it, they put all their luggage in their Maruti 800 and left for Lucknow.

TENDER SETTLEMENT

When they reached Lucknow, Shri Prakash asked Sudhir what the number plate on this car was when Rastogi was kidnapped." Sudhir said, "Bhaiya, it was Delhi's number plate." Shri Prakash said, "What number plate is on it now?" Sudhir said, "Bhaiya, it is Bihar's number plate. I had put the Bihar number plate because here in Bihar, the police stop you once when you see the number plate of another state and ask for more money. Here in UP, no one asks."

Shri Prakash said, "Take off the Bihar number plate and put the Rajasthan plate on it. I will take you to the road next to the Maruti service center before the Chinhat barrier; change the plate in ten minutes." Sudhir said, okay. Shri Prakash turned the car there after a while, and Sudhir got down and put Rajasthan number plates on the front and back of the vehicle. Shri Prakash called the boy sitting next to Kunal and asked, "Just go out and see from B Block crossing to Mazar Tiraha; there is no police checking." He said, "Yes, bhaiya."

Ten minutes later, the boy called, "Bhaiya, there is no checking; at Mazar Tiraha, two policemen are sitting on chairs under the big tree." Shri Prakash reached his house fearlessly. Immediately, they drove the car inside and covered it, took their bags and weapons bags, and went inside the room. Shri Prakash asked the two boys, "Have you ordered food?" They said, "Yes, Bhaiya, I have ordered food for you people too."

Shri Prakash asked, "Where have you brought the food from?" The boy said, "I have brought it from Bhootnath Market." Shri Prakash again asked, "Have you been bringing food from there for four to five days? The boy said, "Yes, bhaiya, I got it from him. I get three meals in the morning and evening, two for these people and one for myself."

Shri Prakash took out his point five pistols and said, "I will shoot the whole magazine down your throat, you, rascal dog. Will you get food from the same place again and again? The police dogs must be sniffing like mad; they ask at hotels and eateries who are the people who have been carrying packed food since the day of the kidnapping till today. If I see you there, I will kill you immediately."

The boy said, "Yes, bhaiya, I made a mistake; I did not have this much idea."

Shri Prakash said, "From now on, you will get your meals from different places every morning and evening. From Quality in Mahanagar, from Karamat wala in Nishatganj, and someday go to Hazratganj and get it from Moti Mahal, do not repeat the food from any one shop. The police must be searching like mad right now."

Then Shri Prakash asked, "Where have the newspapers been from the last five to six days?" He said, "Bhaiya, they are kept here." Shri Prakash said, "Bring them immediately." He ran and brought all the newspapers.

Shri Prakash said, "I will wash my hands and face and read the newspapers; till then, you guys serve the food. Bring my food on the bed; after having food, I will meet that fat bastard. He has been eating sitting for the last ten days."

That boy went to the kitchen to heat the food. Sudhir and Anuj also came out after bathing and, after reaching the kitchen, started taking out their food. Shri Prakash was reading each newspaper correctly; in all the newspapers, the news related to kidnapping was printed on the main page and inside. He took out the English newspapers, kept them aside, and said to Anuj, who was eating there, "Read all the English newspapers and tell me what is written in them." Anuj said, "That's it, Bhaiya; I will read it after having food."

In a while, Anuj finished his food, washed his hands, and started reading the English newspaper. After having his food, Shri Prakash went straight to Kunal's room.

Shri Prakash asked, "Whose numbers do you remember?"

Kunal said, "I don't remember anyone's numbers."

Shri Prakash said, "The police must be listening to all the numbers of the family members. Who is the person who can be called and talked to? You won't be released until you get the money. We have to get the money; if we don't get the money, we will kill you right here and go away." Kunal started crying and said, "No one in my family can give me the money. Papa was the only one who knew about all the accounts and all the money. You killed Papa. Now, where will we get the money from!"

Shri Prakash asked, "Where are your in-laws from?" Kunal started stammering. Shri Prakash said, "Look, it's already too late. If you don't tell us, we will kill you." Kunal said, "My in-laws live in Jugal Kishore Jewellers."

Shri Prakash asked, "What about your father-in-law?

Where is your name?" Kunal told her name; Shri Prakash kept asking for her number, but Kunal did not remember the number.

Shri Prakash said, "It is very late today; I will talk to your in-laws tomorrow. If you don't give the money, your in-laws will give it. No father will let his daughter become a widow. You also eat food and go to sleep."

Shri Prakash called Manju in Kanpur the next day and told her, "Go to Jugal Kishore Jewellers and buy some small items. During the conversation, ask who the owner is. You people are quoting too high a price; I have to talk to the owner. Ask him his name, go to him and talk to him about reducing the price, and see how many phones there are. Get the shop's phone number from the man sitting at the reception."

Manju said, "I don't have that much money."

Shri Prakash said, "Take whatever money you have. I will give it to you when I come." Manju said, "Because of you, the police are searching for me. I live in another house; it will be a big problem if someone recognizes me." Shri Prakash said, "Go, no one will recognize you; I will call you in the evening." Shri Prakash called Manju in the evening and asked her, "What did you take?"

She said, “I didn't take anything, but your work is done. She noted that the receptionist sits at this number, and the owner sits at the cash counter in front of him. The owner has not kept his phone on the table but on the floor. The receptionist transferred the call to him; only then did the owner talk.” Shri Prakash said, “Okay.”

Shri Prakash disconnected Manju’s call and called Jugal Kishore Jewellers. When the receptionist picked up the phone, he asked him to contact the owner by name directly.

The receptionist asked, “What should I tell you?”

Shri Prakash said, “Tell him I am Ashok Singh from Income Tax. He will understand.” Upon hearing the Income Tax name, the receptionist transferred the call to the owner. As soon as he picked up the phone, the owner greeted Shri Prakash loudly.

Ashok said, “Now listen to me carefully. I have your son-in-law with me; arrange for one crore rupees.” Lala said, “Make me talk to my son. I will give you whatever you say.”

Shri Prakash said, “If you try to be too clever, the son will be killed. Keep the cash ready, and remember that our men are watching your shop. Today you are wearing a white shirt and dark brown pants. The top button is open; two thick chains are visible. You are wearing gold-framed glasses, and the phone is kept below. The reception boy with big mustaches is sitting right in front of you. So don't try to be clever and call the police. If you do anything, you will find the boy's body when it is infested with worms."

Lala's face was turning pale. He said, "Yes, sir." Shri Prakash said, "I will talk to you tomorrow evening; keep the money ready." Lala said, "Give me some more time; we don't keep so much cash at home at once." Shri Prakash said, "You think I am a chu@#%a like your customers? I will collect it by borrowing money. I will call you tomorrow evening." Saying this, Shri Prakash hung up the phone. Lala immediately arranged his car and left for home. He sent his man in the car and said, “Go to Kunal's house and tell my daughter to go to her elder aunt's house and call me from another number. It is urgent”. The driver immediately left for Lucknow.

When he reached Lucknow, he told Lala's daughter about Lala's message. When the daughter left for her aunt's house in her car, she saw that a vehicle with two or three people in it was following the car.

She immediately told the driver, "Take me to Rajiv Ratan Shah's uncle's house."

She took the car and reached the house of Principal Secretary, Home, Rajiv Ratan Shah. The Principal Secretary was not at home; his wife was there. Kunal's mother and Rajiv Ratan Shah's wife studied in the same class in the same school. When the security people at the gate saw the car, they allowed it to enter. The news was conveyed inside; Madam immediately said, "Beta, what's the matter? Why are you so worried?" Kunal's wife started crying and said, "Aunty, it has been so many days. Nothing has been found out." Papa called and said, "Talk to someone else; there is something important. When I left home for Bua's place, a car started following me; I felt the police officers were following me to see where I was going. Tell uncle to stop these people so that the matter moves forward." She said, "Okay, sit down; I will tell them."

She immediately called her husband, Shah Sahab, told him the whole thing, and said, "Jugal Kishore has called her for some important matter, but the policemen are following her. Tell the policemen they have been unable to do anything till now; why are they troubling the family now?" After ten minutes, he called again and said, "Tell the daughter she can now go to Bua Ji's place. No policeman will chase her."

Kunal's wife took the car from there and reached Kunal's aunt's house. Aunt and uncle got scared seeing her. She went inside, told them the whole story, and said, "Please let me talk to Papa anyhow." Kunal's uncle said, "Okay, I will let you talk to him from my phone. The police have not questioned us yet; they will not know what you discussed."

Kunal's wife called her father from there; Papa was scared. She told him the whole story of the phone call and that he asked to arrange one crore rupee.

Kunal's wife said, "Papa, please give it to me; nothing is more important than his life." Lala said from the other side, "He has asked us to make arrangements by tomorrow evening; you know that so much cash cannot be kept at home at once."

Kunal's wife said, "Papa, I know you can get one crore rupee from the market in ten minutes." Lala said nothing, saying, "Son, how can I throw money away like this until I talk to Kunal and confirm that he is with him? If you are saying so, I will arrange for the money, but once I talk to Kunal, I will give him the money. Tomorrow evening, you also stay at aunt's place; if he calls, I will inform you." In the evening, Shri Prakash called again. He again told the receptionist that I was Ashok Singh from Income Tax. The receptionist transferred the call. Lala was sitting idle but did not pick up the phone. He asked the receptionist, gesturing with his hand, "Who is it?"

The receptionist roared, "Ashok Singh, Income Tax." The phone was on hold. Shri Prakash heard this and told the receptionist, "If Lala is sitting, why did he not pick up the phone? Tell him to pick up the phone; otherwise, this will be the last call."

The receptionist understood that something was wrong. He put his hand on his mouth and roared, "I am ringing again. Pick up; the Income Tax officer is saying something strange." The receptionist gave me the phone again. This time, Lala picked it up.

Shri Prakash said, "Why are you not picking up the phone? When I told you that our man was there and we were watching you, the son-in-law had just woken up, and you would also wake up. Don't make such a mistake in the future. Pick up the phone. Now tell me whether the money has been arranged or not?"

Lala said, "Bhai sahab, I have arranged for fifty boxes. If Kunal is nearby, please let me talk to him. I will deliver fifty boxes wherever you say."

Shri Prakash said, "It seems you are bargaining for your son-in-law. I told you yesterday that you don't consider me a shop customer. I will take the whole shop. I will give you time till tomorrow afternoon. After that, I will call and tell you the place. Take Kunal's body." Lala said,

"Bhaiyya, I will make all the arrangements by morning, but please let me talk to him once."

Shri Prakash said, "Okay, I will make you talk to him, but remember that he will have a pistol on his head while talking. Even a little trickery will kill Kunal." Saying this, Shri Prakash disconnected the phone. In the evening, Kunal's wife reached Kunal's aunt's house, and his father from Kanpur told her the whole story and told her that tomorrow he would make them talk, and if he made them talk, he would send him the money.

Kunal's wife said, "Nothing will happen to Kunal? The police officers who come here again and again talk among themselves that he is a big thug, he can do anything; I am scared."

At night, Shri Prakash said, "Make preparations in the morning; we will take this bastard somewhere far away and make him talk on mobile; after making him talk, we will bring him back here. If the payment is made, then we will leave him at night. We will decide where to take the payment. Anna knows all the places in Faizabad; we will take Anna along. Anna has been with Kunal for many days. Tell Anna to make him understand; he should not try any trick." Sudhir said, "Okay." Around 11 am, Shri Prakash said, "Anuj bhai, go to Faizabad road and see if there is any checking going on anywhere." He told Anna, "Make Kunal wear dark glasses; put black electrical tape on the inside of the dark glasses. Try wearing them yourself and see that there is no hole left. Make him sit in the middle and keep the pistol pointed at him. If he screams, we will pierce his skull right there and throw him on the road. Let us do this: by the time Anuj comes back from here after checking all the barriers on Faizabad Road, we will clean all the weapons. We will clean all the weapons sitting in front of Kunal. The bastard will think he will be shot at the slightest mistake."

Where Kunal was sitting, Sudhir and Shri Prakash separated the parts of the pistol and AK 47 and cleaned them pistol and AK 47 thoroughly. He also had Singer sewing machine oil with him, which he used to put in the moving parts at intervals and wipe appropriately with a rag. In between, Shri Prakash kept asking Kunal, do you know what this is called? Kunal said, I don't know. Then he told me one by one that this is AK 47, this is a nine mm pistol. This is a point-five pistol. Slowly, he kept telling one or two stories about how Shahi was killed. How Vivek Srivastava was killed. Kunal got scared after listening to his words. After some time, he cleaned all the weapons, wrapped them in a cloth, kept them inside the bag, and told Kunal, "Wear pants and a shirt, and I will make you talk." Kunal asked, "Whom will I make you talk to?" Shri Prakash said, "I will make you talk to the one to whom I have to give money." Kunal said, "Let me talk to my mother." Shri Prakash said, "When I get the money, I will let you go; you can talk to your mother. Kunal became quiet." Everyone got ready and started waiting for Anuj to come. In a short while, Anuj returned with his car, parked it in the portico, went to Shri Prakash, and said, "Bhaiya, everything is quiet; there is no checking going on anywhere."

Shri Prakash said, "These are policemen. After the incident, they shouted that a blockade had been implemented. Checking is being done, but no checking has been found anywhere. All the checking is only on paper and in newspapers."

In the portico, Shri Prakash made Kunal sit in the backseat between Sudhir and Anuj, made Anna sit next to him in the front, and started driving himself. While going towards Faizabad, a little ahead of Raunahi police station, in a very deserted place with no population on both sides of the road, Shri Prakash stopped the car under a big Sheesham tree.

He made Anna leave the car and said, "Keep looking on both sides." Shri Prakash dialed Lala Jugal Kishore's number from his mobile in Kanpur. This time, the receptionist transferred the call to the owner without much questioning, and the owner also picked up the phone.

Shri Prakash asked, "What happened? Is full ransome amount ready?"

Lala said, "Yes, bhaiya, I have collected it somehow; ten is still less." Shri Prakash said, "You mada@#%@d ! This is in your blood; you bargain in everything. Even if your person gets killed, I will take full one corore; I will not take a single penny less. I will take the money and count it completely; only then will I release the boy."

Lala said, "Bhaiya, it would have been better if you had taken the money with one hand and returned it to the son with the other; we would have also been at peace." Shri Prakash said, "You are acting very smart! Do you think that when cleverness was being distributed, you ran away with all the cleverness, and we were left standing with a begging bowl in front of God? Are you mad?"

Lala said, "Okay, bhaiya, whatever you think, let us talk once."

Shri Prakash said, "I will let us talk." Shri Prakash handed over the phone to Kunal. After saying yes and hello, Kunal said, "Papa, give them the money. Otherwise, they will kill me." On the other hand, Lala asked, "How is your health?" Kunal said, "I am fine; how is mummy's health?" Lala said, "She is also fine." Kunal asked again, "How is Ruchina?" Lala said, "She is also fine." On hearing Ruchina's name, Shri Prakash took the phone from him and said to Lala, "Are you satisfied?" Lala said, "Yes bhaiya."

Shri Prakash asked Lala, "Who is this Ruchina?"

Lala said, "She is my daughter, bhaiya; tell me where to give the money?"

Shri Prakash said, "You take the money and come to Faizabad; the entire money should be inside the black bag. When you reach Faizabad, I will tell you where you have to go, and after you take the money, I will give you the address in an hour. Go and get Kunal and go straight to your house."

Lala said, "Okay, I will reach Faizabad." Shri Prakash said, "I will call and ask." Cutting the phone, Shri Prakash drove straight to Faizabad and told Anna, "Tell me a place to stay for four to six hours." Anna said, "I will take you there. It is a big house with a compound, and the car will park comfortably inside. We will stay there and have our meals there, too."

Shri Prakash directly took Kunal from there to the house, as told by Anna. After a while, Anna brought food for everyone. Everyone ate and started chatting among themselves. Shri Prakash estimated it would take about five hours to reach Faizabad from Kanpur. It would be evening, and we would take the payment somewhere on the roadside at night. We would check the payment; if the goods were complete, we would leave the boy on the road. We would tell Lala, and Lala would run away with the boy. Anuj asked, "Bhaiya if the police have put the number on tapping, they must be listening to everything."

Shri Prakash said, "You are educated; you have worked in the airlines, but are you still stupid? The police do tapping by putting a cut in the telephone line or by inserting a wire in the box installed on the pole and sitting somewhere on the side; they do the tapping. When there is no wire in the mobile, how will the police do the tapping? It seems you did not listen. I asked Lala to bring his mobile. Lala also told me the mobile number, where to take the money after coming here, and how it is possible without a mobile. Mobile has become so good that these bastards will never be able to listen." Anuj said, "Yes, bhaiya, you are right."

Shri Prakash called Lala on his mobile to check, and Lala immediately picked up the phone after some time. Shri Prakash asked, "How far have you reached?" Lala said, "I have come a long way from Barabanki. I am about to reach Ramsanehi Ghat."

Shri Prakash asked, "How many people are there with you?"

Lala said, "I am alone, and there is a driver."

Shri Prakash asked, "Did you bring the payment in the trunk or the back seat?"

Lala said, "I have kept it on the back seat."

Shri Prakash said, "When I tell you to drop the driver, you drive the car yourself." Lala said, "Bhaiya, I don't know how to drive properly. I am also nervous; I will not be able to drive."

Shri Prakash said, "Okay, you can inform me of this number. As soon as you reach Faizabad, I will tell you." Slowly, it became seven in the evening. It started getting dark. Shri Prakash got a call from Lala,

“Bhaiya, I have reached the city; you tell me where to come?” Shri Prakash said, “You cross the city and come towards Ayodhya.” Lala said, “Okay.” Lala slowly started moving toward Ayodhya after asking for directions.

Shri Prakash said, “Everyone gets ready; Anna will stay with Kunal. We are going to get the goods.”

Shri Prakash got out of his car and slowly started moving towards Ayodhya. Shri Prakash called and asked, “Tell me your car number and drive slowly.” Lala said, “Tell me your car number and drive slowly.”

He told me his car number and asked the driver to drive slowly. Two and a half to three kilometers before Ayodhya, Shri Prakash called, “I have seen your car. Fifty steps ahead, park your car on the left-hand side of the dirt road and stop a little ahead, I will tell you. You have not locked the rear door; keep the rear door open.” Lala said, “Okay.”

Shri Prakash drove quickly, crossed Lala's car, and went ahead. After going about a kilometer, he came back. He looked in Lala's car with the car's headlights to see if there was any other person. The driver was sitting in the driving seat, and Lala was sitting in the back seat. Shri Prakash quickly drove his car from beside him, went to the right on the main road, and looked carefully to see if anyone was there. Then, as he turned back towards the car, he called, “The car will be parked on the right side of your car; there will be enough space for your door to be opened. Remember, don't try any tricks; a man is sitting with a pistol pointed at your son-in-law's head." Lala said, "What tricks will I use now?" Shri Prakash said, "The car will be parked beside you; I will open your door, keep your bag in my car, and then go ahead. Quietly reverse your car, reach Faizabad city, stop at Metro Hotel, and wait for my call." Lala said, "Okay." After a while, Shri Prakash parked his car right beside Lala's car; there was enough space for the door to open. Sudhir opened the door of his car and quickly opened the door of Lala's car. Anuj got down from his side, stood on the road, and started looking around. Sudhir pulled the bag to the ground but could not lift it even after trying twice or thrice. He called Anuj with a gesture. Anuj and Sudhir picked up the bag and put it in the back of their car. When Shri Prakash moved forward rapidly, Sudhir said, "Bhaiya, this bag is hefty. It seems the bastard has filled the bag with ten rupee notes?"

Shri Prakash said, "Even for a hundred rupees, it will still be quite heavy. Look back. Did the bastard reverse the car or not?"

Anuj looked back and saw that Lala had reached the main road. In a short while, Lala reached the city directly, searched for the Metro Hotel, booked a room, and started waiting for Shri Prakash's call. Even after about an hour, when no call came, Lala called the number from which Shri Prakash used to call, but it was switched off. Lala's breathing became fast. He drank the water in the hotel room and got lost in thoughts, holding his head. After about half an hour, Shri Prakash's call came.

Shri Prakash said, "You have honestly paid the full amount. Go and take Kunal to the Faizabad bus stand. Kunal has also been paid; even if you don't meet him, he will reach Lucknow by bus."

Lala quickly exited, paid the hotel owner, and ran towards the bus stand. He kept looking here and there at the bus stand. After a while, Kunal was seen near the ticket window at the bus stand. On seeing Lala, Kunal hugged him, then, due to fear, he separated from him and started looking around. He said, "Papa, have you brought the car?" "No, sit on the bus; I am scared." Lala said, "No, I have brought the car; let's go by car." Lala took Kunal, went straight to his car, and quickly left. Shri Prakash took out some money, gave it to Anna, and said, "I will send more money after a few days."

When Shri Prakash turned towards the road leading to Patna from there, Sudhir and Anuj asked, "Bhaiya, how did you come here?" Shri Prakash said, "He will reach Lucknow in two hours; as soon as he reaches Lucknow, the police will surround him. They will ask all kinds of questions; they will ask about the place, where he was kept, where he was left, what kind of sounds were heard around the place where he was kept, and when. They will try their best; Lala will also come forward and tell them they have found their son-in-law, and if they are caught somehow, they will get their money back. Lala's mind will be stuck on the money. By the time they reach Lucknow, we will be out of the district. Once we reach Banaras, we will easily reach Patna."

Anuj and Sudhir said, "Bhaiya, it is unsafe to go to Patna with so much cash. If any incident happens in Patna, they thoroughly check the border. They are unlike the UP police; no matter how much is said or ruckus is created, a constable will stand at the border by lowering the barrier. Once he gets a strong warning or sees a red or blue light on the vehicle, he will open the barrier alone."

Shri Prakash said, "We will call Dada before reaching Patna; Dada has set men at the barrier; let us find out whether checking is going on. We have to reach Dada, but in any case, the money will be safe there. Dada has no answer; he has never cheated with money." Anuj said, "Okay bhaiya." Before the barrier, Shri Prakash asked Surajbhan; he asked and said that it was okay to come.

Shri Prakash said, "Dada, I have received the payment for the tender I left to do your work, and I am bringing that. I have to give it to you, where should I come? You will keep it safe, and I will take it later as needed." Surajbhan said, "Okay, come straight home. Our man will meet you near the dhaba and take you outside. It will be quite late, keep the payment here and sleep comfortably in a house here. Then leave in the morning; it is not right to leave at night." Shri Prakash said, "Okay."

Shri Prakash reached Mokama directly. It was pretty late; he met Dada's man at the dhaba, who took him to Surajbhan. Surajbhan was given that black bag. Shri Prakash said, "Dada, the bag has one lakh rupees less; the rest is one crore. Please keep it safe. I will take it later as and when required."

Surajbhan said, "Don't worry. I will send it whenever you say it, or you can come and take it. Now go and rest; I have kept food for three people there. There is also a boy to heat the food; he will give it to you afterward. Sleep after eating, leave comfortably in the morning." Shri Prakash said- "Yes Dada."

AMAZING CHOICE

Getting up in the morning, Anuj said, "Now we have to go back!" Shri Prakash said, "Not now. Sudhir has gone to take a bath. He will return, and I will tell you when we will go." Sudhir also came after some time. Shri Prakash asked Sudhir, "What happened? Did you find out about that doctor?"

Sudhir said, "Brother, I don't want to ask the doctor from Mokama; I haven't found out from anywhere else." Shri Prakash said, "Sudhir, you haven't met the doctor from Mokama; he won't recognize you. Go to him; if he is sitting there, tell him about your illness and get the medicine."

Sudhir said, "Brother, I have just reached Patna; it will be evening by then. Why don't we stay at Dada's Kankarbagh flat? Then we will go to PGI and find out about him." Shri Prakash said, "This idea is good; let's go and talk to Dada right now." After having food, everyone got ready and reached Surajbhan. They told Surajbhan, "Dada, if the Kankarbagh flat is okay, then there is no problem?" Surajbhan asked, "What is the matter?" Shri Prakash said, "Dada, we want to stay here today, but tomorrow, we must shop. Anuj and Sudhir also want to do some shopping. Those guys have distributed many photos in Lucknow; no one will recognize us here."

Surajbhan said, "You don't have any idea about yourself. The work of Braj Bihari has been so big that the whole government is shaken. Don't go to PGI; it has been published in all the newspapers about which room you were staying in and getting your treatment." Shri Prakash said, "Dada, don't worry about that. Whoever has seen me has seen me as a patient. Now, no one will be able to recognize me." Dada said, "Then it is okay, whatever you think. I will tell you that in Kankarbagh, a person will be available to cook food." From Mokama, everyone went straight to the Kankarbagh flat. They parked the car inside, put on the cover, and settled in the room.

Shri Prakash said, "Today, I feel like drinking good alcohol. It has been a long time since I drank alcohol. All the important tasks have been accomplished. Now there will be no problem with money. Whoever is called in Lucknow will pay the money. Lalji Tandon is showing some speed; I will arrange for him, too."

Anuj said, "Brother, it is coming in the newspapers that some STF has been formed, which has been formed only for us. Very carefully selected officers have been appointed in the STF." Shri Prakash said, "The police of the entire state were deployed but could not do anything. Now, what will these four people do? Don't worry; we will only roam in Lucknow and base there. I will see what these bastards do. Find their numbers, too; I will put them under control, too." Anuj said, "Okay, brother."

Then Shri Prakash said again, "Now I will not leave without meeting that doctor. Sudhir, you also wear jeans and a nice T-shirt, wear sunglasses and try not to be seen by many people. The doctor's OPD chamber from Mokama is on the ground floor. Visit her once, then sit outside with the patients. When she comes out after bathing, inform me on the phone. I will surround her there and talk to her. Once I get her name and address, I will see."

Sudhir said, "Brother, the work is risky; why do you get into trouble? You will find many such women in Lucknow." Shri Prakash said, "You cannot understand."

Sudhir went to the market in a short while and brought bottles of liquor. The cook at Surajbhan's flat arranged the rest of the things, and everyone sat down and started drinking. Shri Prakash said, "You people can drink as much as you want; I will only drink beer. A person needs to remain conscious. Dada has also harbored much enmity." Sudhir and Anuj drank to their heart's content. After drinking, they ate and slept. Shri Prakash kept calling someone in between. Shri Prakash woke Sudhir early in the morning and said, "Get ready and go quickly."

Sudhir got ready quickly, went straight to PGI, and reached the doctor's chamber from Mokama by asking for his address. There was a massive crowd of patients; someone stopped him at the gate outside and said, "Where is the numbered slip? First, make the slip, and then come with the number." Sudhir said, "I will come only after getting the slip made; I was just checking whether the doctors are there."

From outside itself, he saw that the doctor sahab was sitting on the main chair and seeing the patients. The same lady doctor was sitting on the chair next to the table. Sudhir understood as soon as he saw that Shri Prakash was saying this. Sudhir sat on the bench outside and waited for the lady doctor to come out. After a while, the lady doctor came out and went straight to the department office, and after a while, she started coming out of the building. Sudhir called and told Shri Prakash, "She is going towards the main gate."

Shri Prakash got out of the car and rushed inside the gate. After walking a little distance, he saw she was going towards the parking. He quickly moved ahead and stopped her, saying Doctor Sahab, Doctor Sahab, the doctor also stopped. She said, "Tell me?"

Shri Prakash said, "Doctor Sahab, you treated me. The prescription has been lost somewhere; I have to get the medicine prescribed again. She said to come to the OPD tomorrow, and now I am returning." Saying this, she left. Shri Prakash said, "Give me your mobile number, I will ask. I will come when you are in the OPD."

The doctor said, "You are crazy; I told you once to come to the OPD tomorrow. How dare you ask for my mobile number?" Shri Prakash said, "What is there to get angry about? I have been waiting for so many days to see you?"

The doctor stood up and said, "If you are very mentally unstable, I will call my brother right away. He will tear you into pieces, and no one will be able to identify him."

Shri Prakash said, "Call him."

The girl said, "Do you even know who my brother is?"

Shri Prakash said, "I don't need to know anyone."

The girl said, “I am Pappu Yadav’s sister. You must know Pappu Yadav. Go away quietly; you will be in trouble if he comes.”

Shri Prakash said, “The same two hundred kilograms, Pappu Yadav, okay, I will deal with him too. Go and tell him that I met Shri Prakash Shukla.”

Shri Prakash saw that two or three more people had gathered around him because this conversation was being held in a loud voice. Shri Prakash turned back, went straight to his car, and left. As soon as he sat in the car, Sudhir asked, “Brother, was any work done?”

Sudhir said, “All the work is done; she is Pappu Yadav’s sister. I will get her home number now and see how she doesn’t talk to me. Now I will ask Dada about Pappu Yadav's house; tomorrow, I will drag him in the car when he comes out." Sudhir said, "Brother, let it be; Pappu Yadav is also a bastard." Shri Prakash said, "I will remove all such people from the way or force them to hold Dada's feet. Dada is fighting for supremacy in Bihar. Once Bihar comes under Dada's control, Dada will be in Bihar, and I will be in UP. Think how much fun it will be. A convoy of fifty vehicles, police saluting at every intersection, and the collector, commissioner touching feet in a closed room." Saying this, all three started laughing and reached the flat in a short while. Shri Prakash asked Sudhir, "Now tell me, have you seen such a girl in Lucknow?" Sudhir said, "Brother, there is no answer to your choice!" Shri Prakash started smiling. Anuj interrupted again, "Brother, you are saying the work is done. Should we leave for Lucknow tomorrow?" Shri Prakash said, "Anuj, I don't understand why you are so scared despite being the son of a police inspector." Anuj lowered his head and started smiling.

Meanwhile, the STF office slowly got organized. The DG installed a desktop computer; the Haridwar Kumbh Mela had ended, and UP Police had bought an Ambassador, three Mahindra jeeps, and a Gypsy for the Haridwar Kumbh Mela. After the Kumbh was over, orders were given from the DG's office to hand over all these vehicles to the STF. All the cars arrived. In the meantime, SSP, STF Arun Kumar, Satyavendra Veer Singh, and Rajesh Pandey got their respective inspectors and sub-inspectors posted in the STF. Now, there were about twenty people in the STF. Every day in the morning and evening, people used to collect their information in Arun Kumar Sahab's room and verify it by calling the concerned police employee officer in the district.

To minimize the use of mobile phones, ADG Law and Order installed a landline phone in the STF office from another office. Everyone used the same landline phone. Everyone decided to call Sultanpur's Dhirendra Pratap Singh, who used to live with Shri Prakash earlier and was an excellent driver, and talk to him separately. By taking him into confidence, find out all the hideouts and, from there, find out about his movements. Rajesh Pandey was responsible for calling and talking to him, and Avinash Mishra kept him in his confidence.

Indrajit Singh Tewatia and Satyendra Veer Singh were given the responsibility of determining if they got any information about the movement and hideouts of this gang in western Uttar Pradesh, then taking that information from Dhirendra and checking its activities in west Uttar Pradesh. After gaining his confidence, Dhirendra Pratap Singh was called to the STF office. At first, he was a bit hesitant and nervous, but later, he came under Avinash Mishra's confidence. Slowly, he started telling the names of Shri Prakash's old hideouts and acquaintances. One day, Rajesh Pandey was talking to him.

In the conversation, he told me, "Shri Prakash has four mobile numbers, and he has bought excellent new mobile phones in Nepal. The mobile numbers are very long, so I don't remember them. These numbers are written on the back of an old newspaper at my home. After the Janpath incident, while taking out his car from Gomti Motors, he had given me these numbers that, after getting a gypsy, call on all these numbers. If you find any one number working, then talk to them. Bring the gypsy to the place I tell you. That newspaper is kept at my home. When you raided my house, I had kept it in the cupboard under the copybook of my nephews. I was afraid you would find out if you got these numbers. Anuj often told me that Rajesh Pandey had good knowledge of mobiles and had been sitting in the offices of Usha Mobile and Essar Mobile for a long time. People from both these mobile companies also know him."

Rajesh Pandey asked, “Will we still get that newspaper there?”

Dhirendra said, “Yes, it must be kept there.” Avinash said, “I will take him to Sultanpur and bring that newspaper from there.”

After a while, Rajesh Pandey told Arun Kumar, who said, “Sure, get it and sit down for a day and explain the mobile system to everyone because if they use mobile phones, it will take much time.” Rajesh Pandey said, “Okay.” Arun Kumar called Avinash Mishra and said, “You immediately go to Sultanpur with Dheerendra, and if you get that newspaper, bring it. From the entire conversation, it seems essential to work on mobile. None of us knows how the mobile system works.”

Avinash Mishra immediately went to Sultanpur with Dheerendra. The next day in the meeting, Avinash brought the newspaper in which four mobile numbers were written. Arun Kumar told Satyendra Veer Singh, “Get the details of these mobile numbers and a detailed report.” Satyendra Veer Singh said, “Sir, give this work to Rajesh Pandey. He knows this work very well and also goes to both mobile companies to get the details. I tried to make Rajesh understand many times but could not.” Arun Kumar said, “It does not matter. Rajesh should do the mobile work, and from now on, if anyone gets a mobile number or wants to get any related information, he should contact Rajesh Pandey only. Rajesh Pandey will tell.”

After looking at the four mobile numbers, Rajesh Pandey said, “Three of these are Usha phones, and one is Essar phone.” Arun Kumar said, “How did you find out by looking at the numbers?” Rajesh Pandey said, '983' are the first three numbers of both the mobile companies, and the one after that has 80, so it is of Usha phone. The one with 90 is an Essar phone. I will go to Usha and get a detailed report from RK Singh and Pawan Diwan in Essar. Everyone will sit and discuss it in the evening." Satyendra Veer Singh said, "See, Sir, I was right in saying I don't understand the mobile phone thing. Only Rajesh will be able to do it." Arun Kumar said, "It is right; now we don't have to sit idly by. Every day, we have to move one step ahead; only then will we be able to reach the target. Rajesh should quickly go and get all the reports; in the evening, we will sit and decide where to go tomorrow." By evening, the detailed reports of all four mobile phones came. Arun Kumar said, "How will we know by looking at this? Rajesh Pandey said it has incoming and outgoing letters written in it. Where did the call occur, and for how long? The last cell ID is given, which tells where his location is. I do not have any information about the cell ID; I will know that only after going to the offices of Usha and Essar phones."

Arun Kumar said, "For now, everyone should take a report and write the STD numbers separately, including the numbers in which cities the call took place. Tomorrow morning, we will go to the offices of both mobile companies; there, we will ask them about the cell ID to find out where he was at that time. According to the call detail report, these four phones have been switched off for two months." Every one searched for the STD numbers of different cities from the telephone directory and wrote down on paper the number with which the call took place in whichever city. Arun Kumar said, "Rajesh should find out if their officers are present in Usha, Essar, then we will go and ask about the cell ID." Satyendra Veer said, "It is too late now, but we can talk tomorrow morning." Arun Kumar said, "No, let's try right now. If we find someone, we will complete this work today to take it forward tomorrow."

Rajesh Pandey called and enquired and told Arun Kumar, "Usha, RK Singh is sitting in the office now. I have told him that SSP and we are coming for some information." RK Singh was also a little hesitant; he said, "You people should not come in police vehicles or park the police vehicles far away in Jawahar Bhawan or Indira Bhawan and come on foot because so many wrong news have been published in the newspapers about mobile phones that the office employees are scared, they will get more scared on seeing the police."

Arun Kumar said, "RK Singh is right. We will park our vehicles in Jawahar Bhawan."

Arun Kumar, Satyendra Veer Singh, and Rajesh Pandey walked towards Shri Ram Tower. Everyone reached RK Singh's chamber after parking the car in Jawahar Bhawan. They told RK Singh their problem, "How can we find out where this person was at that time from the last cell ID written in your CDR?" RK Singh said, "I can tell you this only after asking my engineer."

After a while, their engineer, Mr. Sarkar, arrived; he said, "We decode this cell ID and keep its location separately. Now we will tell where it is from after looking at each cell ID." Sarkar came with his thick file and sat in the same office. Rajesh Pandey kept telling me the cell ID one by one, and Sarkar kept telling me its address. In about an hour, he said all the addresses. He told me one more thing: how does this cell ID come and where does the call end while going from one tower to another? That, too, gets recorded. If you want to know the route and speed of the person carrying the mobile, that too can be told. Everyone was surprised to hear this information.

Rajesh Pandey asked the government, "This is a very good thing; so many people are using mobile; can this information be obtained about all of them?" The government said, "Not many people are using it right now. Currently, mobile phones are less used because their towers have not been installed everywhere; they have been installed only in big cities and towns. These towers will be installed almost everywhere in the next two years, and more people will use them. When more people use them, the call rate will also decrease. Right now, it is so expensive that not everyone can afford it. Outgoing calls are charged at Rs. 17 per minute, and incoming calls at Rs. 10 per minute. That is why, in the report you have gotten, there are not many calls in three months, and the number of calls has decreased.

Now we can tell you about every call." Rajesh Pandey said, "Okay." Taking all the information, everyone reached the STF office with Arun Kumar.

Arun Kumar said, "We have good information; let us also see where Shri Prakash stayed the most. In which area he stayed at night, and which cities he left at what time." After much brainstorming, everyone concluded that according to the information from the mobile phone, Shri Prakash Shukla usually comes to Patna and Mokama. He has been to Lucknow or Gorakhpur for a very short time. There is no call for fifteen to twenty days in between. This means that either his mobile is switched off at this time or he is staying at some place where the mobile tower does not work.

Rajesh Pandey said, “Sir, his last call was from Gorakhpur, and the first call was also from Gorakhpur. It is possible that he was in Nepal for the entire time. A mobile network has not yet come in Nepal. If the details of the people he called on his landline number are sought from BSNL, Nepal numbers may be found. Nepal numbers will be found in the area where he stayed, or if there is no mobile network, then the PCO numbers of that area will be found. This will also clarify where he stayed for about twenty days.”

SSP, STF said, “It is an excellent idea. All the landline numbers in his call details and their information should be sought from BSNL tomorrow. But this information can be seen only by people here at the headquarters. Umesh Singh, Deputy SP, and Anil Singh should be assigned to this work; they should also learn by watching it. Umesh Singh joined from Kanpur three days ago, and Anil Singh has been associated with security here. They will get this detail from BSNL and check which PCOs he has called in these fifteen days, but we will have to leave for Bihar from here tomorrow. His most locations in the CDR are Patna and Mokama.” Everyone said, “Okay, tomorrow there is a train at 11:30 in the afternoon; we will leave for Patna from Delhi Howrah at 11:30.”

The SSP, STF, talked to IG Patna, arranged for everyone's stay, and said, “We will not stay in any circuit house or hotel; we should be made to stay in a guest house where the general public does not come, and there is a telephone.” From there, the IG said, “Come, all arrangements will be made.” As soon as we got down from Patna railway station, there was a zoo in the forest department in the city, and everyone was made to stay in its guest house. The next day, at 8 in the morning, IG Patna came to the guest house to meet Arun Kumar. He told the whole story of the murder of Braj Bihari Prasad and also said that the criminal is from your place; his name is Shri Prakash Shukla.

Arun Kumar said, “Sir, we have the information and come here for the same reason. We should find a local policeman who is well acquainted with Patna and Mokama so that he can tell us about the areas we have found out and where Surajbhan's people frequent." IG Patna was surprised to hear Surajbhan's name and said, "Where did this Surajbhan come from?" Arun Kumar said, "You have learned about Shri Prakash Shukla; how did you not know about Surajbhan? Shri Prakash works for Surajbhan in Bihar." IG Patna said, "The information about Shri Prakash has come from our people's conversation with Rajan Tiwari, but there was no mention of Surajbhan. One more thing was found out from Rajan Tiwari that whatever murders Shri Prakash has committed in Patna or Bihar, after committing the murder, he leaves the spot shouting Jai Bajrang Bali. In the last two years, there have been five such murders recorded in Patna alone, in which the person filing the case has written that the murder was committed by unknown persons, who fled from the spot shouting Jai Bajrang Bali after committing the murder. In the murder of Minister Braj Bihari Prasad, the people present with him had also told this."

The IG, Patna, said, "Chief Minister Lalu Prasad Yadav is very worried about the murder of the minister. Shri Prakash has changed the crime equation here. Shri Prakash has committed all the big murders that have happened recently. What is Surajbhan's connection to these murders? We will also find him afresh. You will get all the help you need, but finishing him and his gang is important. Yes, one more thing: Pappu Yadav will come to meet you; he has also threatened to kill Pappu Yadav."

Arun Kumar said, "Okay, send him; we want to talk to him. First, whether the person threatening is Shri Prakash Shukla or someone else should be proved?" IG, Patna said, "Okay."

Meanwhile, a sub-inspector and two constables of Patna police arrived there in plain clothes. They were made to write down the addresses of mobile towers that Usha Phone had written down. They were told, "You people should go and check all these addresses. Big mobile towers are installed at these addresses. After verifying them on mobile phones during the day, we would like to see them ourselves if you can come in the evening. During verification, you can also find out where people with criminal tendencies visit in this area, whether any political person lives there, and whose place such people visit. After getting all the information, we will call and check the addresses.

Based on the details, we will determine which place our target visits or may visit. This will make our work easier." Taking all this information, the Bihar Patna Police left from there.

Arun Kumar, Satyendra Veer Singh, and Rajesh Pandey once again started reading all the information received from the mobile company. Arun Kumar told Rajesh Pandey and Satyendra Veer Singh, "You read it separately. Guess which area and route he must have visited in the past, as Mr. Sarkar had told me. He gave a chart of where the tower would start while changing and matched it with that. I will also look at it from my side."

The three people could not reach any conclusion while talking to each other when a forest department employee from outside said, "Pappu Yadav has come to meet us." Arun Kumar said, "Keep all these papers in the table drawer; let us see what it tells."

Pappu Yadav came straight inside and touched everyone's feet. Pappu Yadav, who had a hefty body, stood with folded hands and then sat on the carpet after a while. Arun Kumar said, "MLA ji, please sit upstairs."

Pappu Yadav said, "Sir, I am fine here."

Arun Kumar said, "Tell me, what is the matter?"

Pappu Yadav said, "Sir when Braj Bihari Prasad was murdered, this Shri Prakash got admitted somewhere near Braj Bihari ji's room by getting a fake medical certificate made. My sister is a resident doctor at PGI and is not married. Fifteen to twenty days after Braj Bihari Prasad's murder, one day, he came alone to the parking and stood in front of my sister. He started asking for my sister's home phone number and mobile number. When my sister rebuked him, he started misbehaving. When my sister told her that I was Pappu Yadav's sister, he abused her and said, please tell him that my name was Shri Prakash Shukla. My sister returned home and said the whole thing at night. I did not know him; his name was sometimes printed in the newspapers after the murder of Braj Bihari Prasad. I asked people to find out who was saying such big things.

The next day, a call came to the home number, and the caller asked to talk to my sister. My sister often used to get calls from doctors of PGI; she came running and took the phone. The person speaking from the other side started misbehaving with my sister and said he would pick me up. My sister called me and told me that this was the same rude boy who had been harassing me for many days. As soon as I picked up the phone, I wanted to know from him who was speaking. He told me his name was Shri Prakash Shukla; I abused him and said that such Shri Prakash Shukla roams in every street here in Patna, and then he started abusing me badly. In the end, he also said that if you want to know anything, you can ask Surajbhan Dada, DG Police of Uttar Pradesh, or SSP of Gorakhpur, and you will get to know. He also said that you do not have more security than Braj Bihari. It will not take much time to overturn you. Now give the phone to your sister. I disconnected the call."

Arun Kumar asked, "What kind of language was he speaking?" Pappu Yadav said, "Sir, it seemed like typical Gorakhpuri language. It was not the language of Bihar here, but the accent was of Eastern Uttar Pradesh." Arun Kumar again asked, "Then what happened?"

Pappu said, "I started sending my sister by car; I used to send two men along with her. One day, he was again found in front of the PGI gate when my sister was getting down from the car and entering the gate. My sister got scared and started running inside. After going inside, she also shouted, but by then, he was gone."

Pappu said, "Sir, please save me. "The person who killed Braj Bihari Prasad in broad daylight in the presence of hundreds of people can kill me, too. I am very concerned about my sister's honor. Now, I have stopped him from going to PGI, but he tries to talk to her by calling several times a day."

Rajesh Pandey asked, "What does he say while abusing?" Pappu told him. Arun Kumar said, "Okay, you go; we are busy with this." Pappu

Yadav kept saying in a pitiable tone that please save me somehow and then went away. After Pappu Yadav left, Arun Kumar asked, "What do you think?"

Satyendra Veer Singh said, "I think the same. It is Shri Prakash. Otherwise, no one can easily take Surajbhan's name. Secondly, Rajan Tiwari's information is correct. The whole group is the same; Rajan Tiwari drinks a lot. He must have told the whole story under the influence of alcohol, and Pappu Yadav must have also taken information from many places, so this is Shri Prakash Shukla only." Rajesh Pandey said, "One good thing that happened was that Pappu Yadav's telephone number was found. After talking to the IG here, call details of Pappu Yadav's landline number should be taken out, and if possible, the landline should be connected in parallel, and the calls should also be heard. If not possible, then caller ID should be set up by asking Pappu Yadav, and the numbers of all the places where the calls are coming should be found. IG, Patna should be told to continue this conversation with him in any way so that his location and number can be found." By evening, Bihar Police also arrived, and all the mobile tower addresses given to them were verified by going to the spot. Everyone told their side, and after talking to people, they also spoke about the possible routes. SSP and STF had little knowledge of Patna city, so it took time to know this.

The Patna police had not gathered all the information after much hard work. After listening to them, they were allowed to go, and after their departure, there was a discussion again.

Arun Kumar said, "With the hard work of these policemen, we have come to know about an area of two to three hundred square meters in Kankarbagh, where he must have been visiting. Tomorrow, without getting down from closed vehicles, we will try to see those routes by walking during the day, see how far PGI is from there, and see the site of the incident with PGI."

No one was able to understand how is it possible to kidnap Kunal and keep him at some other place and then come to Patna from there and kill Braj Bihari Prasad. How can anyone take such a significant risk that leaves the kidnapped person in someone else's trust and custody, then commit such a big murder here in Patna, and then again go back to Lucknow after committing the murder? This is a very courageous act for any criminal! The following day, all the places where his location was found a month and a half ago were visited by the constables of Patna Police. After this, the place in PGI where Braj Bihari was murdered was also visited. Everyone came back to the guest house of the forest. Arun Kumar called IG and Patna and told them everything about Pappu Yadav's telephone: if caller ID is installed from him and numbers are kept on being received, the work will become a little easier.

Apart from this, IG Patna was also asked which police officer could give more information about Surajbhan. Call the person with the best information about the gang war there so that complete information about him can also be taken. IG said, "When your team came to raid his place, I had sent some people to his place. It is not right to talk to Inspector Mokama; our only information about him is that he is on Surajbhan's payroll. The ASP there is completely new, so he will not have any information. I will send Rural ASP Murari Lal Meena by evening; maybe he will give you some good information."

In the evening, Murari Lal Meena came to the guest house with two other police officers, and Arun Kumar and his team talked to them for about an hour and got much good information. After Murari Lal Meena left, Arun Kumar said, "All the information to be found here has been found. If we had not come here ourselves, we would not have had the information about Pappu Yadav, nor would we have had such in-depth information about Surajbhan. Tomorrow, we will go to Lucknow; maybe by tomorrow, someone will call Shri Prakash or Pappu Yadav's phone, and we will get a new number. When we get a new number, it will be easy to follow him."

The next day, everyone left for Lucknow by train. After reaching Lucknow, everyone again gathered in Arun Kumar's room in the morning. Umesh Singh and Anil gave the information that in those fifteen days when the mobile was switched off, there was a call from Nepal numbers to three business people in Lucknow. Now everyone understands that if there is no call for a few days in the call details of the mobile, it means that he is living in Nepal. Arun Kumar asked OP Mishra and Malviya to go to Gorakhpur and contact the officials of Nepal and find out which areas these numbers of Nepal belong to.

Now, a lot of information has been gathered about mobile phones. The call detail report was received from the mobile company quickly, and the information about where he has been and where he has gone was received well. Meanwhile, data was also obtained from the mobile phone, and he is talking to Bihar numbers from Nepal. Preparations were made to send a team to Patna so that if any number of Patna is found, then an attempt will be made to find out who he is talking to in Patna. So that it can be decided who he is targeting next and what he will do.

Meanwhile, stories about Shri Prakash Shukla started getting published in the newspapers, and the pressure on the police increased. Some newspapers began writing rubbish about the newly formed STF. One newspaper wrote, "STF is proving to be a white elephant; police officers rejected from districts have been posted in it. They can never take action against Shri Prakash." A few days later, another newspaper wrote, "Shri Prakash had come to a wedding ceremony where Rajesh Pandey and Satyendra Veer Singh were present. Shri Prakash shook hands with them, and the officers quietly returned from there."

After reading the newspaper, everyone was stunned. Satyendra Veer Singh and Rajesh Pandey were in Gorakhpur when this incident was reported. The incident was reported to have taken place in Lucknow. In the meeting, Arun Kumar asked who was getting such fake news published. Everyone should find out about this. I will also find out about it. It is possible that some journalist is in contact with Shri Prakash Shukla and is getting such fake news published by him by threatening him. No one needs to be disappointed when I know the truth; it doesn't matter what anyone says or what is published in the newspapers."

Slowly, information started coming that IG Zone, Lucknow, has also formed a team in his office, collecting information about Shri Prakash Shukla, verifying it from the districts, and telling everyone we are very close. We will soon catch Shri Prakash Shukla. Slowly, it became clear that the police itself was involved in such fake and false reports.

They were getting such information published by telling the newspaper people. They thought that if STF reached this gang, Lucknow district police would be defamed, and all the senior officers, including the Chief Minister, would have a bad opinion of Lucknow police. The people who were part of IG zone's team repeatedly told the newspaper people such news.

When Arun Kumar got this information, he also investigated it at his level and found it correct. Arun Kumar went to Principal Secretary, Home Rajiv Ratan Shah. He told him, "The morale of our officers is falling, and I have this information that senior police officers are also getting such false news published in the newspapers."

Rajiv Ratan Shah said, "IG zone comes here and tells something or the other that he is at such and such a place, he has talked to him, who is the next target?" He said, "You people do your work; if someone is talking to the gang alone, what is wrong with it?" Arun Kumar said, "You are right; there is nothing wrong in it, but when completely false and blatantly wrong news is published in the newspapers, the morale of our officers goes down." Principal Secretary, Home said, "Don't worry, I will call the IG zone and make him understand."

OWN GOVERNMENT

Now, Shri Prakash Shukla agreed to kill Pappu Yadav at Surajbhan's insistence. After Braj Bihari Prasad, Pappu Yadav was the closest to the Chief Minister of Bihar. If he is killed, it will be easy to collect money from prominent businessmen and contractors, and minor criminals will also come under his protection.

Shri Prakash told Arun and Sudhir, "Everyone prepares well. This time, we have to take down Pappu Yadav's wicket."

Sudhir interrupted, "Brother, you have done Surajbhan's biggest work. He had done many favors to us; now, don't agree to any other work. Surajbhan Dada should now deal with his enemies himself."

Shri Prakash said, "Look, if Surajbhan comes forward more often, the Chief Minister of that place will go after Surajbhan. People don't think with your mind; you keep blabbering without reason. Surajbhan needs to be strong in Bihar. Surajbhan gets his men to do booth capturing for many leaders in Bihar. They get much money during elections. All the leaders for whom Dada took up booth capturing won the elections of their constituencies. Dada said that by working for these people, they are made MPs and MLAs, and whenever they have to do some work, they have only one answer: I am busy right now, but I will tell you later. If you want to take time to meet them, they make you wait for months, and if you go to meet them at their home, they keep doing some work inside and tell you to come tomorrow."

"It is because of us that people become MPs and MLAs. Our compulsion is to get good money in Vidhan Sabha elections once in five years and Lok Sabha elections once in five years, so our business continues. Dada's idea is correct: wherever we have done the work of capturing booths, we will field our candidates there and do this work of capturing booths for ourselves. Just think that if we have 15-20 MLAs and 3-4 MPs, we will not need to take time from anyone. They will stand up to salute us, and the police, which are harassing relatives and raiding homes, will stand in welcome and salute us. We have done much work in UP now; businessmen are in control, and no businessman leader protests."

"If we have to fix one or two big leaders in Lucknow, they will stop gossiping with the Chief Minister. Right now, this Tandon is catching up very fast; we will have to make arrangements for him too, and this DG Police, who gives a statement every day that he will be caught very soon, he too has to be fixed, then there will be no problem in the next election. Our men will stand, and all the boys we have brought up will be placed with some intelligent person. If these people do the booth capturing, then we will easily win 20-25 seats in Gorakhpur, Deoria, Ballia, Ghazipur, Jaunpur, and Azamgarh, and 20-25 seats means that whoever forms the government, we will get our work done as per our wish and it is possible that if someone is short of 20-25 seats in forming the government, then we will get the government formed on our terms. This thinking of Dada is excellent. Such fielding will be set for Dada in Bihar so that Dada will easily get the same number of MLAs in his state. You think, if we join the government in these two states of India, then gradually we will take over the entire system."

Sudhir said, "Brother, what you are saying is correct. Think how much fun it will be if we are in the government; then, you will get us appointed ministers. We will sit in a white Ambassador car with a red light; there will be a convoy of 30-40 vehicles in front and behind. The district DM and SSP will come to receive him, and the policemen will line up to salute him."

Shri Prakash said, "Now you understand, we can do this work by working a little harder. This is not a difficult task. They win on our strength and form the government; we will do the same work for ourselves." Sudhir and Anuj said, "Yes, brother, you are right, it will be done. Pappu Yadav's work is straightforward. After one bullet hits him, he will not be able to run away; he will fall right there. He will not have to be shot as often as Virendra Shahi."

A significant political murder took place in Uttar Pradesh in 1997. The strong leader of the Bharatiya Janata Party, Brahmadatt Dwivedi, was murdered in a wedding ceremony. Brahmadatt Dwivedi was a leader who did politics of Brahmins in Uttar Pradesh. After his murder, it was speculated that this murder was done for political reasons because Brahmadatt Dwivedi was emerging as a prominent leader of Brahmins in Uttar Pradesh, and his proximity with the national level leaders of Bharatiya Janata Party was increasing. In caste politics, he was seen as an alternative to Kalyan Singh in Uttar Pradesh. In such a situation, his murder started being given a political color.

After the murder of Brahmadatt Dwivedi, the pages of newspapers were full of news, and it was repeatedly indicated that this murder was done by Kalyan Singh's close Sakshi Maharaj and Brahmadatt Dwivedi's home district Fatehgarh MLA Vijay Singh. After all the fingers were raised, Brahmadatt Dwivedi's wife was made a minister in Kalyan Singh's cabinet. Brahmadatt Dwivedi's son, Captain Dwivedi, started preserving his father's political legacy in the area. His father repeatedly called him.

The thought of taking revenge for his father's murder kept coming up as a pain in his heart. He kept making serious efforts for this. Meanwhile, Sunil Dwivedi started searching for people to arrange his meeting with Shri Prakash Shukla. Captain Dwivedi met Ghanshyam Pathak and his companions in Lucknow and asked him to arrange a meeting with Shri Prakash Shukla in any way.

Captain Dwivedi also contacted Mrityunjay Shukla and requested that he arrange a meeting with Shri Prakash. Shri Prakash was informed that Brahmadatt Dwivedi's son wanted to talk. Shri Prakash asked for Brahmadatt Dwivedi's son's mobile number, and then, one day, he spoke to him. Sunil told him that he wanted to meet him and talk. Shri Prakash said he would call him when he was near him.

About fifteen days later, Shri Prakash called Brahmadatt Dwivedi's son to Faizabad. Shri Prakash, Anuj and Sudhir went to meet Brahmadatt Dwivedi's son at a hotel in Faizabad. As soon as he met, Brahmadatt Dwivedi's son told him everything and also gave him his information and said, "My father was murdered by Sakshi Maharaj and Vijay Singh's people, and it can be easily understood why these people got my father killed?"

Shri Prakash said, "Vijay Singh is in jail; nothing can be done about him. But that work can be done once I get Sakshi Maharaj's horoscope." Brahmadatt Dwivedi's son was thrilled. He said, "Shukla ji, this was what I expected from you, and if I can do something for you for this work of mine, then I will do something. I will give as much money as you ask, but this work must be done." Shri Prakash said, "You just think, if we join the government in these two states of India, then slowly we will take over the entire system."

Sudhir said, “Bhaiya, you are right. Think about how much fun it will be. If we are in the government, you will make us ministers. We will sit in a white Ambassador car with a red light; there will be a convoy of thirty to forty vehicles in front and behind. The DM and SSP of the district we go to will come to receive us, and the policemen will line up and salute us.”

Shri Prakash said, “Now you understand; with a little more hard work, we can do this work. This is not a difficult task. They win on our strength and form the government; we will do the same work for ourselves.” Sudhir and Anuj said, “Yes, Bhaiya, you are right, it will be done. Talk to Pappu Yadav; the work is straightforward. After one bullet hits him, he will not be able to run away; he will fall right there. He will not have to be shot as often as Virendra Shahi.”

A significant political murder took place in Uttar Pradesh in 1997. Brahmadatt Dwivedi, a prominent leader of the Bharatiya Janata Party, was murdered at a wedding ceremony. Brahmadatt Dwivedi was a Brahmin politician of Uttar Pradesh. After his murder, speculations were being made that this murder was done for political reasons because Brahmadatt Dwivedi was emerging as a prominent leader of Brahmins in Uttar Pradesh, and his proximity to the national level leaders of Bharatiya Janata Party was increasing. In caste politics, he was seen as an alternative to Kalyan Singh in Uttar Pradesh. In such a situation, his murder started being given a political color.

After the murder of Brahmadatt Dwivedi, the pages of newspapers started being colored, and it was repeatedly hinted that this murder was done by Kalyan Singh's close aide Sakshi Maharaj and Brahmadatt Dwivedi's home district Fatehgarh MLA Vijay Singh. After all the fingers were raised, Brahmadatt Dwivedi's wife was made a minister in the Kalyan Singh cabinet. Brahmadatt Dwivedi's son, Captain Dwivedi, started preserving his father's political legacy in the region. The thought of taking revenge for his father's murder kept emerging in his mind. He also kept making serious efforts for this. Meanwhile, Sunil Dwivedi started searching for people to arrange his meeting with Shri Prakash Shukla. Captain Dwivedi met Ghanshyam Pathak and his companions in Lucknow and asked them to arrange a meeting with Shri Prakash Shukla in any way.

Captain Dwivedi also contacted Mrityunjay Shukla and requested that he arrange a meeting with Shri Prakash. Shri Prakash was told that Brahmadatt Dwivedi's son wanted to talk. Shri Prakash asked for Brahmadatt Dwivedi's son's mobile number and spoke on it one day. Sunil told him that I wanted to meet you and talk. Shri Prakash said that I would call you when I was near you.

About fifteen days later, Shri Prakash called Brahmadatt Dwivedi's son to Faizabad. Shri Prakash, Anuj and Sudhir went to meet Brahmadatt Dwivedi's son in a hotel in Faizabad. As soon as they met, Brahmadatt Dwivedi's son told them everything and also gave them his information and said, "Father has been murdered by Sakshi Maharaj and Vijay Singh's people, and it can be easily understood why these people have killed father?"

Shri Prakash said, "Vijay Singh is in jail; nothing can be done about him. But once I get the horoscope of Sakshi Maharaj, then that work can be done." Brahmadatt Dwivedi's son was thrilled. He said, "Shukla ji, this was what I expected from you, and if I can do something for you for this work of mine, then I will do something. I will give as much money as you ask, but this work should be done." Shri Prakash said, “Don’t worry, I will take the money from you; let me find out for now.” While leaving, Brahmadatt Dwivedi’s son asked, “If I have to tell you something important or if I suddenly need something, how can I contact you?" Shri Prakash said, "I will keep talking to you myself; you need not worry."

The three left from there and reached Gorakhpur. At night, Shri Prakash asked two new boys from Gorakhpur to prepare Sakshi Maharaj's Kundali and told them to prepare his complete Kundali within a week or ten days. After the conversation, Shri Prakash told Anuj and Sudhir, "It seems that God is also kind to us that we got this work; we did not have to make any separate effort. This Chief Minister says in his daily speech that criminals will either be in jail or outside the state. His mind will also cool down. Sakshi is his closest person, and once Sakshi's work is done, this Chief Minister will also be under his control. Once the Chief Minister is under his control, we can do all our work comfortably in Uttar Pradesh, just like Suraj Dada has made a place for himself in Bihar."

Sudhir said, "Brother, look at the other side of this; once Sakshi's work starts, the police will go crazy. Right now, these people have made life miserable. Our relatives are in jail, and even those who are distant relatives, the police pick them up every day, beat them up, and then let them go. Now, the police have started disrespecting even the women of the house. After Sakshi is not there, will they make it difficult to even go on the road?"

Shri Prakash said, "You are right; the policemen have made our life miserable; they have beaten up elder brother a lot. They pick up their father and take him to the police station daily. I am very grateful to SSP Gorakhpur.

When RK Singh was threatened, he started whining that we could not do anything. An STF has been formed for this purpose; the STF people are doing this job of arresting people."

"This STF has not come from London; the DG of the police is its owner. Now, the DG will have to be tightened. This DG is a baniya, so he cannot take on a heavy load. I will tighten him someday. Daily, relatives send news that the police are troubling them a lot. If this DG still does not listen, then I will finish off the STF people. One advantage of killing RK Singh is that if any policeman is found on the way during checking, he understands as soon as he is shown the AK and immediately salutes and lets the car go. By killing the STF people, no one will come on the road, nor will anyone kidnap family members, and those who are left in the STF will also run away." Anuj said, "One day, I talked to Papa, and Papa told me to be very careful with the STF people. Arun Kumar, Satyendra Veer Singh, and Rajesh Pandey are of the same temperament; they will risk their lives and don't care much about anyone."

Shri Prakash said, "Some boy called me from Lucknow and told me these three are scoundrels. The rest of them make tall claims and tell tales to their officers. I will have to deal with these three, too, but you don't worry, first I will deal with them, and then I will take Sakshi's wicket down. After Sakshi's wicket falls, no matter how much the Chief Minister shouts, no policeman will come out on the road."

Anuj said, "Yes, brother, this has to be done. Now, there is not much work left to do; get the police in shape once, and we take Sakshi's wicket down, and no one will say anything. The rest of the work will be handled by the time the elections come. Before the elections, please decide who will contest from where."

Shri Prakash said, "I have decided everything and have told everyone over the phone to make their preparations. Identify the booths with the most voters in your area; you must go to many places and work hard. We will select the booths with the most voters; our man will go easily.

MINISTER THREATENED

The next day, Shri Prakash called to know what was published in the morning newspaper. He was told that Lalji Tandon's statement had come again, that we would finish Shri Prakash and his gang very soon, and that businessmen need not be afraid. If any goon is collecting tax from a businessman, he should directly contact STF and inform them.

Shri Prakash asked, "In which newspaper has this been published?" He was told that it was in 'Jagran.' Then he asked, "What is printed in other newspapers?" The news of each newspaper was read out separately. This statement of Lalji Tandon was printed in almost all of them. For the English newspaper, he asked Anuj to understand it from him and tell him. When Anuj talked to him, he said that some journalists in 'The Times of India' had written even worse. Shri Prakash asked Anuj, "Which is this newspaper of Deepak Sharma? What is written in it?" Anuj said that nothing is written in it; there is no statement from Lalji Tandon in his newspaper 'Pioneer.' Yes, it is written that Shri Prakash Shukla's terror has spread in Bihar as well.

Shri Prakash said first, let me deal with Lalji Tandon. Then he said, "Give me Deepak Sharma's number, I will talk to him. He seems like a good man; he writes the right thing, and his newspaper is read extensively in Delhi."

After saying this, Shri Prakash hung up and dialed someone in Lucknow. When he dialed the number, he got angry and started shouting, "I had asked you to get Lalji Tandon's kundali, but you did not tell me to date. Do you think that I will leave you, you bastard? I always give you as much money as you ask. Now, do not make me angry. If I get angry, I will also put a bullet in your head."

He started saying, "Bhaiya, how can I inform you? I don't have your number; you had said that I would call and ask, but you didn't call and ask. I have got your entire kundali ready." Shri Prakash said, "If I hadn't called, you would have told Omprakash bhaiya in Gorakhpur. You could have told Dhannu Pathak in Jaunpur; I would have called immediately. Don't be so careless in the future." Shri Prakash said, "Narbadeshwar, you know I give you much work, and whenever you need money, I get it for you. Don't be careless in your work. Now tell me where you are today." He said, "Bhaiya is in Lucknow today. I had gone yesterday; there was a meeting in the evening at the stadium in the square, and the traders from all over Lucknow had gathered. It was someone's birth anniversary celebration. I don't remember his birth anniversary, but many people garlanded him." Shri Prakash asked, "Did all the people who garlanded him were from above, or did people from below also go?" Narbadeshwar said, “In the beginning, he was being called by his name, and people from below also brought garlands and put them on him. Then, after that, people started standing in a line and putting garlands on him on their own.”

Shri Prakash asked, “How many people would have put garlands on him?”

Narbadeshwar said, “Bhaiya when the garlands were filled around his neck, and they started getting stuck in his neck, Tandon would take off his glasses and get all the garlands removed. After taking out the garlands, some were kept on the table in front of him, and then later, he would give the garlands to someone behind the stage. After some time, the same garlands would come down, and people would again take them in their hands and walk. When people put garlands on him, I also took a garland of marigold and put it on him to see it closely.”

Shri Prakash asked, “What clothes were you wearing then?”

Narbadeshwar said, “Bhaiya, I wore jeans and a light blue T-shirt. I was wearing white sports shoes.”

He said, “Bhaiya, when many people came, Tandon refused. He called the person managing the stage and said, I have to go to another meeting, then Lalji Tandon started speaking. After speaking, newspaper people were standing below when he came down from the stage; there were four TV cameramen also.” Someone had asked, “In your rule, businessmen are being harassed so much. Businessmen are paying goonda tax out of fear, and the government is not doing anything about it."

Lalji Tandon asked, "Who is such a big goon that the businessmen of Lucknow are afraid of him?" Someone from the crowd of reporters said, "Shri Prakash Shukla." Then Tandon said that the police were going to wipe out the entire gang very soon. Bhaiya, I got scared after hearing this and left.

Shri Prakash asked, did you go alone, or was there someone with you? Narbadeshwar said, no, Bhaiya, I went alone. You have already told me that one should be alone while getting someone's Kundali done. If you take someone along, the news gets leaked somewhere or the other."

Shri Prakash asked, "Was there anyone there who recognized you? Or did you meet anyone?" Narbadeshwar said, "Bhaiya, I have just come from Deoria and was admitted to BA four months ago. No one knows me in Lucknow; neither did I meet anyone, nor would anyone recognize me." Shri Prakash said, "That is fine; now tell me, what is his program for today?"

Narbadeshwar said, "As per his program published in the newspaper today, he will go to a conference of PWD employees at 11 am in Visheshyya Hall in front of Raj Bhavan. After that, the program is in the Secretariat itself." Shri Prakash said, "Excellent; please tell me his office and home numbers. Have you found out who answers the office and home phone?" Narbadeshwar said, "Yes, Bhaiya, I have discovered everything." Narbadeshwar noted down the office and home phone numbers.

And he also noted down who picked up this number.

Shri Prakash said, "You have a good Kundali, but you are not telling me on time. I will check everything now. I will call you in the evening and tell you how much money is to be received from where." Narbadeshwar said, "Bhaiya, may your blessings continue."

Shri Prakash disconnected Narbadeshwar's call, dialed Lalji Tandon's landline number, and told the person who picked up the call, "Satish,

I am BJP District President, Mau, let me talk to the Minister for a minute; it is a fundamental matter."

Satish said, "Hold on for a minute." After a while, he said, "I am giving the line to the Minister."

When Tandon ji picked up the phone, Shri Prakash said, "Tandon ji, don't hang up; listen to me carefully."

Tandon Ji said, "Who is speaking?"

Shri Prakash said, "I am Shri Prakash Shukla speaking."

Tandon said, "Who is Shri Prakash Shukla? I don't know?"

Shri Prakash said, "Tandon ji, you know everything. I am the same person who shot Virendra Shahi with 150 bullets in Lucknow. I am the same person who shot 10 bullets in the head of Inspector RK Singh in the crowded market of Janpath. If you remember something, it is okay. Otherwise, I will tell you more. Listen to the whole thing and don't hang up; otherwise, it will be very costly. Then, Shri Prakash started speaking fluently. He said that today a statement has been published in the newspapers that your police will kill us, so Tandon ji keep in mind that I know your police, if they had that much strength then they would have killed us already. But I will kill you in a week.

I would have killed you yesterday, and all these hundred men who walk with you with toys would have run away. If you don't believe me, then find out: Braj Bihari Prasad was a minister senior to you, and when he was killed in Patna, he had more than a hundred armed men with him. When we killed him and left, twenty minutes after that, these bastards started firing in the air. So don't talk about the police. Yesterday, I also went to the program you went to at the stadium near the square. I went there because you are shouting businessman and pressurizing the Chief Minister. First, I will deal with you, and then I will deal with the police.

Yesterday, when you went to the program at the stadium, the people on the stage garlanded you, then brought garlands from below and garlanded you; I also went on the stage and garlanded you. At that time, two pistols were tied to my waist; I wore jeans, a blue T-shirt, and sports shoes. I also touched your feet after garlanding you. I felt like shooting ten bullets in his chest right there, but I thought I should tell you first and then kill you. I have never killed anyone without telling them. Ask anyone in Gorakhpur. I had told Virendra Shahi that I would kill before Holi, and I did kill before Holi. Ask for the photos of yesterday's program and see them; when you left from there and headed towards your car, I came back. Today, I read in the newspapers that before sitting in the car, you told the police officers that our police would finish off Shri Prakash Shukla and his gang very soon. After today, I will not call you but come directly to you. Keep preparing to go to Bhainsa Kund." Lalji Tandon's face turned pale, and he said, "What do you want from me?" Shri Prakash said, "Stop making statements and do your work. You repeatedly deceive the Chief Minister in the name of businessmen; if this appears in any newspaper again, count a week from that day. I have nothing more to say than this." Shri Prakash disconnected the call after saying this.

Putting the phone down, Lalji Tandon told everyone, "You all go; I am going to get ready; I have a meeting." Everyone left from there. Lalji Tandon immediately called his PA inside and whispered, "Bring all the photographs of the program held in the stadium yesterday. Look at them and tell whether any boy is in jeans, a T-shirt, or sports shoes. Also, he said that these photographs should come by the time I get ready." The PA said, "Yes, Sir!"

The coordinator of that program and the party people talked to Tandon's PA, found out the name of the photographer, and asked him to send a car and bring the photographs immediately. He also instructed that all the pictures of the stage in the program are needed. From the arrival of the minister till his departure. I should get all these photographs in half an hour. Lalji Tandon quickly bathed, prayed, and got ready in an hour. When he came out, his PA said, "Sir, have breakfast. There is a meeting at Visheshyya Hall at 11 am." Lalji Tandon asked, "First, tell me whether you got those pictures?" The PA said, "They are coming in a little while. The man has gone to the photographer's place. He will bring them directly from there."

Lalji Tandon said, “Now I will not meet anyone. Bring the photos when they arrive. Till then, I will have my breakfast.” The PA said again, “Sir, that meeting of the PWD people?”

Lalji Tandon scolded him loudly, saying, “You cannot hear what I am saying. Get the photos first, and do not discuss anything else until the photos arrive.” Now that the PA understood that it was a serious matter, the minister does not insist on anything like this and he usually neither asks for photos of any program nor wishes to see them. The PA sat in his room and kept calling people repeatedly to ask how long it would take for the photos to arrive. Whoever he talked to, everyone told him that it would take just five minutes. It had been almost half an hour while he was saying this. The PA also started getting irritated; he understood it was a grave matter. If the photos were not received soon, he would have to face much scolding; he sat down holding his head.

About fifteen minutes later, the minister's orderly came inside with photos in a packet. The PA snatched the packet from his hand. He quickly looked at all the images individually, separated five or six pictures from them, and went straight into the minister's room. On seeing him, the minister asked, "Did you get the photos?" The PA said, “Yes, I got them.”

The PA kept the envelope containing the photos aside, placed four or five photos taken out from it in front of him, and said, “Sir, these are the photos of the people who garlanded him on the stage.” Lalji Tandon started looking at those photos carefully. On seeing two or three photos, his face started changing. He called his PA and said, “This photo of the boy in jeans and a T-shirt is not taken from the front; only half of his face is visible. Give this photo to us and try it with the photographer. Let us know if he can find a photo of him from the front.”

He also told the PA to park the car; I will not attend the meeting now. Tell them to start their program. I will arrive at noon and then go straight to the secretariat. On reaching the secretariat, Tandon ji called the DG Police directly and said, “You reach the secretariat immediately and bring the SSP and STF with you.”

Tandon Ji told his staff members that DG, SSP, and STF people will be coming until they came.

I will not meet anyone. After half an hour, DG Police and Arun Kumar reached Lalji Tandon's room. On their arrival, the minister signaled you people, go to the restroom at the back; I will come. DG Arun Kumar went to that room. Tandon called his PA and said, "Till I talk to the DG, neither give anyone's phone nor let anyone in; anyone means anyone!" Saying this, Tandon went to a separate room.

On seeing him, DG Police said, “Sir, you seem a bit worried.”

Tandon said, “Yes, I am worried.”

Urban Development Minister in Uttar Pradesh Government Lalji Tandon told him, “In the morning, I got a call from Shri Prakash Shukla. He talked to me for a long time and told me that tomorrow I would have killed you in the program at the Chaak Stadium. He also revealed his identity and said that you should get the program photo and identify him. I also got a photo of the program, and I brought it. SSP, STF, you look at this and tell me whether he was saying he is correct. Is the man in the photo Shri Prakash Shukla or not? And if he was Shri Prakash Shukla, this is a grave matter. Whenever you people are asked, you people say that we will catch or kill him very soon. I am a senior minister in the government and the oldest man of Prime Minister Shri Atal Bihari Vajpayee; if even I am not safe, then what is the meaning of such a large police force?” Saying this, Lalji Tandon angrily threw all the photographs in front of DG Police.

DG Police kept all the photographs before Arun Kumar and told the minister, “Sir, please give us some time; I will show him to those who know him closely and then tell you. His face is visible from the side in these photographs, so it is difficult to identify him immediately.” Lalji Tandon said, “Okay, tell me by this evening.”

DG asked SSP Arun Kumar, “Arun Kumar, what do you think? Is this Shri Prakash or not?” Arun Kumar said, “Sir, I have also seen the photograph, but I have not seen him from the front. It is difficult to say anything if he is seen from the side. We have a person who has seen him closely for a long time; let us get him to identify him.” DG said,

"Arun Kumar, this matter is grave. You will have to tell me by evening at any cost." Arun Kumar said, "Okay."

After seeing off DG Police in his car, SSP STF Arun Kumar left for the office in his car. On the way, he called Rajesh Pandey and asked, "Where is Dhirendra Singh right now?" Rajesh Pandey said, "He is with us." He said, "You reach the office immediately; there is vital work." Rajesh Pandey said, "Yes, I am reaching."

After some time, Rajesh Pandey was present when Arun Kumar reached the STF office. Arun Kumar took five photographs from the diary and gave them to Rajesh Pandey. Showing the photo of a boy in a T-shirt and jeans, he said, "Show it to Dhirendra and find out if this is Shri Prakash Shukla or not?" Rajesh Pandey said, "I will tell you right away."

Rajesh Pandey left from there, went to Dhirendra with Avinash Mishra, and showed the photo to Dhirendra. Dheerendra said, "The clothes and shoes look like he is the same, but his face is not clear enough. His hair is the same as he used to keep short, but his nose looks a little different. Avinash Mishra insisted, "Look at it repeatedly and tell me clearly whether this is Shri Prakash Shukla or not?"

Dhirendra looked at the photograph several times and said, "Can't you say it clearly? There is a slight difference in the face; the rest of his gait and clothes look like his. If there is a front photo, then it can be told." Rajesh Pandey asked again, "If he had called and told me to identify the photo and see I am garlanding the minister, then how much truth would there be in this?"

Virendra said hesitantly, "If he has told me, then it must be true." After much questioning, Rajesh Pandey again went to Arun Kumar and told him the whole thing. Arun Kumar became slightly worried; Rajesh asked, "Is it a serious matter, Sir?" Arun Kumar said, "It is severe."

Then Arun Kumar told Rajesh Pandey the whole thing. Rajesh Pandey said, "Even after seeing him a lot, Dhirendra cannot recognize him properly, nor can he deny it. This clearly shows that this could also be Shri Prakash. It has been seven or eight months since Dhirendra saw Shri Prakash." After listening to the whole thing,

Arun Kumar called the DG Police and said, "The person who recognized him was shown, he too is not able to say clearly either 'yes' or 'no.' There is a fifty percent chance that this could be Shri Prakash Shukla."

From the other side, the DG said, "Telling this to the Minister is not without danger. If he is angry, he will immediately say, you people have been telling the story every day for so many days, yet you have not identified him correctly. I think it will be appropriate to tell the minister that it seems the same."

Arun Kumar said, "Sir, whatever you feel is right."

In the evening, the DG again met Lalji Tandon and told him the same thing he had told Arun Kumar. Lalji Tandon's face turned pale; he composed a little and said, "This man is hazardous. This means that I got saved yesterday. To increase security at my house, I will cancel all the programs in the coming days. Now, do something about him quickly; otherwise, a big incident will happen someday."

The DG kept listening to everything with a police smile and then left.

At night, Lalji Tandon called his private secretary, sat with his son and family, and mentioned the incident; the whole family got scared after listening to him. Someone said that you should go to Bombay, and someone said that you should not go out of the house for a few days. Lalji Tandon said, "Look, I am a political man. I can stay outside for a day or two, but I cannot stay inside the house for a long time or stay outside the state for a long time. People will start criticizing, and this is politics. If I leave the state even for fifteen days, someone else will take my place. After so much penance, I have reached here."

The family members said, "But the way he came in front of you while chasing you, he can harm you anytime." Lalji Tandon said, "Only one thing is coming to my mind: I should get admitted to KGMC Medical College on some pretext. I will get a room in the private ward there. Two rooms next to it will also be vacated, and a telephone connection and PA room will be made there. I will be able to talk to important people; I will also be able to meet people who need to meet me. No one will come to ask for a program, and even if someone comes, the doctors will tell him that he is not fit to go out. If a month or two passes there, the police will either arrest him or kill him by exerting pressure. The Chief Minister is stringent; no one can defend him, nor can the police be lenient."

The family members said, "Absolutely right, this idea is correct. But there is a danger in this that if the doctors have even the slightest doubt that he is admitted to the medical college on the pretext of illness, then this news will get out, and there will be unnecessary defamation." Tandon said, "First, let us call Doctor Malviya and take his advice on what illness can be mentioned to get him admitted there. It would not be right to talk about a more serious illness. People in our area will start saying that he has got such an illness now and he will not get well soon. This is public; it will start looking for new people. Therefore, we have to say something: the doctor also knows that she will be fine in a month or two, and there is no doubt that she will be admitted without any illness."

It was agreed that tomorrow, Dr. Malviya would be called, and everything would be understood, and then after getting his recommendation, he would be admitted. Dr. Malviya was called the next day, and Lalji Tandon talked to him in private. Dr. Malviya said, "You already have a little problem with your appendix, and saying that there is an infection in your appendix, I will do all the pathology tests and all the tests. I will prescribe the medicines and keep the record with me. You call the principal of KGMC and give him a hint." Tandon said, "Okay."

The next day evening, Lalji Tandon reached the hospital and was admitted to the private ward. The next day, all newspapers published that Minister Lalji Tandon had fallen ill and had been accepted into the medical college. All the newspapers also wrote that, according to sources, the minister is suffering from some serious illness. Therefore, no doctor is ready to say anything about his illness.

When Shri Prakash called in the morning to get the news, he was told that it had been published in the newspapers that Minister Lal ji Tandon was admitted to the hospital due to some illness. When he told Shri Prakash this news, Shri Prakash started laughing loudly.

After talking for a while, Shri Prakash hung up. After hanging up, Anuj asked, "Bhaiya, today, after a long time, you were laughing out loud."

Shri Prakash said, "I will tell you right away." He started calling Narbadeshwar. When Narbadeshwar picked up the phone, Shri Prakash said, "Narbadeshwar, tell me, what reward do you want? You made a very amazing kundali for Tandon. Yesterday, he was admitted to the hospital." Narbadeshwar also started laughing.

Shri Prakash said, "Tomorrow, you go to Shakti Jewelers in Alambagh. There, you will find a fat man named Roopchand. Tell him that Ashok Singh has sent you. He will give you ten thousand rupees." Narbadeshwar said, "Yes, bhaiya, ten thousand is too much." Shri Prakash said, "You have done a great job. Keep it; I will not give you money for a few days. Go and watch a movie and have fun." Narbadeshwar said, "Okay, bhaiya."

Shri Prakash looked at Anuj and asked, "Did you understand? Why was I laughing so loudly?" Anuj said, "I understood." Then Shri Prakash said that now only the police are left. If I remove a prominent police officer, the police will never even take my name. Their DG and the Chief Minister will keep shouting. The police will not move from their place, so my work will be done. See, in the next election, I will make both of you contest; all my candidates will win, and then it will be fun. The Chief Minister is acting over smart; we have also got a job after doing which the Chief Minister will be threatened. That work has to start tomorrow as well."

Sudhir said, "Bhaiya, this will be very good; you will be in the government in Uttar Pradesh and Surajbhan Dada in Bihar."

Shri Prakash interrupted, saying, "Suraj Dada also has one work left; if his work is also completed, then there will be no one left to face him, and he will easily dominate Bihar; there will be no one left to challenge him."

Anuj said, "I understand, bhaiya; if Pappu Yadav's work is done, only Dada will be left in Bihar. Over half of the tenders and government work have now come to Surajbhan Dada. After dealing with Pappu Yadav, no one can come before Dada for tenders." Shri Prakash said,

“You have identified correctly, now only his work is left. Now tell me whether Dada's work should be done by going to Bihar or the work here should be done first?”

SAKSHI KUNDALI

Sudhir said, "Bhaiya, have you thought about how to deal with the Chief Minister?"

Shri Prakash said, "I am not that stupid; the Chief Minister has Black Cat commandos. They are not khaki police, and they run so fast on seeing our AK that they look back only after going a kilometer ahead. Black Cat commandos have weapons better than AK. Even if somehow the bullet hits the CM accurately, none of us will survive, and then our battle for supremacy will remain incomplete. The most important person of the Chief Minister is Sakshi Maharaj, who has to be dealt with. Once he is dealt with, the Chief Minister will also think he can deal with anyone, and our work will be done. But to deal with Sakshi, we will have to go to Delhi.

Anuj said, "Bhaiya, don't take up such a big task right now. Let's go to Bihar first. Let's finish Suraj Dada's work, and then we will go to Delhi."

Shri Prakash said, "No, let's finish the work here first, then we will go to Bihar. Anuj, you go to Delhi and rent a good flat there near Sakshi's ashram. Buy the stuff for the flat and settle in the flat. When everything is ready, Sudhir and I will also come. Then Sakshi's Kundali will be taken out there, and from there, our work will become easy."

Anuj said, "Okay, bhaiya, I will go to Delhi with the seal. If I go to see the flat with the seal, there will be no problem getting a good flat."

Shri Prakash said, "Okay, you can arrange a flat. Anyway, the work in Lucknow is mostly done now; we will have to do something in Delhi. After Syria Pehlwan's death, the places there were over, and there was no need to go there. There will be good work there, too. You must not have seen Syria Pehlwan's Delhi office in Panchvati Colony; he was great fun and a friend of friends. After his death, we have almost stopped coming to Delhi place; if he were here now, we would have got a good flat for rent with just a phone call."

The next day, Anuj left for Delhi in his blue Cielo car and stayed at a hotel in Chanakyapuri. After getting all the Hindi and English newspapers, he would note down the address and telephone number of the flat in all the advertisements of flats for rent in his diary. After talking to the flat owners throughout the day, he would see the flat. One day, per the newspaper advertisement, Anuj called the telephone number in a house in Vasant Kunj. He told him to come to Vasant Kunj D Block, and he would take him there. Anuj saw the flat. It was a good flat. The door of the flat was not in front of any door of the other flat on that floor, and one could quickly go to that flat by lift without anyone knowing. One could soon jump from the back balcony to the balcony of the lower flat.

Anuj asked him, "What does the owner of this flat do?" He told him, "He was the PA of a former Prime Minister. He has many such flats that he has rented out. The person who rented the flat earlier was a bank manager, and he has been transferred to Himachal Pradesh, so this flat has been vacant for two months." Anuj said, "Okay, I will talk to him tomorrow and give him whatever advance is required for this, and if you want to get an agreement signed, I will sign the agreement as well."

Anuj returned to the hotel and called Shri Prakash in the evening to tell him that the flat belonged to an influential person. The police will not come here quickly; even if the police come after us, then we can jump onto the balcony of the flat just below our flat without any significant risk, and from there, we can get down and run away. He asked for Rs. 4,500 as rent for the flat, and I agreed. Shri Prakash said, "Excellent. Sakshi's ashram will also be nearby there. Pay the advance for it tomorrow and sign the agreement." Anuj said, "Okay."

The next day, that flat was rented, and Anuj also bought three to four mattresses, sheets, and small kitchen items. After four days, Shri Prakash came to Delhi with Sudhir in a Zen car, and after coming to Delhi, he kept his luggage and all the weapons in that flat. For two to three days, he used to go for a run in the park in the morning wearing a tracksuit in the colony, and for three days, he got information about the people living there. He saw that there was no one there who recognized him, nor was there anyone from Gorakhpur. After being wholly assured, after three days, Shri Prakash, Anuj, and Sudhir reached Sakshi Maharaj's ashram.

The people in the ashram said that Sakshi Maharaj meets in the morning during Satsang; one has to come at six. He does not meet anyone in the afternoon and goes to different places for Satsang or discourse in the evening. Hearing this, all three of them returned and reached there the next day at six in the morning. The volunteers posted at the gate asked for their names and addresses and searched them by touching their hands. There was a crowd in the morning, and Sakshi Maharaj was not visible from the gate from where they entered. They had to go to the satsang hall after taking a walk. All three of them went inside the hall and sat there. Meanwhile, all three of them correctly observed the way to exit and the way of Sakshi Maharaj. All three of them also saw that many of Sakshi's security guards, who looked like veterans, were present around the hall.

On returning, Shri Prakash said, "If we carry the weapon in the bag, we may get into a scuffle with the people checking here. If we get into a scuffle as soon as we enter inside, it won't be easy to reach Sakshi. It is the month of August; it is not getting cold yet. When it gets cold, it will be easy to go inside by covering ourselves with a blanket. Sakshi's work will be done once all the weapons are taken inside. We think we should go for a day or two more and see the route, which room Sakshi comes out from, which room he goes to, and where he goes out in the afternoon; we will also see this. If we find a place on the way, we will do it right now, and if we cannot find a route, we will wait for winter to come. Until then, we will set up the fielding for Dada's work and finish Bihar's work. We have a flat here, so there will be no problem coming and going."

Sudhir said, "Bhaiya, when we used to go to Patna from Gorakhpur, Lucknow, or Faizabad, we used to go comfortably in our car. It is difficult to go to Bihar from Delhi by car." Anuj said, "When I came, there were police barriers at twenty places; there can be some difficulty." Shri Prakash said, "I have come in my car with all the weapons; no one stopped me." Sudhir said, "Bhaiya, there is no question about stopping us. Who will stop us? But going to Patna from here will take fourteen to fifteen hours. We will have to stop at Lucknow before going to Patna. We will go from here to Lucknow, stay in Lucknow for a day or two, then from there, we will go to Bihar." Shri Prakash said, "Yes, this is correct." Shri Prakash told Anuj, "Buy ten SIM cards from Delhi, find someone in the market who can activate the SIM card without any identification, and give it to you. It will be great to get ten SIM cards by giving the fake driving licenses you have, and everyone gets three or four phones for themselves. No one must make more than one or two calls on any mobile. How did these policemen find out about everyone in Patna? Where did all of us go? No one can spy on Patna; no one has the information except Dada." Anuj said, "Okay, I will bring them." Anuj brought four new mobiles and ten SIM cards the next day. All the SIM cards were checked by putting them in the mobiles, and all three were very happy that they were working.

Shri Prakash said, "After the work of Sakshi is done, the police will also become light, and no leader will say anything, and if everyone is made to stand in the election, then we can easily field our candidate on twenty-twenty-two seats. As Surajbhan Dada told us, we will field our people in the areas with booth-capturing boys, but each candidate will have to pay about one crore rupees so that food and drink can be arranged for the booth-capturing boys. Almost everyone has weapons, and no one will have any problem with them. To travel in the area for ten days, one must hire a car and pay for the expenses. According to this, we should have twenty-five to thirty crores. At least one crore will have to be given to each candidate. Expenses of banners and posters are also very high." Anuj said, "Bhaiya, we will not be able to get out; the police will kill us; who will do this work?"

Shri Prakash said, "Tell me how many people in Bihar fight elections from jail, and all of them win. Surajbhan Dada has given this idea that we will appear in court six months before the elections by making arrangements, and the nomination form will be filled from the jail itself, and we will fight the elections from the jail itself. Dada has made this program for Bihar; he has finalized the names of his candidates." Anuj said, "Okay, it is possible, but where will we get twenty-twenty-five crores?"

Shri Prakash said, "Everything will come; the railway tender will give ten crores. No one from Shahi goes to Gorakhpur to get tenders now. Harishankar Tiwari will have to be dealt with, and it will be very easy to deal with him. Now, I will call him three times a day; I have put my boys on duty, and they will tell me his daily horoscope in the evening. I will contest from Chiluatal only; Harishankar Tiwari will not file his nomination. Arrangements have been made for everyone else, too. The rest of the Lucknow business people will neither go to anyone nor come on the road. All those whose horoscopes we have, all of them have one or two crores each. Everyone will give the money without making a fuss. Now we will keep the money with us. We have finalized a hotel in Viratnagar, which has 20 rooms. He has agreed to give it for 25 lakh rupees. We will take that hotel, all our boys will look after the hotel work, all the money will be kept there, and we will give money to everyone from there."

Anuj said, "Bhaiya, this is an excellent idea."

THE DGP THREATENED

At 9:30 at night, Shri Prakash called someone to inquire about Gorakhpur; he said, "Bhaiya, today the police have taken Om Prakash bhaiya to the Cantt police station. They have also taken the women and girls of the house, and the police inspector there said that the police have beaten the women and Om Prakash bhaiya very badly."

Shri Prakash said, "Keep the phone; I will tell you right now."

Shri Prakash called SSP Gorakhpur and spoke to him very harshly and said, "I am in Nepal. I will come in four hours, and first of all, I will kill the policemen standing outside your bungalow with rifles, who keep rubbing tobacco in their hands with their rifles resting on the wall. All those who are seen in uniform inside will be killed, and no matter which room you are in, you will also be shot in the throat. How dare you touch women?"

The SSP said, "We are not aware of it; this is the Lucknow team, and the STF people from Lucknow are doing all this." Shri Prakash said, "Okay, so everyone is under the DG of police? I will talk to the DG right now."

Shri Prakash dialed the DGP office and told them that the honorable minister, Amarmani Tripathi, wanted to talk. The DG came on the phone line.

Shri Prakash said to him, "DG sahab, why are the women of our house being harassed? If I lose my temper, your entire police force will be troubled."

The DG said, "The entire police is already troubled; what more trouble will you cause?"

Shri Prakash said, “Okay, you will not agree like this, I will come myself, you have no idea how many dead bodies will be lying there in the DG office!” Saying this, Shri Prakash disconnected the phone.

The DG called Arun Kumar and told him, “Just now such a call came, see from where he is calling, find out the details.” Arun Kumar said, “I will find out right now; there is no need to panic; he is not so daring that he will come to the DG office.”

The DG (Director General of Police) called a meeting of the officers of the DG office and told them that this was the call from Shri Prakash Shukla. He was very agitated because his family members were called to the police station and some were arrested and he said that he would deal with the matter as soon as he came to the DG office and disconnected the call. Some officers posted in the DG office said that even if he does not come here, the arrangements in the DG office should be very strong. In the meeting, everyone was told that this matter should not go out, otherwise it will have an adverse effect on the morale of the police.

The next day the entire DG office, which houses the DG Police, was converted into a cantonment. The journalists and outside officers who visited daily were left trying to find out the reason why so much police force was deployed in the DG office. Several companies were deployed inside and outside the DG office. Almost all the newspapers also published the news that a large number of police force was deployed in the DG office, but no clear reason was written in any newspaper, everyone just made their own guesses.

The next day, when Shri Prakash called for news, the boy called and told him that it was published in today's newspapers that a lot of force was deployed in the DG office. On hearing this, Shri Prakash started laughing loudly. The boy asked, "Bhaiya, what happened?"

Shri Prakash said, "Nothing happened; read what has come out in the English newspapers and tell it to Anuj; he will tell me." After disconnecting the phone, Shri Prakash told Sudhir and Anuj that now our work is done; after dealing with Sakshi Maharaj, no one will be left who can even look at us. Sudhir said, “Get bade bhaiya, bhabhi, and the girls of the house released from the police station; the police are beating them a lot."

Shri Prakash said, "Don't worry, the DG has been given a dose. He will release them on his own, we will find out in the evening."

In the evening, Shri Prakash called Gorakhpur again to find out, the caller told that the family members are hiding somewhere, Om Prakash bhaiya has been beaten badly, a doctor has been called to the police station to get him treated. Shri Prakash got furious, he immediately called all the three ministers of Gorakhpur one by one and told them to go and talk to the Chief Minister directly, if the family members are not released by tomorrow, then be ready to face the consequences.

Everyone told him, hey, don't be so angry, we will go and talk to the Chief Minister tomorrow morning. Shri Prakash called all the ministers again in the morning and told them that he will call in the evening and till then talk to the Chief Minister and get them released. If they are not released then I will not call again, I will come myself and see which policeman saves whom.

All the ministers understood the seriousness of the matter and unanimously took time from the Chief Minister. When so many ministers asked for time together, Chief Minister Kalyan Singh, understanding that there is something serious, gave time to all to come to the office at one o'clock. Along with the three ministers from Gorakhpur, three more ministers also went to the Chief Minister's chamber. When everyone reached together, the Chief Minister asked, "What happened that all these people have come together?"

The most senior minister started the conversation, "The police are committing excesses in Gorakhpur; the women of Shri Prakash's family have been made to sit at the police station, and they have been tortured. What do you have to do with the women and men of the house?"

The Chief Minister said, "Why not? His brother is taking all the benefits and contracts, so why he has nothing to do with it? If you people have come to get him released from the police station, then let me make it clear: he will not be released at all. You people should have thought before coming for this work that whose case are you pleading for? I am unable to understand why you, such senior ministers, are pleading for this? The police will not show any leniency towards Shri Prakash Shukla or his family members. I also request the DG to send all of them to jail and also bring the family members of the people who are in his gang to the police station and interrogate them and send them to jail under the sections that give protection to criminals. I am hurt by your recommendation to show leniency towards the criminal. It will be better if you people leave."

The faces of all the ministers turned pale. Some people said, "Chief Minister, we are sorry." All the other ministers got up and left. The Chief Minister was very angry. He immediately called the DG, "What is the matter? Have the family members of Shri Prakash Shukla been brought to the police station? Why are they still being held? Why haven't they been sent to jail? You tell the officers of Gorakhpur that no leniency should be shown to them. That criminal has created havoc in the state, and some of our own ministers had just come to plead for him; you tell me in the evening whether they have been sent to jail or not? Apart from this, he sent the family members of his other gang members to jail as well. Only then will these criminals understand that this is our government. Our attitude towards criminals and their associates is very clear."

All the ministers who got up and left the Chief Minister knew what answer they would give if Shri Prakash called them in the evening. All of them decided that if he called, they would tell him that today, the meeting with the Chief Minister could not happen.

The meeting has not been possible; we will meet tomorrow. At four in the evening, Shri Prakash called again and asked, "Honourable Minister, my family members have not been released from the police station yet; what happened? Did you people meet the Chief Minister or not?" The minister clearly refused and said, "He has many programs today; we could not meet today. We will try to get time tomorrow."

Shri Prakash said, "I know, it is beyond your control, I will have to do something."

Shri Prakash was calling many people in Gorakhpur in anger when someone told him, "Bhaiya, the Cantt police has sent bhaiya, sister-in-law and all the adult members of the family to jail. All these people have been admitted to jail at six in the evening, and I have heard one more thing that today, four-five ministers met the Chief Minister, and the Chief Minister scolded these people a lot and told the police officers to send everyone to jail. Along with this, raids have been conducted at everyone's houses. The police have also taken away Sudhir's brother. Police raided Anuj's house in Faizabad as well. It is being told from the police station that now everyone's family members will go to jail."

Shri Prakash said, "There is no truth in this news; the Chief Minister did not give time to the ministers today." That boy said that "These people are lying. The PA of the Health Minister told me that five people had gone, and the Health Minister was not aware of the whole matter. He went with the other ministers with the greed that if he got to meet the Chief Minister, he would get an order to provide a gunner to his brother. But seeing the Chief Minister's anger, he apologized and left. Whoever told you has not told the truth. All these people had gone and stayed with the Chief Minister for about thirty-five minutes."

Shri Prakash said, "Okay, I will see now."

Shri Prakash again called the senior minister from Gorakhpur. On picking up the phone, he said, "Why are you lying to me? You five people went there, and we talked for thirty-five minutes. Apart from you three, you had taken two more ministers along; they also apologized to the Chief Minister there. Do you think that I will not find anything? I have my men in the Chief Minister's office as well." Hearing this, the minister was stunned.

The minister said, "Bhaiya when the Chief Minister refused, what would I have told you? Now I will threaten the officers and get them released." Shri Prakash said, "You think I am a fool? While fooling the public, you have also considered me as your dumb voter? The police sent everyone to jail; why haven't you threatened the officers yet?" The minister could not utter a single word.

Shri Prakash said, "I will not talk to you cowards anymore, but you be ready to suffer and face the consequences now." After this, Shri Prakash disconnected the phone. Anuj and Sudhir sat there, listening to Shri Prakash's entire conversation.

Sudhir said, "Bhaiya, I have also discovered that my brother has also been arrested. Thankfully, my sisters were not at home; they had gone to the market. When they reached the house, they found out that a lot of police had arrived, so they ran away from there to their relative's house. Otherwise, the police would have insulted us a lot today."

Shri Prakash said, "I feel like going right now and directly dealing with the Chief Minister, but to reach there, I will have to do a lot of fielding. I will have to stay in Lucknow for a long time and will have to get the Kundli every hour." Sudhir said, "Bhaiya, all the family members will be in jail by then."

Shri Prakash said, "Don't worry, from tomorrow we will meet Sakshi Maharaj again, now it is very important to kill Sakshi. When Sakshi turns back, all the minister's anguish will end. Sakshi and the Chief Minister belong to the same community, and Sakshi has many men, and all of Vijay Singh's men work for Sakshi. This is the reason why the Chief Minister is upset. Let's try for two or three days. Now Sakshi will have to be dealt with; otherwise, we will suffer much loss." Sudhir said, "In two days, we have seen that the people who are with Brajbihari Prasad were all loose-lipped, but those who go with Sakshi are more alert." Shri Prakash said, "Sakshi is in danger from Brahmadatt Dwivedi's people. Sakshi knows this very well, and that is why he never goes to Fatehgarh, even by mistake. If Brahmadatt Dwivedi's people find him before us, they will kill him. He has also increased his security a lot by telling the Chief Minister. But it doesn't matter, let's try for three-four days, otherwise we will go in blankets in the winter and deal with him there itself." Shri Prakash was apprehensive about his family members going to jail. For the first time, he felt under pressure. He felt that his pleas were not heard even after doing so much. Now, something bigger has to be done; this way, the police will not be able to do anything, but our family members will be troubled. Whenever this thought came to his mind, he would call someone or the other and get information about Gorakhpur. What happened to Sudhir's bhai, was the bail application filed or not? He started talking to the lawyers directly that get him bail in two-three days; I will deal with all this later. Sudhir and Anand were also getting worried; the police also took away their family members. Shri Prakash told Sudhir and Anand, "It is essential to do the witness work in two-three days, otherwise this police will trouble you a lot." Sudhir said, "Bhaiya, there is no use in listening to the ministers, the inspector and constables do the work, it is their direct servants.

If they are suppressed, they will not trouble anyone."

Shri Prakash said, "Didn't you see how the Chief Minister is adamant? No one will dare to do so if the Chief Minister gives any order. The police officers do not want to leave their police station or their district, and the DG does not want to leave his post. Whoever wants to save his post will obey the orders of the Chief Minister in whatever way he wants. Do you think that I did not talk to Inspector Cantt? When I dialed his number, he started crying and said, "Bhaiya, we are being oppressed from both sides; if we don't listen to you, then one day someone will shoot us inside the police station and go away; if we don't listen to the higher authorities, we will be suspended, our children will come on the streets. I am also yours. Will you like that child come on the streets and beg?"

I asked him, "Whose pressure is this? Why are you talking like this? He said straight away, "Bhaiya, the Chief Minister directly talks to the STF and the STF itself picks up the accused and brings him to the police station. They tell the DIG, IG that they have caught him and handed him over to the police station, now it is the police station's job to extract the truth from them. Tell me bhaiya, if someone brings him to the police station and hands him over, how can I remove him from the police station, I will get him suspended immediately."

Shri Prakash said, “You know I talked to the SSP. The SSP was also saying the same things and it seemed that he would cry.” Sudhir interrupted and said, “Bhaiya, it seems that this Chief Minister talks directly to the STF. That is why the STF people are catching up faster. Why don’t we make arrangements for these STF people? Once the STF people get out of our way, the police will never touch us.”

Shri Prakash said, “I also think that these STF people are chasing us the most. By the way, once the Sakshi work is done, the Chief Minister will reduce the pressure, then the STF people will also get a chance, they will stop touching. But you are right, these STF people will also have to be fixed, so it is more important that the Sakshi work is done first, two birds will be killed with one arrow. Brahmadatt Dwivedi’s son’s work will also be done and the Chief Minister will also be respected. So let's wait here for two-three days, after that we will go to Lucknow. In this battle for supremacy, family members are being harassed, who are not interested in this battle, so something has to be done."

The next day Shri Prakash, Anuj and Sudhir started going to Sakshi Maharaj's ashram from 6 am in the morning in a queue. They got up in between to gather information about the routes and other details. Shri Prakash said, "If we had called the Kundali boys from Lucknow, the work would have been done by now. These boys had done such accurate Kundali that the whole work would have been done. We have stopped doing this work, that is why we are facing difficulties. The whole day was wasted but we did not get much success." The next day when these three again reached Sakshi's ashram, this time they brought all the luggage in the car.

Shri Prakash was very impatient to do Sakshi's work. As soon as they reached the gate of the ashram, the gate was locked. The man present at the gate told, “Maharaj has gone out, he will come after a week.” Anuj said that it was very important to meet Maharaj, where has he gone? If you tell us, we will go and meet him there. The man from the ashram said that if Maharaj had not informed us, he would have either gone to Fatehgarh or Lucknow. All three returned disappointed.

FACE TO FACE

Meanwhile, Shri Prakash contacted prominent builders and business magnates in Lucknow for financial assistance. When he contacted Sanjay Seth of Sarna Marble, the response was fearful. Seeking support, he also connected with Satyendra Veer Singh and Rajesh Pandey to explain the situation. Having installed caller ID, Sanjay Seth quickly discovered that the number calling him originated from a mobile linked to Delhi.

Acting swiftly, a team was dispatched from Lucknow to trace the source of the SIM card. Their investigation revealed ten SIM cards had been registered under a single driving license. Upon visiting the address associated with the license, they found both the name and location to be fabricated. The details for all ten numbers were extracted in Delhi, uncovering several linked to Lucknow, Gorakhpur, and Bihar.

Arun Kumar then suggested the formation of a dedicated team in Delhi to monitor these mobile numbers closely, emphasizing the urgency of tracking the number with the highest call frequency. The assistance of local law enforcement became necessary to obtain mobile details in Delhi and establish surveillance. Arun Kumar reached out to the DCP of the Crime Branch, who promised full cooperation.

Additionally, Inspector ACP PP Singh, an acquaintance of Satyendra Veer Singh, served at the Azad Mandi police station in Delhi's Crime Branch. He offered comprehensive support and arranged the necessary setups to listen to the calls. The call detail report revealed that Shri Prakash was not using a single mobile device but kept switching numbers. To identify all the mobile numbers registered in Lucknow and Gorakhpur, two STF teams were dispatched to gather information from the local mobile provider, with a two-day deadline to compile the names and addresses of the mobile users. Meanwhile, the Delhi team confirmed that the signals still emanated from within the city.

Upon learning that Sakshi Maharaj would be away for a week, Shri Prakash returned to his flat and addressed Anuj and Sudhir, saying, “It's time to go to Lucknow. We need to take care of Sakshi's issue—now, no one can protect her. Let's first handle the STF.” That evening, they loaded their weapons into a car, leaving their Seelo vehicle behind in Delhi, and returned to Lucknow in a Zen.

Arriving in Gomti Nagar's Viram Khand, they reached the spacious house where Shri Prakash had placed his father for safety in light of police scrutiny. The property was registered in Anuj's mother's name and was surrounded by residences of senior IAS officers.

Shri Prakash suggested, “First, let's gather the horoscopes of Arun Kumar, Satyendra Veer Singh, and Rajesh Pandey to determine their daily movements. We need to make some adjustments; otherwise, their family members will start to worry.” He continued, “In the meantime, I've noticed an increase in checks at the Zen. An open Jonga jeep belonging to the army is parked at Pawan Pandey's house with a Syrian wrestler inside. Let's take it for a spin; no police officer would dare stop us if they saw us in the army jeep. We won't even have to venture into the cantonment area.”

Sudhir returned with the dust-covered open Jonga jeep from Pawan Pandey's place an hour later. “Get it serviced at Munish's service center in Indiranagar,” Shri Prakash instructed. “We'll use this jeep to move around tomorrow.”

Sudhir hesitated, “Bhaiya, the Lucknow police are vigorously searching for us. It's risky to travel in such an open vehicle.”

Shri Prakash reassured him, “They only have my picture. I've told you before that people can't recognize someone just by a photo in a crowd. However, someone familiar who has been seen before is easily identifiable. So, relax; the police won't stop you or recognize us.”

After getting the Jonga jeep serviced in Indiranagar, Sudhir drove back to Gomti Nagar. Inside the jeep, Shri Prakash took the wheel, with Anuj beside him and Sudhir in the back seat. They discreetly carried all their weapons in a cricket bag.

They headed to Hazratganj, where they paused at a Woodland store for a brief break. Afterward, they went to the Capital, Tiraha, to see Arshad Mushtaq, who ran a PCO near the Shiv Sena office. There, they conversed with Arshad, gathering information about various individuals.

Shri Prakash headed toward Mahanagar and remarked, "Let's check out the STF office."

Sudhir quickly warned, "Bhaiya, we shouldn't go there. The STF has Dheerendra in custody, and if he recognizes us, we could be in serious trouble."

Shri Prakash replied defiantly, "If I come face-to-face with Dheerendra, I won't hesitate to shoot him down right then and there. He's leaking our whereabouts to the police, tipping them off about our hideout."

Sudhir insisted, "Bhaiya, the police have already tracked down a location that Dheerendra is unaware of. It seems they might be gathering information through phone surveillance."

Meanwhile, the team in Delhi informed Arun Kumar, "These individuals haven't been in Delhi since the evening of the day before yesterday. The mobile company confirmed they are moving around in Uttar Pradesh, and we can only trace their roaming details within that state." Arun Kumar relayed this information to Rajesh Pandey and asked, "How do we find them?"

Rajesh responded, "Sir, we'll have answers in about half an hour. I'll contact Rajendra Singh at Usha and Pawan at Essar; they can pinpoint our location." About an hour later, Rajesh Pandey updated Arun Kumar, saying, "Sir, Rajendra has confirmed that Shri Prakash has been in Lucknow since yesterday morning. His movements have been traced to Gomti Nagar, Hazratganj, Kaiserbagh, and Mahanagar, and he's currently in Gomti Nagar."

Arun Kumar quickly summoned Satyendra Veer Singh, Rajesh Pandey, Umesh, and Avinash to the office, instructing, "Everyone should head out to different areas. Once we locate the target, set up a barrier there and conduct checks with assistance from the Lucknow Police."

Rajesh Pandey suggested, "I'll bring Dheerendra along; he can confirm any suspicions we have." Arun Kumar agreed, "All right, take him with you." The following morning, the team dispersed to patrol various regions. Around 2 PM, Rajendra Singh reported that the target's phone had been active near a tower in Vikas Nagar an hour earlier, but it had since been turned off. Umesh Singh began scouring the main road in Vikas Nagar, but after two hours of searching, they found nothing. By 5:30 PM, Usha received another update indicating that the phone's location was now pinpointed back to Viram Khand in Gomti Nagar.

In Gomti Nagar, Rajesh Pandey suggested they check at the Mithai Wala crossroads. Dheerendra replied, "There's no need for all that. Just park the car on the side; I'll keep watch and can recognize those three even in the dark."

Rajesh was driving the jeep with Dheerendra in the front seat, while two STF commandos equipped with AK-47s accompanied them. "You're right, Dheerendra. Let's head to that crossroads by the vegetable shop," Rajesh said. "We'll park the jeep there for a clear view of the traffic coming and going. Watch; we'll call the others over if you spot them."

As Rajesh made a U-turn from the petrol pump to return to the checkpoint, he noticed a few vehicles filling up with petrol and diesel. Suddenly, when the jeep's headlights illuminated an army's open Jonga vehicle, Dheerendra ducked and urgently whispered, "That's him, that's him!"

Rajesh, confused, asked, “Which one?” Dheerendra pointed toward the vehicle in front but struggled to speak due to panic. As they approached the few cars at the pump, the army's Jonga quickly reversed without refueling. “Are those the people in the open vehicle?” Rajesh asked Dheerendra, who remained crouched and confirmed, “Yes, that’s the same guy.”

Just then, the Jonga sped off toward the Polytechnic crossing. Rajesh backed up slightly and accelerated after it. Light rain began to fall, engulfing the road in darkness as Dheerendra cautiously lifted his head to get a better look.

Rajesh Pandey turned to Dheerendra and said, “What was the point in being so afraid? You’re carrying two AK-47s with you! Why didn’t you mention earlier that the open vehicle was an Army Jonga? I was focused on the Maruti 800 and the Safari that were refueling. We could have caught them if you had told me sooner that the Army Jonga was there.”

Rajesh pursued the vehicle for about five minutes until Shri Prakash turned off his backlight. He hurriedly reached the Polytechnic crossing and called Satyendra Veer Singh, Ajay Kumar, Avinash Mishra, and Umesh to inform them. Everyone rushed to Gomti Nagar, surrounding the area from all sides and searching for the army's open Jonga throughout the night. As dawn broke, they still hadn’t found anything. Disheartened, they returned to the office.

For the first time, the STF team confronted Shri Prakash Shukla. Arun Kumar inquired about the entire incident, expressing frustration towards Rajesh Pandey. He said, “When you had the chance to see him in the headlights, you should have opened fire with the AK-47. Maybe only one or two civilians would have been caught in the crossfire!”

Rajesh listened quietly while other officers said they would have ensured Shri Prakash didn't escape. Finally, Rajesh spoke up, “Dheerendra was the first to spot him, but as soon as he did, he ducked under the dashboard. I was trying to hastily turn from the petrol pump to get to the Mithai Wala crossroads. Dheerendra lowered his head and started making 'hmm hmm' sounds, which drew my attention. I asked, 'What's wrong?' Dheerendra said, 'It's him.' When I asked, 'Which one?' I had already pulled out my pistol. I even yelled, 'Which car?' but no words came out of Dheerendra's mouth. I couldn't fathom that he would be in an open jeep. In an instant, they took off toward Faizabad Road. When they were far away, Dheerendra finally raised his head and mentioned three people in the open jeep. When I tried to catch up, they had already made a significant distance and turned off their backlight. I can't understand why Dheerendra panicked so much."

A heavy silence fell over the room as everyone absorbed the situation. Since early morning, attempts have been made to trace the location of Usha's and Essar's phones, but the response remained the same: the phone was switched off, and no location could be found since 7 PM.

Arun Kumar contacted the SSP of Lucknow and deployed teams across the district to search for the army's open Jonga vehicle. The teams were instructed to check where the car might be hidden, even in large bungalows around Gomti Nagar. Despite a full day of searches, there was still no breakthrough.

Meanwhile, Shri Prakash, Anuj, and Sudhir stayed vigilant at the window throughout the night. The Jonga was concealed within a garage, its shutter secured. Shri Prakash had sent his father upstairs to keep watch, instructing him to shout if any police vehicle or personnel approached the gate, allowing them to prepare for a swift escape.

All night long, police vehicles drove by, horns blaring. As morning approached and police activity subsided somewhat, Shri Prakash remarked to Anuj and Sudhir, "How did the police reach the petrol pump within ten minutes of us leaving? Something doesn't add up. Someone from Indiranagar, where the servicing was done, tipped them off, or someone else fed them information. The moment the headlights fell on us, the Gypsy started tailing us. Had it not been for the darkness on the road, we would've been forced to fire."

Turning to the group, Shri Prakash asked, “Did anyone get a good look at who was in the car?”

Sudhir responded, “Yes, bhaiya. I was right in front of them. When the scooter driver left after filling up, I caught a glimpse in his headlights. Rajesh Pandey was driving, but the passenger seat beside him was empty. Two men were sitting in the back with AK-47s.”

Shri Prakash stated, "I had the same suspicion that it might be Rajesh Pandey. They must have communicated something over the phone. Rajesh manages our telephone communications and is the only one with the guts to stand up like this. Consider this: whenever shots are fired, they inevitably come from Rajesh Pandey. Who else has the nerve? Didn’t you notice how, when we were returning from Hazratganj yesterday evening, there was a checkpoint at Gomti Barrage? That hefty police inspector asked us to roll down the window; I merely showed him the AK-47, and he immediately took four steps back, saluted, and opened the barrier."

Sudhir interjected, "He’s in charge at a police station nearby. Two days ago, his picture was published in the newspaper; he’s quite rotund, with a prominent belly."

"Yes, that’s him," Shri Prakash confirmed. "Let’s keep this car in the garage and lock it up from both sides. The police will be searching for it frantically. It’s no longer safe for us in Lucknow. Those bastards have started tailing us. There’s something off; how else are they hitting every location we go to?"

Anuj added, "I had asked for the contact number of the person from whom I bought the SIM card and phone in Delhi to recharge my mobile. Once, I even recharged it by speaking with him directly, telling him, ‘I’ll pay you when I come back.’ He called me recently to say that the police had been here, troubling him about who had taken the ten SIM cards."

Shri Prakash replied, "We need to call someone for another vehicle. First, we must leave this place and head to Viratnagar. It’s crucial to find out who’s tipping them off. From now on, we’ll only communicate through PCOs. No mobile phones will be used because the person who provided the SIM card doesn't have a PCO, and no PCO was used for that transaction. These guys have infiltrated a mobile network somehow, allowing them to track our movements."

Anuj announced, "There's a new Tata Sumo parked in Faizabad. I'll call for it right away. It should arrive in about two hours; we can use it to head to Viratnagar." He placed the call and arranged for the Tata Sumo, which arrived by evening. The driver was instructed, "Park the Tata Sumo at the Polytechnic crossing near the bus stand. We'll meet you there, and on our way out, we'll drop you off at Rakabganj in Faizabad." As darkness fell, all three of them left the house. Before departing, Shri Prakash advised his father, "You leave for Deoria in the morning to visit your uncle, but stay away from Gorakhpur." His father replied, "Okay."

Once they moved, the three took a tempo to the main road. They disembarked directly at the Polytechnic crossing, drove to the Tata Sumo, and parked far from the bus stand. Anuj instructed the driver, "First, hand over your mobile and sit in the back. We'll drop you off at Rakabganj." Shri Prakash took the wheel, driving swiftly away toward Faizabad. After dropping off the Tata Sumo driver at Rakabganj, they continued to Gorakhpur, reaching their old place in Viratnagar by morning. Upon their arrival, they felt a wave of relief wash over them. Shri Prakash remarked, "Things have gotten too heated. Even our family has stopped visiting. The STF has started tailing us, and we need to take action."

Everyone was exhausted, so they had breakfast and went to sleep. Shri Prakash was at a loss for what to do next; they couldn't even find a witness for their case. While they could have gone to Lucknow to eliminate one or two of the STF officers or anyone outside their office, that plan was also off the table. Frustrated, he mused, "Can't we figure something out?"

Shri Prakash left the hotel the following day and called Rajesh Pandey's home number from a nearby PCO. At that time, all STF officers recorded their landline calls using tape recorders equipped with caller ID, ensuring they could track incoming calls.

At 6:30 AM, when Rajesh Pandey picked up the phone, still groggy, he immediately switched on the tape recorder. The voice on the other end said, “This is Shri Prakash Shukla. Do you recognize my voice?”

Rajesh Pandey, now alert, replied, “I certainly recognize you.”

Glancing at the caller ID, he noticed the number was from Nepal. "You left for Nepal in a hurry," Rajesh said. "I thought you were brave, but now you're just a coward."

Shri Prakash retorted, "Do you think I came unarmed? I saw you in the beam of my scooter's light; I had an AK-47."

Rajesh Pandey replied, “We weren't exactly sitting around unarmed either. We were men, so why did we bolt like scared dogs? If the road had been well-lit, your story would have ended yesterday.”

Shri Prakash shot back, “Those two boys with toy guns wouldn't even get a chance to pull the trigger before I empty an entire magazine into you. But enough of that—what's done is done. Tell me, why are you pursuing me?”

Rajesh Pandey said, “You've been stirring trouble for us in Lucknow. Of course, I'll chase you down. Why don't you surrender? If you don't, the day I spot you, you won't even be able to reach out to your AK-47. I will pump bullets in your every body part."

Shri Prakash angrily said, “Don't think I'll go down alone; I'll take you and a few others with me. It's not easy to shoot me; even big police shooters will not dare even attempt shooting at us. We've dealt with major players before; even those who wielded ten or twenty rifles were shot dead like a dog. Don't you remember my record?”

Rajesh Pandey countered, “Why didn't you stop at the petrol pump? You had a chance to fight; why did you run away like petty thieves?”

Shri Prakash continued to hurl insults, “Your daughter rides in a blue gypsy to Loreto school every morning. There are two guys in the back with toy guns. You think that's enough to protect her?”

Rajesh Pandey declared, “Save those tricks for the baniyas and the businessmen; it might work on them, but not on me. Just tell me your address in Nepal. I’ll come, find you, and kill you. You know our address, too; feel free to drop by if you’re brave enough. Why are you hiding in your mother’s petticoat, fleeing to Nepal like a coward?”

After this, Rajesh Pandey began to hurl insults back at Shri Prakash. About thirty-five minutes had passed by that time, and Shri Prakash abruptly disconnected the call. Once the line went silent, Rajesh Pandey noticed that his children, sleeping beside him, were awake and visibly frightened. His wife had also roused from sleep and appeared equally alarmed.

"Oh, you two are up early today?" Rajesh Pandey said, attempting to lighten the mood. Both kids remained silent. His wife interjected, “Why were you using such abusive language?” He replied, “He was insulting my mother and sister—there’s no way I could just sit back and tolerate that.”

His wife frowned and continued, “From tomorrow, I won't be sending our children to school. I heard everything.”

Without missing a beat, Rajesh Pandey informed Arun Kumar, “I just received a call from this number in Nepal. It was foul language, and I’ve recorded the entire conversation.”

Arun Kumar responded, “I’ll be at the office by nine o’clock. Bring the cassette; we’ll gather everyone to listen to it.” The Gorakhpur team was then instructed to head to Nepal immediately to trace the PCO associated with the number. Inspectors Malviya and OP Tripathi were already in Gorakhpur, and they set off to Nepal with two additional constables.

When they provided the number to the police stations along the Nepal border, the officers there promptly informed them that it belonged to Viratnagar. Inspectors Malviya and Tripathi made their way to Biratnagar, arriving by evening. After extensive searching, they located a PCO that night.

They approached the PCO operator and asked, “Was a call made to India at 6:30 this morning? Can you tell us to which numbers?" The operator showed them the register, confirming that Rajesh Pandey's home number was indeed listed. Malviya relayed the news to Arun Kumar, “We found the PCO, and the call was made to Pandey Sahab this morning.”

Arun Kumar instructed, “If there’s a nearby place to stay, book a room for the night. He’s likely to return to the same PCO again.”

Malviya hesitated, prompting Arun Kumar to challenge him, “Are you scared of dying? There's also a chance your bullet could take him out.” Malviya replied, “Sir, that’s not feasible in Nepal.” Arun Kumar pressed on, “Anything is possible. If it comes down to it, shoot without hesitation; we’ll all be there. We’ll coordinate with the Nepal Police. Right now, he has the largest bounty on his head in Uttar Pradesh.” Malviya responded, “Okay, Sir!”

The team settled into a small hotel far from the PCO. They decided that one person would monitor a nearby shop from when the PCO opened until it closed, watching for Shri Prakash's arrival, identifying him by appearance, and following him wherever he stayed.

On the third day, around 7:30 AM, Shri Prakash returned to the same PCO alone in a Tata Sumo. When he entered, the PCO operator asked, “Will you be calling Lucknow?”

Shri Prakash replied warily, “How do you know?” The operator explained, “Four people came asking about the call you made the day before yesterday morning. They looked like UP policemen.” Upon hearing this, Shri Prakash dashed out, jumped back into the Tata Sumo, and sped off. By the time the officer monitoring from a nearby tea stall grasped what had transpired, the Tata Sumo was already gone.

He rushed back into the PCO and inquired, “Where did the man who just left intend to call?” The operator replied, “That’s the same person who called two days ago. When I told him the police were asking about him, he jumped in his car and fled without making a call. I noted his Tata Sumo's number; you can have it if you want.”

The officer on surveillance rushed back to the hotel to relay everything. Malviya immediately called Arun Kumar, who was visibly furious. "I told you he would come! You couldn't keep a proper watch for even two days. If you had been alert, we would have caught him today. Please find the details on this Tata Sumo, such as where it's from and who owns it. He won't return there again. Head back to Gorakhpur, and if you receive a call from anywhere, I'll inform you."

Meanwhile, Shri Prakash reached the hotel in the Tata Sumo, quickly rushed to his room, and began packing his belongings. He instructed Sudhir and Anuj, "Get the luggage in the car immediately. We need to leave in ten minutes!"

Sudhir and Anuj were taken aback. "What trouble has come upon us here in Nepal? We've been fine so far!"

As they hurriedly loaded the luggage into the Tata Sumo, Shri Prakash drove away from Viratnagar, steering toward Bihar via Raxaul. Once they crossed Bihar, Sudhir turned to him and asked, "Bhaiya, what happened in Nepal? We've never faced any issues here before."

Shri Prakash replied, "I can't understand how the police are tracking us. He's even stopped using his mobile. When I got to the PCO, the operator told me that the police had come asking about the number I called the day before yesterday."

Sudhir pressed, "What description did you give? Who did you talk to that day?"

"I spoke to Rajesh Pandey," Shri Prakash said, frustrated. "But the description the PCO operator gave doesn't match Rajesh. I can't figure out whose appearance he was referring to. He mentioned that those policemen were from UP."

Shri Prakash continued, "They broke into our old house in Lucknow, took the gypsy, and many of our belongings. We barely escaped in Mokama. That day, that jerk Rajesh Pandey came to the petrol station in Gomti Nagar. We came to Nepal hoping for some peace, to devise a strategy for our future, and to see what happened in just two days.

I can't understand how they're getting such precise information. Only the STF knows about these places; the local police never do. We can't go back to any of our old contacts, and from now on, we will avoid talking on mobile phones. We should only use the PCO if it's essential."

Anuj suggested, "This is going to be tough. We should buy fifteen to twenty more SIM cards. No one should use the same SIM for more than an hour; tracing the numbers will take longer. Also, I'd recommend we talk in the car after driving ten to fifteen kilometers away."

Sudhir chimed in, "Now I understand how they caught and killed Anand Pandey. He was always on his phone after coming to Delhi. They managed to pin down his location, and those thugs got him. We have to be especially vigilant now."

Shri Prakash nodded, "It's not just Rajesh Pandey who is involved in this. The Chief Minister and the SSP of the STF are in cahoots. They don't heed anyone else; whatever they decide, their goons below carry it out. Remember how five ministers couldn't do anything to help after we went to see the Chief Minister? Our bhaiya and sister-in-law ended up in jail.

It was sheer bad luck that those goons spotted us at the petrol station. Otherwise, we were supposed to head to the STF office right after fueling up. If we had parked outside the office and waited, we would have encountered someone we knew. It would have kept us busy for a few days if we dropped off a couple of people.

Now, we don't have much going on. The witness work would have been wrapped up in a month or two, and then we planned to head to Bihar to handle Dada's business. After completing those two tasks, we would make arrangements to surrender just in time for the elections. But for over a month now, nothing has been straightforward. It seems like everyone we called in Lucknow for money gets our numbers and starts tracking us. If we're going to talk to our contacts from now on, we need to do it from somewhere they can't reach us for a day or two."Sudhir said, "Let us look for a place in

Bihar to talk and reach Patna. By the time they all find the PCO and reach there, we will reach another place." Sudhir said, "Bhaiya, we have come this far, so let us go via Araria. We will find a place to stay there and get a PCO." Shri Prakash said, "Okay."

Shri Prakash headed toward Araria. Upon arrival, the group searched for a decent hotel, but their efforts were unsuccessful. Ultimately, they settled in a small establishment called 'Prakash,' where everyone expressed their intention to stay the night.

The following day, Shri Prakash took Sudhir with him in search of a PCO. In the primary market of Araria, they found a row of PCOs. Sudhir remarked, "There are plenty of PCOs here."

Shri Prakash replied, "It's too close to the hotel; we can't talk from here. Tomorrow, we'll scout around more and find a safer spot. Let's get out of the city."

After traveling four or five kilometers, they located a PCO at a roadside dhaba along the highway. Shri Prakash instructed Sudhir to stay in the car. "Keep an eye on the people coming and going while I make the call," he said.

From there, Shri Prakash dialed Surajbhan. After a few rings, Surajbhan picked up. "Dada, I've been worried these past fifteen to twenty days. The STF seems to be everywhere," Shri Prakash confessed.

"What is STF?" Surajbhan inquired.

"It's a special task force formed by the Chief Minister, targeting us specifically," Shri Prakash explained, frustration evident in his voice. "You know we've been operating quietly for a long time; the police couldn't find us even months after the incident. Now, they're showing up within half an hour of us moving. I called to let you know I'll switch off my mobile. If something important arises, I'll call you from a PCO or use a new SIM card. Just make sure to pick up my calls."

Surajbhan asked, "Where are you right now?"

"I'm in Araria, just back from Nepal," Shri Prakash replied.

Surajbhan's tone shifted as he announced, "The deal for the hotel in Viratnagar is finalized. The money you have will be used to buy it. The paperwork is ready; I need to hand over the cash to the owner, and I'll have the hotel registered in the name of one of your brothers. Once he receives the money, he'll vacate the premises. I'll also need two to four people to help with the transition. We're looking at around ten to twelve lakh rupees for painting and whitewashing. After that, the hotel should be operational. The previous management didn't take care of it properly, and the number of people staying for free kept increasing, which is why it wasn't sustainable.

"With the hotel under our control, we can be sure that no one stays for free. Gradually, we can also buy up the three small hotels nearby. Establishing a permanent presence in Nepal is crucial. Since the demise of Mirza Dilshad Beg, his men have just been wandering around, and the police have ramped up their activity. Lalu Yadav has also been unpredictable since Braj Bihari's murder.

Shri Prakash said, "Dada, you mentioned a task in Araria a while back."

Surajbhan replied, "Yes, you're right. That man has been a thorn in our side, causing trouble for our people who smuggle goods across the Nepal border. His office is based here in Araria."

"Get me someone who knows him; we'll take care of him immediately," Shri Prakash insisted.

Surajbhan cautioned, "You're in a precarious situation. Come to Mokama, rest for a few days, and then plan your next move."

"No, Dada, I can't go now. If I sit idle, the STF will take advantage and escalate things further. I need to act now. It feels like Kamakhya Mata is displeased with me; I haven't performed a human sacrifice in a long time. She demands a sacrifice," Shri Prakash exclaimed.

Surajbhan responded, "But if you're not using your mobile, how will anyone reach you?"

"Have your man wait at Ghantaghar crossing and ask what clothes I wear. I'll pick him up myself. I'll call you again in half an hour," Shri

Prakash instructed. After a lengthy discussion, he hung up and gestured to Sudhir at the PCO gate, asking, "Is there anyone nearby?"

Sudhir signaled back, "You can go now."

Shri Prakash quickly returned to the car and accelerated away. He drove soon for fifteen to twenty kilometers on the main road. Sudhir asked, "Bhaiya, where are we headed after leaving Anuj?"

"I'm not going anywhere specific; I must find another PCO. I won't return to this one. The person I need to speak with has asked me to call back in half an hour. Let me know if you spot a PCO ahead; I'll be watching, too," Shri Prakash replied.

After a short drive, he stopped at another PCO, got out, and called Surajbhan again. Surajbhan informed him, "There's a shoe shop a little from the clock tower. A man is waiting outside; I've alerted him. He'll be wearing a red comrade cap, and his name is Chandan. He'll provide you with the information you need."

Shri Prakash said, "Okay, Dada," then headed straight to the clock tower. He spotted a man wearing a red cap standing outside a shoe shop. Shri Prakash parked the car and approached him. "Are you Chandan?" he asked.

"Yes," Chandan replied, adding, "Are you Ashok Singh Bhaiya?"

"Yes, let's go by car. Do you know what we need to do?" Shri Prakash asked.

"Of course, Dada has briefed us. Follow me," Chandan responded.

After Chandan climbed into the car, they drove about a kilometer until they reached a large sand and cement shop where a few people sat. Chandan gestured inside the vehicle, "This is his office; he's sitting in a chair out front."

"Which one is he?" Shri Prakash asked as the car moved forward.

Shri Prakash said, "Let's go further and turn around. Make sure to give me a heads-up."

Chandan described the target, saying, “Bhaiya, he’s wearing a kurta and pajama with a towel around his neck. He’s sitting right in front, and two or three guys are in jeans and T-shirts next to him. They likely have weapons.”

“Understood,” Shri Prakash replied. He returned to the same road after driving three or four kilometers ahead. “Look carefully!” he instructed Sudhir.

Shri Prakash looked closely and asked Chandan, “What vehicle does he drive?”

Chandan replied, “He drives a white Bolero, sometimes with a red light on top. He heads toward the Nepal border once or twice a week. Also, be aware that his aim is excellent; he’s a very bold man with a reputation for committing multiple murders. The police don’t raid his place out of fear. He spends most of his time at this shop, surrounded by ten to twenty people.”

“Got it,” Shri Prakash affirmed. After dropping Chandan back at the clock tower, he headed straight to the hotel. Upon arrival, all three men ordered light snacks. Afterward, Sudhir and Anuj slept, but Shri Prakash found it hard to rest. His mind was preoccupied with thoughts of someone trailing him and tipping off the police, leading to their swift responses. His paranoia kept drifting back to Sudhir and Anuj.

Shri Prakash reflected on the situation. He realized that no one knew his movements except for Sudhir and Anuj. However, he quickly dismissed that notion; they didn’t know the address of the PCO in Viratnagar. He had gone there alone without mentioning it to anyone. If Sudhir or Anuj had been informing him, the police would have shown up at the hotel instead of the PCO. Yet, he couldn’t fathom how the police managed to find him at the petrol station in Gomti Nagar.

After much contemplation, he concluded that few people in Lucknow own an army that opened in Jonga. It was possible that someone recognized the vehicle and reported it to the police, especially since it was reported in the newspapers two days later that Shri Prakash had been seen in Lucknow in an Army Jonga. In this web of thoughts, he concluded that completing Surajbhan's task would appease Kamakhya Mata. Perhaps she was displeased with him for not performing a human sacrifice for so long.

Suddenly feeling the urgency of his situation, he woke Anuj and Sudhir. "Put all the luggage in the car; we must leave immediately. Let's settle with the hotel owner," he commanded.

"Bhaiya, it's evening, and driving at night isn't safe," Sudhir cautioned.

"Just do it; I'm not feeling great about staying here," Shri Prakash insisted. Sudhir and Anuj quickly washed up, gathered their belongings, and loaded the car. Shri Prakash again headed down the same road where Chandan had identified their target.

About half a kilometer from their destination, Shri Prakash told Anuj, "Take out the AK and roll down the windows entirely." Anuj, sitting in the backseat, complied.

"Sudhir, lower your front window halfway, just enough," Shri Prakash instructed. "If you lower it fully, the AK cartridges could spill out the back window. You'll need to be able to shoot from your seat without standing up to hit the target more accurately."

"Got it, bhaiya!" Sudhir responded.

Shri Prakash continued, "I will slow the car and stop right in front for only five seconds; we need to get it done in that time."

"Okay," Anuj agreed, his expression serious.

Shri Prakash followed the same course of action. The target was seated in the middle when the car came to a stop, and Anuj immediately opened fire. The target remained sitting, unable to rise. Other individuals jumped up, attempting to flee, but stumbled as they tried to escape. Before anyone could grasp the situation, Shri Prakash accelerated the car and sped toward the highway.

"Why didn't you shoot?" Shri Prakash asked Sudhir.

"Bhaiya, not a single bullet from Anuj bhai hit outside. All twenty-five struck him directly; he couldn't even move. I saw it, so what's the point of wasting ammunition?" Sudhir replied. Shortly thereafter, the car reached the highway. Shri Prakash asked Anuj, "Is there a car behind us?"

"No car is in sight. That fool probably hasn't even started his vehicle yet," Anuj answered. Shri Prakash then turned left and headed straight for Nepal. Sudhir asked, "Do we have to go back to Viratnagar?"

"No, we won't be heading there directly. The police will be stationed there for months. We're going straight to Delhi instead," Shri Prakash replied.

"All right, but it'll take about fifteen to sixteen hours," Anuj remarked.

"That's manageable," Shri Prakash said. The trio arrived in Delhi the following morning around nine o'clock. "Anuj bhai, please fetch food for all of us. We'll freshen up and then sleep after we eat; we're exhausted," Shri Prakash instructed.

"Okay, I'll take care of it," Anuj responded.

By the time Anuj returned with the food, Sudhir and Shri Prakash had already bathed. Anuj then took his turn, and the three of them sat down to eat. They kept the bag containing their weapons hidden under the bed before they all slept. The next day, Shri Prakash announced, "From now on, we won't be using any phones. While in our flat, no one should use their phone or go to a PCO to talk. If we need to discuss anything, we'll drive ten to twenty kilometers away and park on the side of the road to talk."

"Bhaiya, we need to communicate with the boys who do Kundli and the newspaper delivery guy daily," Sudhir pointed out.

"Of course, we will. Let's head out for breakfast now, and after that, we'll drive twenty to twenty-five kilometers away to talk somewhere in the car," Shri Prakash replied.

After a short while, the three of them left. Following breakfast, they drove to the Delhi Mathura Highway, parked before a dhaba, and started discussing matters with the boys. Shri Prakash asked, "Is there anything special to report?"

The newspaper boy shared, "Yes, DG's statement has been released, stating that our STF is actively working on dismantling this gang, and we can expect success soon. There's also a small piece of news published in 'Pioneer' that a prominent leader from Araria has been killed with an AK-47."

Shri Prakash asked, "So this news has made its way to Lucknow?"

"Yes, it has been published in Lucknow," the boy confirmed.

"Okay," Shri Prakash replied thoughtfully. He turned to Anuj and asked, "What's the name of that journalist from 'Pioneer' who accurately reports on us?"

"His name is Deepak Sharma," Anuj answered.

"I had asked you to get his number; do you have it?" Shri Prakash prompted.

"Yes, I have it," Anuj replied, providing the details. A short while later, Shri Prakash called Deepak Sharma. "You report the facts correctly, and I have some news for you. Please publish it," he stated.

"Tell me," Deepak responded eagerly. Shri Prakash detailed the entire incident that had transpired in Araria. Deepak asked probing questions as Shri Prakash explained every moment of the event.

"Bhaiya, what has happened has happened. Now, what about the future? Who is your next target?" Deepak inquired.

"The next target is significant; it will shake the entire government," Shri Prakash replied.

Deepak pressed, "Can you give me some hints about who it might be?"

"In response, Shri Prakash asked, "Will you write it?"

"Of course, I will write it. Whatever you tell me, I will publish. It's my livelihood, and the newspaper needs stories to sell," Deepak assured him.

Shri Prakash said, "I can't reveal the name again. Just understand that this individual is the closest to the Chief Minister."

"Give me a few more hints; it's possible I might piece it together," Deepak suggested.

Shri Prakash laughed and said, "Deepak bhai, we have some sense too. I may not be highly educated, but I've learned a thing or two. Just don't ask me his name. Eventually, you will come to know as he is closest to the Chief Minister."

"That's perfectly fine," Deepak replied, understanding the situation.

Shri Prakash said, "I promise that after hitting the target, I will tell you first. Otherwise, many people are sitting around; they will start getting their names published in newspapers to get their name stuck." Deepak said, "Okay." Shri Prakash disconnected the call.

Sitting in the car, Anuj immediately expressed concern when the call with Deepak Sharma ended. "Bhaiya, why did you make this mistake? These are newspaper people; you can't trust them. They could easily tip off the police. If they do that, they can trace your number, too. The police will be here before you know it; mobile phones are off. Every time I call, the police somehow show up shortly afterward. I even spoke to some officers in Gorakhpur about how police can record phone calls without wires. Since mobile phones don't use wires, how do they manage it? They told me it was the STF. When I asked who handles that in STF, I learned that Rajesh Pandey has the equipment to listen in on mobile numbers."

Shri Prakash brushed off the concerns, responding, "That's nonsense. No one can tap a phone without using a wire. Mobile phones don't have wires so that nobody can tap them. Stop worrying."

Sudhir chimed in, "Still, let's change locations. If you're done talking, let's head back."

Shri Prakash turned the car around without hesitation and returned to their flat. Meanwhile, as soon as Deepak Sharma ended his call with Shri Prakash, he dialed Rajesh Pandey. “Where are you?” he asked.

“I’m at the office right now. What’s going on?” Rajesh replied.

“I’m heading to Wireless Crossing in Mahanagar; you should come there too,” Deepak said.

Rajesh pressed, “If you’re coming, just come to the office.”

“Bhaiya, I can’t come to the office; it’s important,” Deepak insisted.

“Fine, just reach there. I’ll be at Wireless Crossing. I’ll park my Tata Sumo after turning it to the right,” Rajesh instructed.

After waiting a long time, Deepak finally approached the parked Tata Sumo and signaled the driver to open the door. Once inside, he signaled the driver and gunner to exit the vehicle. Once they had stepped out, Rajesh looked at Deepak and asked, “What’s the matter, Deepak bhai? You seem a bit worried.”

Deepak began, “Yes, bhai, I just received a call from Shri Prakash Shukla.” Rajesh Pandey asked, “Do you have his number?” Deepak replied, “Yes, he called the office landline and spoke for quite a while. We installed caller ID just ten days ago. As soon as the call ended, I asked the telephone operator where this call originated. He gave me a mobile number, which I’ve brought.”

Rajesh quickly noted the phone number in his diary and asked,

“What time did the call come?” Deepak shared the time with him. Rajesh then inquired, “What was the purpose of his call?”

Deepak explained, “He mentioned that he committed a significant murder yesterday in Araria. As he shared the details, I realized Patna had already published this news. I felt there was no point in writing it again. Driven by my curiosity for exclusive content, I asked him who his next target was. What he told me shook me to my core.” He then recounted the entire conversation to Rajesh.

“This is a serious matter, Deepak bhai,” Rajesh said gravely. “I need you to come with me right now. Arun Kumar is in the office, and I was hoping you could tell him everything. He might need to know more from you.”

Initially, Deepak resisted. “Rajesh bhai, I don’t want this to get around. Shri Prakash has many supporters in your police department. If anyone finds out... he warned me that if I meet Arun Kumar, he’ll have me killed without a second thought. I was riding my motorcycle yesterday; I don't even carry a knife for self-defense!”

Rajesh reassured him, “Deepak bhai, no need to worry. When the conversation is only between us, it stays that way. I’ll inform Arun Kumar that I’m bringing you along, so it’ll just be the three of us. I’ll also tell him that your name should not appear in any reports or discussions.”

After a moment of contemplation, Deepak relented. “Okay, Raju bhai, if you insist, let’s go to him. I’ll leave my car by the paan shop and accompany you. Just drop me off here.”

“Fine,” Rajesh replied. He then called Arun Kumar to inform him of their arrival. Once their conversation concluded, they made their way to the STF office.

Rajesh led Deepak into Arun Kumar’s office. Deepak immediately relayed the number from which Shri Prakash had called and shared every detail regarding the next target. Arun Kumar asked, “He didn’t mention any names?”

“No,” Deepak confirmed. “I tried to get him to divulge it, but he didn’t gave any hints. He said he would tell me the name after the job is done to prevent others from getting wind of it and potentially revealing names prematurely.”

Listening intently, Arun Kumar’s expression grew troubled as he absorbed everything Deepak shared. Deepak said, “Sir, we should leave now; it’s not wise to linger.” He added, “Please, you can discuss this wherever you need, but my name must remain confidential. You all know what could happen to me if it gets out.”

Arun Kumar assured Deepak, "You know I'm true to my word. Your name won't come up anywhere." Rajesh Pandey interjected, "Sir, I will drop Deepak off where he left his car." Arun Kumar nodded, agreeing, "Drop him off and come back here." After taking Deepak to the Wireless crossing and dropping him there, Rajesh returned to the office, arriving within five minutes.

Once back, Arun Kumar said, "This is a grave matter, but who could this target be? If something happens, the government will panic, and no one will believe us if we reveal anything. We need to identify the target and secure them, or perhaps we should inform the Chief Minister; he might understand the gravity of the situation."

Rajesh Pandey responded, "Sir, I'm not sure who this person could be. Only the Chief Minister might have insights. If he suggests four or five people instead of just one, security can be provided to all. But who will relay this to the Chief Minister? How will we present this information if Deepak's name remains confidential?"

Arun Kumar replied, "No one will ask about the source of the information. If pressed, we can say it was overheard in a phone conversation, but we don't have a recording." Rajesh expressed skepticism, "They won't be ready to believe that!"

"It's my job to convey this information," Arun Kumar stated bluntly. "It's up to them to believe it or not. In my opinion, we shouldn't delay too long. This needs to be communicated as soon as possible. Additionally, provide this number to the Delhi team and check its location first. Knowing the number's location will help confirm if he indeed executed the Araria incident or if he's boasting." Rajesh nodded in agreement, "That makes sense."

The next day, in a meeting with the STF officers, Arun Kumar reported, "According to the number we received yesterday, the gang's location is currently in Delhi. The call originated from near a market on Delhi Mathura Road." Satyendra Singh asked, "Who was the call made to?"

Arun Kumar explained, "The call was made to someone we know who provided this number. The phone arrived in Delhi a day prior. Before that, it passed through UP via Nepal, then Araria, Bihar, and Banaras before reaching Delhi—this phone number is credible."

Someone interjected, "Sir, there's a very popular program on Zee News called 'India's Most Wanted.' It features dramatizations of crimes committed by wanted criminals, followed by an appeal for public assistance. The program has gained significant viewership. A local journalist from Lucknow mentioned that Jamshed, their reporter, will be visiting Lucknow in two days. We might obtain more information if we provide him with details about Shri Prakash Shukla."

Arun Kumar considered this idea. "There's no harm in that. If they ask for details, we can provide them with photographs of a few major incidents in Lucknow. This program likely has a wide audience in the Hindi-speaking region so that it could yield useful information. However, we mustn't entirely rely on television. The Delhi team must investigate the location of the call yesterday."

Satyendra Veer Singh agreed, "We'll certainly check it out. If the location is confirmed in Delhi, we should consider going there and setting up base." Arun Kumar emphasized, "First, we must secure the location for a day or two. The longer this goes on, the higher the chance he targets someone next, and that's when a major scandal could erupt. We shouldn't remain idle in the office; we must be out there. Wherever we get a lead or location for a day or two, that's where we'll go. Even the cleverest criminals make mistakes eventually."

The Delhi team spent the entire day searching along Delhi Mathura Road with no success. The trio left in their car the following morning, connecting with teams in Lucknow and Gorakhpur. After stopping for breakfast, they proceeded further down an alternate road. Eventually, they parked the car on the side of the road and began discussing their next steps, the tension and urgency palpable as they strategized on their next moves.

Sure! Here's a rewritten version of the paragraph:

Someone informed Shri Prakash, "Today's newspaper features ten to twelve incidents along with your photo, stating that all these events are related to you, yet the police have still failed to apprehend you."

Curious, Shri Prakash asked, "What incidents are mentioned?" The informant then read through the newspaper articles one by one. Shri Prakash inquired, "Is there a date listed for each incident?" The reply was, "Yes, bhaiya." Shri Prakash prompted, "Check the date for the incident concerning Moolraj Arora." He was told it was recorded as May 13, 1997.

"All right, that's noted," Shri Prakash responded.

He then turned to Sudhir, asking, "Do you have Moolraj's number?" Sudhir flipped through his diary and replied, "Yes, there are three numbers." Shri Prakash requested, "Give me any one of them." Sudhir provided one long number, but it was switched off. Shri Prakash then dialed another number, and to his relief, Moolraj answered.

Shri Prakash greeted Moolraj, asking, "How have you been?" Moolraj responded, "Everything is all right, Bhaisaab." However, Shri Prakash's tone turned harsh, "Get ready because you haven't repaid the remaining money, and the people you mentioned have also failed to deliver. They were all swindlers."

Moolraj retorted, "Bhaisaab, you should consult someone else. Everyone I mentioned to you is wealthier than I am. You must not have pressured them properly; otherwise, they would have given me double the amount." Shri Prakash replied sternly, "It's been over a year since your escape; you've been deceiving me for far too long. You will repay the money—don't even think about evading payment, or I will kidnap your daughter."

Moolraj pleaded, "Please forgive me, Bhaisaab! I'm already in dire straits. I plan to move to another city and start anew for the sake of my children. The entire city regards me with suspicion now."

Shri Prakash said, "You're trying to deceive me again. Wherever you run off to, you must first repay the money. With interest, it has now doubled to fifty lakhs, and you owe me one crore. I won't give you much time this round."

Moolraj responded, "Bhai sahab, please check my situation. None of my projects are operational now; all my previous ventures are finished. I've sold all my properties except for one flat where my family and I reside. Even if I sold that, I wouldn't gather enough funds."

Shri Prakash countered, "You've built several Asha Apartments; none have sold for less than twenty-five lakhs. Please don't assume I'm unaware. I won't back off this time, even if you need to borrow money."

Moolraj argued, "Bhai sahab, currently only one person is progressing in this field. The old builders are out of business. Politicians and goons have taken over, and we're losing our ground." Shri Prakash insisted, "You keep working; no politician or thug can touch you—I'll handle them."

Moolraj replied, "Bhaiya, we have no financial strength left to pay any ransom to you. On my request, please look into Arif Builders. He's acquired a large piece of land along the Gomti River in Nishatganj and bought the site of an old paper mill. His project is underway; he's constructing a city called Metro City. I saw the advertisements in the newspaper. Moreover, he owns the Arif Castle Hotel, across from National College in Hazratganj, and hotels in Nainital and Dubai. With just one phone call, he can arrange everyone's share. If you want, I can provide you with his number, too."

Shri Prakash said, "Okay, tell me, I will see where he lives?"

Moolraj said, "He lives in an ancient and luxurious mansion in the Cantt area."

Shri Prakash said, "Yes, that is okay."

As soon as he hung up, Sudhir said, "Bhaiya, this guy Moolraj is a bastard. He seems to have given you another fake story to make you happy without paying any money. You got outraged initially, and later, your voice became very low and polite."

Shri Prakash said, “You are right; there is no one more rascal than Moolraj bastard in entire Lucknow. Whatever he has told me about Arif Hotel, I will give someone the job of getting his Kundali. Just get his Kundali and bring it. If his statement is true, we won’t have to work hard. He will give enough money for the election. If he cannot pay the full amount for the election, he will be taken away, the hotel will be sold, and the money will be given.”

Sudhir said, “Yes, bhaiya, first find out, there is no trust in what Mulraj says. Look, it has been one and a quarter years, he left for half the money, and a long time has passed, till now, he has not sent even a single penny.” Shri Prakash immediately dialed the number and told the whole story of Arif to a new boy and said, “First get the complete details of the hotel in front of National College, then find out where he lives in the cantonment and you will get the complete list in a week.” A voice came from the other side, “Yes, bhaiya.” Shri Prakash disconnected the call and switched off the phone. Shri Prakash said, “Let’s go to Noida today, and we will have lunch there. At this time, all the builders are opening their shops in Noida; let’s go there too; maybe we will find someone there too!” Anuj said, “Okay, he is right, bhaiya, it is essential to change the place. Don’t know which Shani Charan has come; as soon as we leave the place, the STF people come.” Suddenly, Anuj said, “Bhaiya, we have come to the same road where we parked the car and talked the day before yesterday morning.”

Shri Prakash said, “We talked. So, does the photo also get saved on the mobile phone? Why are you getting so worried?” Anuj said, “No, bhaiya, how can the photo get saved? I was telling you.” Shri Prakash said, “Don’t worry, now I will not slow down the car anywhere before UP Gate.” Anuj said, “Okay.”

After a while, Sudhir said, “Hey bhaiya, look, where we talked in front of the ice cream parlor, the police have blocked the entire road and are checking, and there are many police around as well.” Shri Prakash turned his neck to the right and looked, and his speed immediately increased. After going four to six kilometers ahead, Shri Prakash told Anuj, “Look, is any car coming from behind?”

Anuj looked back and said, “No, no vehicle is coming.”

Shri Prakash said, “These policemen may not be looking for us.” Anuj said, “Bhaiya, when I used to work at East-West Airlines, our office was three to four kilometers away; I used to come and go from here four times a day. I have never seen police here. Sometimes, the patrolling Delhi Police constables were seen parking their motorcycles and eating ice cream here, but so many vehicles and policemen never came.”

Shri Prakash said, “No one except us three knows about coming here and talking on the phone. How can the police come?” Anuj said, “Bhaiya, something is wrong with this mobile phone. No one can tell correctly, nor is it understood. If you go to the PCO, someone comes immediately, and if you talk on the mobile, someone comes there after some time, too.”

Shri Prakash said, “It could be so.” After this, the three reached Noida, sat at a newly opened restaurant, and had dinner. Shri Prakash asked Sudhir, “This Suman lives in Noida. Whenever he visited the Syrian wrestlers, he talked to Suman and sent beautiful girls. Let me see, maybe Suman's number is also in my diary!” Sudhir said, “Bhaiya, how did you suddenly remember Suman?” Shri Prakash said, “You are not understanding; I have been very worried for the last ten-fifteen days that the police are following me. I cannot concentrate anywhere, and I wake up even at night. Once I get to know who is informing, I will shoot him with not less than two hundred and fifty bullets! There will be so many holes that half of the holes will stop bleeding. What Anuj told me just now is that the police are standing at the place where the call was made while sitting in the car. If what Anuj says is true, it will be difficult to get out of here. That is why I remembered Suman. I will talk to him now. It is essential to make arrangements for the night.”

Sudhir said, “Bhaiya, call him now, and you will stay here for the night. We will come and pick you up tomorrow morning.” Shri Prakash said, “No, that will not happen. We will stay together wherever we stay.” Anuj said, “Bhaiya, you know I have no attachment to all these things.” Sudhir said, “Bhaiya, I also stay far away from these matters.”

Shri Prakash said, "It is no big deal. I will call you at some market near the flat and take you to the flat itself. You people sleep in the outer room; I will stay in the inner room and drop you in the morning." Anuj and Sudhir did not say anything. The woman picked up the phone after Shri Prakash called Suman on the number in the diary. While talking on the phone, Shri Prakash asked, "Syrian wrestlers used to order goods from your place only. Do you remember anything?"

The woman from the other side said, "We remember everything, but a year ago, police dogs raided Noida. I left the house there and bought two flats in Mayur Vihar. First, you tell me what you want?"

Shri Prakash asked, "Will you get Russian?"

Suman said, "Everything will be available at our place, but you must come to Mayur Vihar."

Shri Prakash said, "I cannot come to Mayur Vihar; I will take you to my flat."

Suman asked, "Where is your flat?"

Shri Prakash said, "It is in Vasant Kunj, Sector D." Suman said, "It is very far."

Shri Prakash said, "No problem. You can bring it to a nearby place; I will pick them and then drop it off in the morning." Suman said, "Okay, sir, can you pay for such expensive stuff?" Shri Prakash said, "I will pay as much as you want."

Suman said, "Okay, come to Super Shopping Mall at 8 o'clock. I will take all the money there, take the girl, and drop her off on time. Make sure that her mobile is neither switched off nor you snatch her."

Shri Prakash said, "You know me very well; I don't break my promise." Saying this, Shri Prakash took everyone towards Vasant Kunj. As soon as they reached there, Anuj and Sudhir said, "Bhaiya, if you have to bring her, you go alone and bring her; we will stay here."

Shri Prakash said, "No, Anuj will come with us. Sudhir, you will stay here in the flat." Anuj said, "Bhaiya, you know I will not get into this mess." Shri Prakash said, "Who is asking you to get into this mess? Come along. While returning, sit quietly in your seat and come back. Sudhir will drop her in the morning."

Sudhir and Anuj both remained silent. At seven, Shri Prakash took Anuj in his Cielo car and left for a super mall as decided on call. By ten, Shri Prakash returned to the flat with the girl. While returning, he stopped before a liquor shop and asked Anuj to bring liquor. Anuj quietly went and got the liquor and sat in the car. Shri Prakash did not even eat dinner, and Anuj and Sudhir did not even dare to ask Shri Prakash if he wanted food. Sudhir brought food for three people. He kept the food in the cupboard, and both of them ate and went to sleep.

At four in the morning, Shri Prakash woke Sudhir and said, "Take him and drop him there; I will call Suman." Sudhir said, "Okay." Sudhir told the girl, "You go down by the lift; I am coming down the stairs."

Sudhir dropped her at Mayur Vihar and came back. He returned and saw that Anuj was awake and Shri Prakash was sleeping. Anuj and Sudhir came out to the balcony and started talking. Anuj told Sudhir, "This habit of Shri Prakash will get us all killed someday. Till now, it was fine; he used to go out and have fun and return at night. This is the first time he has visited the flat with a girl. You know, all the big mafias who have been killed have been killed because of girls. If Virendra Shahi had not gone to that woman's house alone because of that woman, we would not have been able to kill him. When Virendra Shahi was killed because of this habit of his, the same will happen to us too."

Sudhir said, "There is no other option. Anand had left us with great courage and ran away; he was killed within two or three months. We are very hopeful that it was bhaiya who got him killed. Don't you remember that after Anand left, suddenly he started talking a lot to the police officers and never talked in front of us? We think Anand would be no novice if it were not for the information he provided to the police. I don't know why he has been worried for the last fifteen days. Even in such a state of worry, he doesn't forget the girl."

Anuj said, "Sudhir bhai, let things go as they are. Nothing can be done right now. Our family is in jail, and many members of your family are also in jail. We have no other option but to live with him. Now, he has taken over the entire kingdom. It took Anand three months to die; he will get us killed in three days. The police are in so much contact with him that he will not have to do anything; he will tell the police, and the police will chase and kill us. The boys who make horoscopes have become so trained that they will get our horoscopes made in four to six hours."

After this long conversation, both of them became silent. They came from the balcony and again lay down on the bed. Sudhir said, "Rest; we cannot even go for breakfast alone. He has been awake the whole night; he will wake up late. Wait for him to wake up; only after he wakes up will we bathe and go for breakfast." Then, both of them went to sleep; Shri Prakash woke up around one o'clock and said to Anuj, "Didn't you guys go for breakfast?" Anuj said, "Bhaiya, we were waiting for you." Shri Prakash said, "Oh, it's one o'clock now; you guys go and have breakfast; I will have breakfast later." Sudhir said, "No problem, bathe and get ready; everyone will go together." Shri Prakash got ready quickly, and all three of them left.

Shri Prakash said, "Let's all have food; there is no time to have breakfast. We haven't talked since morning, so let's go talk to someone." First, all three of them went and ate food at a roadside eatery, and after leaving, they parked their car on the roadside and started talking to the boys from Lucknow. As soon as he picked up the phone, he said, "Today, it has been published in all the newspapers that the Uttar Pradesh government has announced a reward of two lakh rupees on you. The same reward, i.e., two lakh rupees, is on Brajesh Singh; there is no more reward than this on anyone else. There is a reward of twenty thousand rupees each for Sudhir and Anuj. Other people's names are also written, on whom the government has announced a reward of ten thousand rupees each. Your photo is printed in all the newspapers, and it is written below that the Principal Secretary, Home, Uttar Pradesh, has announced this reward. This reward will be given to the person who gives information or gets you caught."

Shri Prakash asked, "Which photo is printed? Is it the same old or a new one?" He was told from the other side, "The same one in jeans and a t-shirt, only the old photo is printed; there is no new photo." Shri Prakash disconnected the phone and said to Sudhir, "Now, let's go straight to the flat. Now let us rest for a few days or talk to Pandit Ji from Kolkata; there is some bad planetary position. It is going on. Otherwise, I have never felt so hopeless!" Sudhir asked, "What happened?"

Sriprakash said, "Today, this news has been published in all the newspapers of Lucknow, and the government has put a maximum reward of two lakh rupees on us and a reward of twenty thousand rupees on both of you. I cannot understand why the bounty is higher on you and us. A reward of ten thousand or five thousand has been put on everyone else. Neither Pawan Pandey's nor Narendra Pandey's nor Akhilesh's nor Hem Singh's name is there. Whoever is informing is giving accurate information that only the three of us are going together. Let's go straight to the flat, eat and then sleep, in the evening we will walk in the colony park. We will not talk to anyone, neither will we go out and talk, nor will we talk from the flat. After two or three days, we will take Panditji of Calcutta's opinion about why the police have been hovering around us for fifteen days. Wherever we go, they reach there. What is this matter?"

Sudhir asked, "Is a reward of two lakhs a lot, bhaiya? Your photo is also almost identical; we will be trapped and troubled if anyone sees it. Now that we openly stay in hotels and roam around on the streets, this is not right."

Shri Prakash said, "Only Brajesh Singh and Tribhuvan Singh have a reward equal to ours. Briju Bhaiya is far ahead of us and also more significant. Now, he has done work worth billions. Briju Bhaiya's reach is far and wide. These guys have deliberately kept a reward of two lakh rupees.

While talking about all this, the three of them reached the flat after having food. For a long time, we talked about how the police had reached the place immediately after we had left. The police reached the place where there was no plan, and no one knew about it; only three people knew about it.

Anuj said, "Bhaiya if you notice, wherever we have used mobile or PCO, the police have reached there. I am not able to understand this either. I had brought all the SIM cards and mobile phones together. This time, I had brought five SIM cards from Patna; I don't know if the police reached the SIM card shop in Patna or not! But there is something that is tied to our telephones. I have tried everything else, and there is no way we can get an idea of why and how the police are following us! Believe it or not, this STF man, Rajesh Pandey, always sits at the mobile company. He is regularly seen at the mobile company people's places.

Narbadeshwar said that even Lucknow's police are terrified of him and don't know how he listens to mobile conversations. That is why Arun Kumar respects him a lot, and Arun Kumar is also a very tough officer; when it comes to his reputation and prestige, he does not even care about his life. Bhaiya, you must know that no police officer ever passed in front of Mukhtar Ansari's house. This Arun Kumar had imposed a curfew in Ghazipur and had Mukhtar Ansari's property confiscated. Mukhtar Ansari and his bhaiya Afzal Ansari are the most influential people in Purvanchal; no one has more influence than them. Arun Kumar had climbed the house with the entire force and was throwing fridges, TVs, and boxes from the third floor on the road as if throwing vegetable peels. He did not listen to anyone and had even stopped picking up the phone of the minister and the chief minister. He picked up everyone's phone only after confiscating Mukhtar and Abbas." Shri Prakash said, "Okay, yes, you reminded me. This is the same man whose name makes Mukhtar's soul tremble. During the election, Pappu Yadav's convoy of hundred men was stopped while coming from Bihar to Uttar Pradesh, and when Pappu Yadav's men were being a bit unruly, they were thrashed like sheep and goats. Everyone ran away, leaving their vehicles and weapons behind. Pappu Yadav's vehicles and weapons rotted away in the police station for many years." Shri Prakash took the conversation forward and said, "Well, now I understand; this STF has been formed by gathering all the bastards. Anuj, your point seems to be true. These guys must have found a solution to the mobile, but what can be done? It won't work without talking. Even if we get a good hold, how will the tender collection be done without a phone?" Anuj said, "Bhaiya, it cannot be stopped completely, but it should be used only when it is very necessary, and in my opinion, wherever we live or go, we should talk from a PCO only after going at least fifty kilometers from there and never go to that PCO again. It is also not good to stop at a PCO for too long. One should only talk once from a PCO; as far as I understand, mobile use should be stopped."

Shri Prakash said, "How can the mobile be stopped? You are right in saying that we should not use mobile wherever we stop. Mobile should be used only while traveling in the car, but the problem is when the car is moving at high speed, the mobile gets disconnected every few minutes, and then we cannot talk for a long time. But you are right; something has to be done. These years have troubled us a lot. Now, let us rest for two or three days, let our minds become a little stable, and then we will talk. We will also talk to Guruji in Calcutta only after two or three days."

CENTURY OF HUMAN SACRIFICE

Three days had passed since their last conversation, and in the morning, Shri Prakash said, "I feel a little lighter now. I haven't been able to focus on the newspapers for the past few days. And the boy who asked about the Arif Hotel owner's horoscope—he must have gotten it done by now. I need to talk to him. Also, I must make some calls in Gorakhpur, or people will think I'm dead."

He turned to Sudhir. "Find out if Nisha is back. Her parents sent her away, and I have to talk to her. It's been too long. If I don't, she might do something drastic."

Sudhir hesitated but said, "Bhaiya, if you don't mind, I have something to say."

Shri Prakash looked at him. "Say it. Don't hold back."

Sudhir took a deep breath. "Maybe you should lay off the girls for a while. You've been saying these are tough times, and these girls can't be trusted. Who knows how many of them are mixed up with others? If the police come, they'll crack and start spilling everything in a second. It'll be just a matter of months. You said you'd surrender once you finish the three big tasks you've planned. You've already made arrangements. After that, you'll go to jail, but at least you can focus on the election from there. Jail won't be a problem. The people there are like street dogs—show them something, and they'll follow you. Everything will fall into place once you're inside."

Shri Prakash's face darkened. "Enough. Don't bring this up again."

Sudhir nodded quickly, "Yes, bhaiya."

Shri Prakash's irritation showed. "No one talks to me about this again. Only I know how thrilling it is to untangle these messes of beautiful girls."

Sudhir fell silent. The three of them got ready quickly and left for Old Delhi. They parked the car near Nizamuddin Railway Station and walked to a PCO outside the station. They made a call to Calcutta. Half an hour later, Guruji's disciples from Calcutta called back. They asked to meet at a different PCO.

Shri Prakash left for the new PCO and started asking about the latest news in the newspapers.

The boys told him, "There's news that you've gone to Singapore for plastic surgery and will return after the procedure." Shri Prakash burst into laughter. "That's correct," he said with a smile.

Then they added, "Other newspapers are saying you've grown a beard and are walking around Lucknow, but no one can recognize you." Shri Prakash nodded, pleased. "Good," he replied.

He moved on to the next PCO and called the boy working on the Arif Hotel owner's horoscope. "Did you get the Kundali?" he asked.

The boy replied, "Yes, bhaiya, I've got the full Kundali."

He explained, "The Arif hotel owner is about to launch a huge multi-story apartment project in three locations around Lucknow. He owns big hotels in Dubai, Nainital, and Lucknow. High-ranking officers from the government often visit him. Every evening, there's a party at his house. One of his sons lives in Dubai, and the other is probably studying elsewhere."

Shri Prakash listened closely, then said, "What his son is doing isn't important right now. Did you get his phone number or not?"

The boy replied, "Yes, bhaiya. I got eight different numbers for him—some are from the hotel; some are from his home. He doesn't come to the hotel much. Most of the time, he stays in Nainital or goes to Dubai."

Shri Prakash asked, "Where is he now?"

The boy replied, "He's been in Lucknow for three or four days."

Shri Prakash nodded. "Alright, write down all the numbers." The boy quickly jotted them down.

After the call ended, Shri Prakash returned to the car where Anuj and Sudhir were waiting in the parking lot. Anuj asked, "Bhaiya, did you make more than one call from any PCO?"

Shri Prakash replied, "No, I made only one call from each of three or four PCOs. I still haven't been able to reach Guruji in Kolkata. He told me to call back in half an hour. But I'm not sure I dare to go to another PCO now. If you want, we can call him from here on the mobile. After talking, we can leave. Even if the police come, it will take them at least an hour to get to Nizamuddin parking."

Anuj said, "Yes, bhaiya, the police will come. The sooner we finish talking, the better. Anyway, I think you should relax. I can drive, or Sudhir can. You sit in the back, and we can talk while we drive. The call won't disconnect in the city. It only drops when we're on the highway."

Shri Prakash shook his head. "No, I don't trust either of you to drive well. I'll talk from here. We'll turn off the phone and leave afterward."

Sudhir and Anuj fell silent, understanding he had made up his mind. Shri Prakash then dialed Guruji.

Guruji answered the phone. After greeting him, Shri Prakash said, "Guruji, I don't know what's happening. For the past 15-20 days, everywhere we go, the police show up almost immediately. I feel like Kamakhya Mata might be angry. Just ten days ago, a human sacrifice was made in her name. Since then, nothing else has happened, but I can't shake the feeling something's wrong. The police arrested all our family members, insulted my sister-in-law, and even arrested my companions' families. There's a huge bounty on my head. Twice now, we've even come face-to-face with the police. You told me that I'd win in the fight for supremacy, and until now, everything was going well, but for the last few days, nothing is working out."

Guruji's voice was calm as he replied, "I told you that once you complete the century of human sacrifice at Kamakhya Mata's feet, you would be unstoppable. After that, no one would be able to defeat you. Mrityunjay himself would bless you, and you would be immortal. But I think you haven't completed the century of sacrifices yet, and that's why these problems are coming up. When someone is close to completing the century, dark forces try to stop them. It seems like you are very close to reaching this century, and that's why these bad planets and demonic forces are blocking your path. Don't worry; complete the sacrifice soon, and everything will be fine."

Shri Prakash said, "Guruji, I haven't counted, but I must have completed my century of human sacrifices by now."

Guruji's voice was firm. "That's not possible. Sit down and think again. You haven't reached your goal yet. If you had, you wouldn't feel the confusion you're experiencing now. You have the blessings of the Mother, and you are meant to be invincible. Just complete the worship of Maa Kamakhya."

Shri Prakash sighed, "Okay, Guruji."

Guruji added, "Recalculate and let me know how much is left."

Shri Prakash nodded. "Okay, Guruji." He bowed his head and hung up. Immediately, he started the car and drove out of the railway station parking lot.

Shri Prakash said, "Even if the STF (Special Task Force) gets here quickly, it'll still take them half an hour. Let's head to Connaught Place for breakfast."

Anuj shook his head. "No, bhaiya, it's too crowded there. It's better to go to a dhaba or head towards the highway. We shouldn't stop around here."

Shri Prakash increased the car's speed, driving quickly toward Gurgaon, about ten kilometers outside Delhi. There, they stopped at a dhaba and had breakfast. As they left, Shri Prakash said, "Let's use the PCO here. All the money is with Dada in Patna. We may need four, six, or even ten lakhs, and we must arrange that too. Arif will talk to the hotel owner. We'll ask him for the money here in Delhi."

Anuj said, “Bhaiya, not many people have the Delhi address. It’ll be easier to get the money in Lucknow.”

Shri Prakash didn’t respond immediately. He drove up to a PCO near the dhaba and stepped inside. He dialed the numbers for the hotel owner’s office. Someone picked up the phone from one of the house numbers and asked, “Who’s speaking?”

Shri Prakash replied smoothly, “I’m the PA of Honourable Minister Amarmani Tripathi. The Honourable Minister would like to speak with you.”

The voice on the other end said, “I’ll hand over the phone right away.”

A few moments later, Arif came on the line. “Sir, Namaskar!” he greeted.

Shri Prakash wasted no time. “Arif, where exactly are you planning to build those flats in Lucknow?”

Arif said, “Sir, I’m starting work at two or three locations. I’ve already begun at the paper mill. If you have any issues, let me know. I’ll come to meet you personally.”

Shri Prakash responded coldly, “I am Shri Prakash Shukla. I’m sure you’ve heard of me.”

Arif replied, “Yes, I’ve heard of you.”

Shri Prakash’s voice grew sharper. “Listen carefully. You need to pay Rs. 50,000 for each flat you’re building on the paper mill colony land. If you don’t, you know what will happen.”

Arif hesitated. “Sir, it will take some time for the flats to be completed. Once they’re built and sold, then I’ll make money. Right now, I’ve put all my savings into this project.”

Shri Prakash scoffed. “The booking for those flats is for ninety units. Not one of them costs less than Rs. 20 lakhs. Do you think you’re clever? Why are you trying to destroy your future?”

Arif tried to argue, "But who keeps that much cash lying around these days?"

Shri Prakash's tone remained icy. "I want the booking money for all the flats within the next two days. I'll tell you the rest later. You even booked two flats just yesterday."

Arif said, "Yes, I did."

Then he asked, "Where should I send the money?"

Shri Prakash answered without hesitation, "Give the money to Bablu Shukla in Lucknow jail."

Arif froze. "I can't go to jail."

Shri Prakash said, "Send one of your men. I'll give you the date and time. Tell me which one of your men will go, and I'll tell you who to meet in the jail and who to give the money to."

Arif replied, "Okay."

After the call ended, Arif quickly checked his tape recorder to see if the conversation had been recorded. He found that the entire call had been taped. Arif immediately dialed the ADG of Law and Order and said, "Sir, I need to meet you urgently."

ADG Ajay Raj Sharma responded, "Come right away."

Arif reached his office in half an hour. He was visibly nervous. He told the whole story, explaining that the caller introduced himself as Shri Prakash Shukla. At the end, he added that he had recorded the call.

Ajay Raj Sharma asked, "Have you ever received any call where you were told to record it?"

Arif shook his head. "No, sir. No one told me to record any calls before. But after the news broke that Shri Prakash had kidnapped Moolraj Arora, and Moolraj had named the big builders of the city, we all knew that Shri Prakash was calling and threatening people, extorting money. We held a meeting, and it was decided that everyone should attach a recorder to their phones to capture every call. Some people had already paid money after receiving fake calls. Later, it turned out that Shri Prakash Shukla wasn't behind those calls. So, I should record this one. I'll follow your instructions once someone listens to the recording and confirms it's his voice."

Ajay Raj Sharma said, "If you've brought the cassette, give it to me. If not, I'll send Rajesh Pandey to your place. He'll listen to it and immediately tell if it's Shri Prakash's voice."

Arif replied, "Sir, I didn't bring the cassette because many people came into the office. Are you talking about Rajesh Pandey from STF?"

Ajay Raj Sharma nodded. "Yes, the same Rajesh Pandey who was the CO of Hazratganj. He's now in STF, and he knows voices very well. Go home now, and Rajesh Pandey will come to your house soon to listen to the recording."

Arif left for home right away. Ajay Raj Sharma called Arun Kumar to explain the situation as soon as he went. He said, "Send Rajesh Pandey to Arif's house immediately. He should listen to the recording and identify whether it's Shri Prakash's voice. It was just an hour ago, so there's a chance we can get an immediate location."

Arun Kumar responded, "Rajesh Pandey is with me in the office. I'll send him right away."

Arun Kumar instructed Rajesh Pandey to note Arif's address. "Go there and listen to the recording. He must also have a caller ID if he's using a recorder. If you find the number, let him know over the phone. We won't waste time; the Delhi team will help separate the truth from the lies."

Rajesh Pandey called Arif. "ADG Law and Order has asked to meet you. Where are you now?"

Arif replied, "I'm at home. I'll give you my address."

Arif shared the address, and Rajesh Pandey said, "I'll be there in 20 minutes."

When Rajesh Pandey arrived outside Arif's house, several of Arif's guards were standing at the gate. When they saw Rajesh, they opened the gate and led him to the dining room. Arif was sitting with his family inside. He asked everyone to leave the room and switched on the tape recorder connected to his landline phone.

Arif switched on the tape recorder and said, "Sir, this conversation continued for a while. Please listen to it and tell me if it's him or someone else."

As soon as the tape started playing, it became apparent within the first minute that it was Shri Prakash's voice. Rajesh Pandey listened to the recording and asked, "Did you install a caller ID?"

Arif replied, "Yes, I installed it but don't know how to read the numbers. After this call, many other calls came in. You can check them if you want. I've noted down the time. A meeting was held with everyone else who received his call, so I had already set up the recorder and caller ID to be safe."

Rajesh Pandey grabbed the caller ID device connected to the phone line. He found the number for the time of the call, then noted down the two numbers that came before and after it in his diary. The number was a mobile phone; the first four digits indicated a Delhi area code.

Rajesh Pandey reassured Arif, "Don't worry, this phone belongs to him. We're very close now, and your problem will be solved soon."

Arif asked, "He's asked me to call him the day after tomorrow. What should I say and do now?"

Rajesh Pandey replied, "Keep talking to him. Just take your time so we can track more locations."

Arif hesitated, "I don't dare to talk to him. You heard how dangerous his tone was. If I talk to him the day after tomorrow and delay the conversation, he'll curse or hurt me. If you want, send an expert from your team to sit with me. I'll explain everything, and if he talks, it'll be in a better way."

Rajesh Pandey responded, “From our conversation, I can tell you use many colloquial Urdu words. If I send someone else, he’ll immediately know you’re not the one speaking, and the conversation will end. That would block our way forward, forcing us to take a dead-end route. I’ll try to send someone from STF to you. We have one Muslim head constable; he’ll come to you tomorrow if he's available. Explain everything to him. If the call comes, he’ll handle it. You can keep recording the conversation; we’ll listen to it later. If anything goes wrong, we’ll fix it next time.”

Arif agreed, “Okay.”

Rajesh Pandey got into his car and called Arun Kumar, giving him the phone number they had identified. “According to the time, this seems to be the number. It’s a Delhi number. I’ve also noted down the numbers before and after it.”

Arun Kumar immediately recorded the number and instructed the Delhi team to gather the call details and see how many other numbers were involved in the conversations.

A little while later, Rajesh Pandey returned to the STF office and reported everything to Arun Kumar. He said, "Arif is now too scared to talk to Shri Prakash. I told him I’d send a Muslim officer because, from the conversation, I could tell that Arif speaks fluent Urdu with perfect pronunciation. If I send anyone else, Shri Prakash will immediately recognize it’s not Arif and stop talking. Then we’ll be back at square one, waiting for a new number to call. It’s a matter of money, and he will call the day after tomorrow. That will give us a location. You said we could head to Delhi if we hold out for a few days. We can go there if the locations are from today and the day after the match. Let's send Head Constable Fazrullah to Arif’s place. His voice and tone are almost identical to Arif’s. If anyone can talk to Shri Prakash convincingly, it’s him."

Arun Kumar replied, "That's a great idea. Let's see where Fazrullah is." He picked up the phone and called a colleague outside the office. "Check which team Fazrullah is with," he instructed. The response was, "Fazrullah is in the office, sitting with Avinash Mishra in the back room."

"Send him in right away!" Arun Kumar ordered.

Fazrullah immediately came inside the room. Arun Kumar and Rajesh Pandey explained the whole thing to him. Rajesh Pandey called Arif and told him, "Head Constable Fazrullah Khan, whom I was asking to send tomorrow, I am sending him today itself. Please explain the whole thing to him. Day after tomorrow

He will be on your phone from morning onwards."

Arun Kumar told Fazrullah, "You should leave now. Talk to Arif, understand everything, and if that cunning man calls you, talk to him smartly and try to postpone the conversation for two to four days so that we keep getting the numbers."

By evening, the Delhi team informed us that the location of this number was in Delhi; this number had been opened after a long time. Earlier, this number had talked for a long time to three numbers in Gorakhpur. Out of this, a very long conversation occurred on one number late at night.

Arun Kumar noted down those three numbers and made Gorakhpur DIG A.S.N. Singh note down these numbers and told him to make arrangements to listen to these three numbers and as soon as any call comes on these numbers, get it recorded and send the number from which the call is being made to STF immediately so that further work can be done. The DIG said that we had made all the arrangements to listen to the telephones at our residence, and two employees of the telephone department stayed there. If the phone number is not from a rural area, then arrangements will be made to listen to it from the DP box. Arun Kumar said, "Sir, as soon as you start getting calls, just tell me which numbers have been listened to." The DIG said, "Okay, I will tell you immediately."

Fazrullah had understood the whole thing and was present at Arif's bungalow at 7 am that day. Around 10:30 am, Shri Prakash's call came. Arif's servant picked up the phone, and as soon as he said,

"Tell Arif that it is Ashok Singh's call," he immediately understood and signaled Fazrullah. Fazrullah picked up the phone and started talking to him. Meanwhile, Arif went to the other room and called Rajesh Pandey to tell him that Fazrullah was talking to Shri Prakash.

Rajesh immediately informed Arun Kumar. Arun Kumar immediately told the Delhi team to go to the Crime Branch or meet PP Singh and find out the location from where this call was taking place. The Delhi team also reached out immediately and, within half an hour, told that this call was taking place from the tower near Azadpur Mandi, but this phone was switched off just ten minutes ago.

Arun Kumar called Fazrullah and asked, "At what time did the call stop?" Fazrullah said, "Ten minutes ago." Arun Kumar told Rajesh Pandey to call Satyendra Veer, Avinash Mishra, and Tewatia; everyone should get ready in half an hour. I will also get clothes, but we must leave for Delhi immediately. His location has been in Delhi for three days. Today's call also came from somewhere near Azadpur Mandi in Delhi. I have just spoken to the Crime Branch, and they say that this call was not made from a densely populated area, but the phone was switched on on the road and switched off immediately. This suggests that he must be living somewhere nearby.

Everyone will go by a bypass road. Waiting for the train will waste time. In forty-five minutes, the entire team was ready with the vehicles, and everyone, along with Arun Kumar, left for Delhi in their cars. On the way, Satyendra Veer Singh talked to PP Singh and arranged everyone's stay. Arrangements were made for everyone to stay in a hotel near Azadpur Mandi.

Satyendra Veer Singh told Arun Kumar, "Sir, we will stay nearby so that everyone in the crime branch can remain alert to find out the number and location." Arun Kumar said, "That's fine."

Everyone reached the following day, and PP Singh said that our crime branch had also made arrangements to listen to mobile phones. For the last three months, we have heard the criminals' calls by diverting them to mobile phones. The phone on which this listening is being done is connected to the two wires of the speaker near the ear by adding two more wires to it and connecting it to a small tape recorder. Whenever a call comes, the recorder is turned on. The whole conversation is heard and recorded as well.

Arun Kumar said, "We will give you two mobile phones, remove the wires from them, and arrange a small tape recorder so that if we start listening to his phone, our work will become easy. Right now, we have to find out who called from the call details, then find out his address and verify it on the spot. If we start listening to his phone directly, all these problems will be solved immediately.

PP Singh was given two old model Sony Ericsson phones, and in just two to three hours, he removed the wires from them and made a lead to be used in the tape recorder. Rajesh Pandey went to the market and brought a small tape recorder that used small cassettes. PP Singh said that a request letter from your side will have to be sent to the mobile company regarding the numbers to be listened to on the mobile, and they will forward the call.

THE WILD CAT GETS KILLED

Everyone was sitting in the hotel; the Delhi team also arrived, and they were asked which numbers they had verified in the last four days. In Lucknow, Umesh Singh was also asked which numbers had received calls the previous week. He emphasized the details of the number from which Arif was called.

Four numbers were taken out, and Arun Kumar made a request letter on plain paper in his handwriting to listen to these four numbers directly on surveillance. PP Singh took that letter and left. After getting it forwarded from the Delhi Police Head Office, he gave it to the mobile company. After an hour, calls started coming. Calls were coming from different numbers, and as soon as the call came, its recording was started by pressing the recorder button. One by one, everyone heard Shri Prakash's voice directly on the call. It was a thrilling experience; Shri Prakash's voice was heard directly. The tape recorder was played again; the voice was evident in that, too.

Arun Kumar said, "Rajesh will do the work of listening and recording it, and Rajesh Pandey will find out which location the call was made."

Arun Kumar said, "Tomorrow is 20th September 1998. Navratri will start from tomorrow. It seems that we will be successful in our work during Navratri itself. I also fast on the first day; Rajesh fasts for nine days. There is no need to put any other effort into listening to the mobile. There was some difficulty in the first two days of Navratri, but there were other people, too. Wherever there is a need, everyone will go together."

Rajesh said, "Tomorrow, on the first day, it will take some time for the puja rituals; for that time, I will give this listening job to Satyendra Veer Sir; after that, there is no problem." Arun Kumar said, "Okay."

After saying this, everyone went to their respective rooms. In the evening, a call came from someone other than Shri Prakash. He wanted to talk to the inquiry at the airport, saying, "Three tickets were for Ranchi in the morning but could not go on that. Can these three tickets be transferred to the Delhi - Ranchi Indian Airlines flight on the 22nd?"

The employee at the inquiry said, "For this, he will have to come to the inquiry center with the tickets. Although there is no transfer provision, we will look into it if you come." Anuj gave his reference that he had worked for some days at East-West Airlines in Mumbai and Delhi and said that this ticket could be transferred.

The person at the inquiry said, "As far as I know, this is impossible for Indian Airlines. Still, you come to the inquiry; we will investigate it." This information was essential, so Rajesh Pandey ran and told Arun Kumar about it. Arun Kumar said, "Everyone will go to the airport; if Anuj comes, we will try to identify him. We will talk to the airport's DCP security. At the general inquiry counter where people come and tell their problems, the employee sitting there will be told that if anyone comes to enquire about the future dates of the air ticket, then they should be informed about him. We will track him from there and catch him outside the airport. Our work will be done tomorrow. He may also come to the Indian Airlines counter for a new ticket. However, the possibility of this is very low. He can go to the nearby travel agent and book the ticket for the new date. Out of all the tickets booked for Ranchi on the 22nd, if three tickets are booked together and the age is between twenty to twenty-five years, they will be marked and checked among the people coming to the airport. We will more or less identify Shri Prakash and our work will be done there. It is the first day of Navratri, Rajesh; if you have done the Puja, let's go now. Otherwise, get Satyendra Veer Tewatia and Avinash ready. It seems we are reaching very close to the target." Rajesh said, "Sir, I am just coming after bathing and doing Puja. From today, I am fasting for nine days. Mother Vindhyavasini will bless us, and we will succeed in this Navratri." Saying this, Rajesh hurriedly ran to his room and quickly told Satyendra Veer Singh Tewatia and Avinash the whole thing.

Satyendra Veer Singh said, "It has been a long time, Rajesh; even the bullets of the pistol are getting excited. Find the location quickly; it has been a long time running around. We are getting ready in ten minutes, Pandit ji. Don't waste much time in Puja; come quickly, let's go."

Rajesh Pandey laughed, "Sir, the bullet is coming from my pistol also. I am tired of running around; I am leaving right now. Today is the first day of puja, and work will be done." Saying this, Rajesh Pandey ran to his room. After a while, Arun Kumar came out of his room and asked Satyendra Veer, "Rajesh Pandey must be doing puja? You have a recording phone. Have you received any other calls?" Satyendra Veer Singh said, "There is no other call." Arun Kumar said, "Everyone is ready." Satyendra Veer noted that everyone was ready, and Rajesh was coming in five minutes. Arun Kumar said, "Let's all go down. Rajesh will also come in a little while."

Everyone reached the airport directly. After reaching the airport, Arun Kumar took the number of DCP Airport Security and talked to him; he said he was sitting in his office. Arun Kumar went straight to the airport DCP office, told the entire story, and said, “He is the biggest criminal in our state of Uttar Pradesh, who has the highest government reward on his head.”

DCP Airport Security assured full help, immediately called his two sub-inspectors, and said to introduce this UP team to the reception person and the person sitting at the Indian Airlines counter. Try to keep one person around at both places and as soon as any person comes to get such information or to buy a ticket, he will be identified. Keep in mind that CCTV is installed there. No one should be caught there; whatever action the police have to take should be done outside the airport only. After telling everything, everyone came out. By then, another call came from Shri Prakash, who spoke to Surajbhan from another number. Shri Prakash told Surajbhan, “We missed our flight today; I could not wake up in the morning. Anuj tried a lot, but he could not change it. We have booked a flight on the morning of the 22nd. All three of us will reach Ranchi by 10 in the morning.” Surajbhan asked, “How will the luggage arrive?”

Shri Prakash said, "I have sent the luggage by road from Zen car; that is why I called. If that vehicle does not reach the airport, please provide your vehicle. We will pick you up from the airport and drop you wherever you have arranged to stay. By the way, I explained to the boy that he should reach the place by vehicle. I do not want to use the phone after reaching there. Nowadays, wherever you call, I don't know how the police reach there."

Surajbhan said, "It is no problem; the boy who knows you will reach there with the vehicle."

Rajesh Pandey finished playing the cassette and played the call to Arun Kumar. Arun Kumar told Satyendra Veer Singh, "Call Tewatia and Avinash. Also now there is no use in staying here. Now everyone will come on the morning of the 22nd of September, at the time of the flight. After checking, we will bring all three from there. They will not have any weapons; we will quietly pick them up and bring them here, and then our work will be done."

Everyone's face was filled with joy, and listening to the phone was so beneficial; all the information was being received instantly. Otherwise, the whole day would have been spent here at the airport. Arun Kumar said, "Let us talk to DCP Security as soon as we get them from where on the 22nd!"

When Arun Kumar talked to DCP Security on the phone, DCP Security said, "Sir, I have talked to my Joint CP, and he has told us that we have CCTV cameras installed all over the airport. We cannot permit any police force from outside to arrest any person. Please tell us if any criminal has to be arrested, and we will arrest him. Give us a copy of the FIR against him and the warrant issued by the court; we will arrest him and present him before our magistrate. After that, you can take him wherever you want. We will not be able to allow the arrest of such a person from within the airport."

Arun Kumar tried very hard to convince them how dangerous a criminal he was and how much we needed him, but all the efforts to persuade him failed. DCP Airport Security outrightly refused, citing the reference of Joint CP. Arun Kumar said, "Let's all go to the hotel;

we will sit there and find a way. When he is arrested and handed over to us and presented in court, we will not get any benefit. We will not even be able to interrogate him."

Then everyone left for the hotel disappointed. After reaching the hotel, everyone concluded that 'there was no benefit to us from arresting anyone or taking any action inside the airport. Whatever we have to do, we will do it outside the airport. One thing was clear from the calls: these people had decided to go to Ranchi on the morning of September 22nd by Indian Airlines flight. So, STF will have to arrest him outside the airport at any cost. Now we have no other option except this. First, we have to get the list of all the passengers on the flight and guess which ticket is for Shri Prakash, Anuj, and Sudhir from the three tickets booked together.'

Rajesh said, "Sir, what will be the use of this? This will be needed only when he enters the airport in this name. We cannot take any action there. We will have to take action before he enters the airport. We will have to stand at the first barrier of Delhi Police on the way to the airport and see if any CCTV is installed there. We will have to keep an eye on all the vehicles coming. He will not come in his car at all, so the car cannot be identified here in the parking. He will come in a taxi. We will try to identify the three people in the taxi, of whom we have the photo of Shri Prakash Shukla, or we will ask them to get down if we see the three young boys in the taxi, apart from the driver, for questioning. If those three are found, we will quietly put them in our car."

Satyendra Veer said, "They will not go without weapons; some boy will accompany them. They will give their weapons to him before getting out of the taxi and going to the airport, who will return by taxi." Rajesh said, "If he brings someone else, he will bring his car. Why would he take the risk of coming by taxi? They will bring weapons in the cars; as soon as they reach the safe zone, all three will enter the airport, and that boy will return with the car." Rajesh Pandey said, "In the recording of the conversation with Surajbhan, Surajbhan had asked for luggage. Shri Prakash had said he had been sent to Ranchi by road from Zen. This means that he has sent his AK 47 and carbine and two-three small weapons by car, but till the time he is here, he will have some pistol with him." Satyendra Veer said, "One pistol will not make any difference; even if all three have pistols, it will not. We are eight to nine people, and we have three AK 47s. Where will he run away?"

Arun Kumar said, "I agree with Rajesh Pandey that he might have at least one or two pistols because VIP activities occur almost every day at the airport, and vehicles and people are strictly checked when a VIP arrives or leaves. He will not come to the airport with many pistols. Yes, there is a possibility of one or two pistols. There will not be much difficulty in operating there at that time. We have a full day right now. Tomorrow, we will go again and check the checking point once again. Most of the calls have been made from a radius of ten to twelve kilometers of Vasant Kunj. It seems that he is living somewhere on that side. The way to reach the airport from that side meets the airport road before the barrier. We will not have much difficulty. We can also do our checking before the first barrier at the airport. I will ask the DCP to give us one or two constables from Delhi Police; we will check that road first, and it will be easier for us there."

After a while, calls started coming. Rajesh Pandey picked up the phone, turned on the tape recorder, and indicated it was his call. Shri Prakash was talking to the girl from Gorakhpur. After talking for a long time, the phone was disconnected; everyone was sitting in Arun Kumar's room, and that call was played on a tape recorder. Everyone was listening; that girl repeatedly said I would run away from home and come to you. Every morning, mummy and papa go to Durga temple for Navratri puja; I will take some luggage and reach Delhi railway station, come there, and take me. Shri Prakash repeatedly said I was not in Delhi; I am now in Jaipur. There is no need to come now. I will tell you when I come to Delhi, but that girl was not ready to believe it. Then, both of them kept talking about their love for each other for a long time. Then Shri Prakash started obscene and lustful conversation while talking. Arun Kumar said, "Disconnect, wait for the next call."

PP Singh was asked to find out from where the call was made. After a while, he said the call was made from Connaught Place. Everyone was sitting and talking when the call came again. Rajesh again indicated through gestures that it was his call. After a fifteen-minute conversation, the call was disconnected, and then, in front of everyone, everyone listened to the call on the tape recorder. This time, Shri Prakash had made this call to Harishankar Tiwari. Harishankar Tiwari was repeatedly saying, "Why are you after me? What have I done wrong? Today, neither I nor any of my men have any contract for railway, PWD, or irrigation. Everything is with you and Sujar Bhan's men."

Shri Prakash said, "You kept roaming around with my father for a month, Panditji; what did you get? And now you have bought two minibusses, twenty people travel in the front and twenty people in the back minibus. You sit in three cars in the middle by changing cars. What did you think that I don't know?" Harishankar Tiwari said, "I also have many enemies."

Shri Prakash said, "Don't lie; we have killed your enemy. Now, who is left to have enmity? You take fifty people or five hundred people; I will blow you up with a rocket launcher. You know rocket launcher, right?"

Hari Shankar Tiwari said, "What do you want?"

Shri Prakash said, "I will just kill you; you have done enough hooliganism. Think, when I put a rocket launcher in your ass... and you will fly upwards, and when your dhoti will open, then think what will happen?" Shri Prakash started laughing loudly while saying this. Shri Prakash said, "How many days will the goat's mother be happy? You count the days; remember that I will also come to eat puri on your thirteenth day."

Shri Prakash disconnected the call after saying this. Everyone laughed when the conversation ended; PP Singh called the crime branch again and wanted to know the location. After half an hour, DIG Gorakhpur SN Singh called and said that Shri Prakash was currently talking to that girl. He also made Arun Kumar write the number shown here. Arun Kumar disconnected the call and said to Rajesh Pandey, "Didn't you get the call on your phone? How did this call come there?"

Rajesh Pandey said, "We have made only six calls; he may be talking from some other phone, and it is also possible that he has given a different number to that girl, which is used only to talk to the girl; that is why the call regarding this conversation is not coming on our mobile." Arun Kumar said, "Yes, this is a possibility."

After a while, PP Singh said that this call was made near New Delhi Railway Station but not from the railway station. Then he said, "The distance of that place from the hotel is about forty kilometers. Otherwise, it can be checked right now."

Arun Kumar said, "He is talking to a girl; he will not finish the conversation soon. He is used to talking for a very long time. You should reach near the railway station because DIG Gorakhpur is saying that a wedding ceremony is happening nearby from where he is talking. Thunderous songs are playing, giving the impression that he is stationary there, not moving anywhere. There is no harm in taking a chance." PP Singh immediately left for New Delhi Railway Station with one of his constables and a sub-inspector.

Arun Kumar called DIG Gorakhpur and said he would inform us as soon as the call ended. Sitting there, everyone estimated that it would take PP Singh about fifty minutes to reach there. If this call continues for an hour, PP Singh will come close to it. The weddings will not be held at ten or twenty places; the two or four weddings that will take place will either be in a car or a hotel or restaurant.

About half an hour later, DIG Range Gorakhpur called and said the call had ended. Arun Kumar told PP Singh that the call is not working now, but you should still ask for the tower location from the crime branch to see where the wedding is taking place and whether there is a hotel or restaurant there. PP Singh said, "Okay."

PP Singh reached the spot and investigated a lot; weddings occurred in three or four places. He went to all the places and saw many small hotels; almost all the hotels had restaurants downstairs. PP Singh told

Arun Kumar the whole thing. Arun Kumar said, “Come back now; there is no use.”

In the evening, when everyone sat together and discussed, it was decided that it was just a matter of tomorrow; by the day after tomorrow morning, we would reach the airport, and it was possible that we would succeed before entering the airport. Everyone was very excited, and we seemed to be very close to our target. The next day, at 9:30 in the morning, DIG Range Gorakhpur said, “I am talking to that girl right now.” He also noted down a number. On enquiring from the Crime Branch, it was found that this number is of Greater Kailash 2; the address was also given.

Then, after a while, DIG Range Gorakhpur said that this call had been disconnected. This girl is adamant that tomorrow, at some time, she will leave the house and go directly to Delhi Railway Station by train. DIG Range Gorakhpur also provided the name and number of the train.

DIG Gorakhpur told Arun Kumar I would also send a person who identified the girl by the same train. When she gets off the train, if your team meets her there, we will follow this girl to her destination, and Shri Prakash will inevitably come to meet her. According to the number of calls the girl heard here, she has a very intimate relationship with Shri Prakash; if he comes to meet us, our work will become easy. Arun Kumar said, "Okay."

Meanwhile, Arif called from Lucknow. He told Rajesh Pandey that Shri Prakash was talking to Fazrullah. He was threatening a lot today. Rajesh Pandey immediately contacted Umesh Singh in Lucknow and asked the number from which Arif was called. The number Umesh told was the same number from which Shri Prakash talked to Nisha in Gorakhpur. Arun Kumar said, “He is still there. Greater Kailash is also a half-hour journey from here; we all go there. He has been talking for so long, it is difficult to talk for half an hour, but we will get to know his appearance once we go there.”

AK Gupta's team in Lucknow is working on this, spreading rumors and getting news published in newspapers. Three days ago, news was published that he had grown a big beard and had plastic surgery done in Singapore. At least if the PCO from where he is calling is there, then if the PCO person is shown the photo and asked, he can tell whether it was this man or some other man. This will make it clear whether he has changed his appearance or not.

Arun Kumar said, “We will go to the airport. Once again, we will see where to check on the roads leading to the airport and understand where we can easily catch him.” Everyone sat in a jeep and a car of Delhi Police and started going to Greater Kailash 2 after asking for the address. Rajesh Pandey said, “Sir, only Dheerendra will be able to get the correct description of Anand and Sudhir. Both of them may be together, so it will be better to take Dheerendra along; he can give good information about the appearance.” Everyone left immediately, and while enquiring about the address of Greater Kailash 2, they had reached halfway when Arif called to say that the call was over. Arun Kumar said, “Okay, we have the number; we are trying.”

Just then, DIG Range Gorakhpur called again, “He has called again; he is talking to the girl again, and the number is the same on which he was talking earlier.” Arun Kumar said, “Drive the car fast. He is still talking to the same girl. It will take us ten to fifteen minutes to reach, and we will find him talking to the girl.”

We reached that posh area of Greater Kailash. While looking at the house number, both the cars stopped in front of the gate where the house number was written. It was a small shopping complex in the residential area. After getting down, Satyendra Veer, Tevitaya, and Rajesh Pandey went inside, and they saw a PCO on the ground floor on the right-hand side. Satyendra Veer asked the PCO operator, “When did the person who just spoke to Gorakhpur and Lucknow leave?”

The PCO guy said, “The bus is just leaving; it has left since you people have come.”

Before Satyendra Veer could ask the PCO guy anything, the sub-inspector driving the jeep came running and said, "Sir, Dheerendra is saying that three people have just passed in a blue Cielo." Everyone ran and reached their respective vehicles; Dheerendra said that the car was seen on the straight road until the red light, which had been only two to three minutes.

Driving the car fast, an attempt was made to go beyond the red light and look, but the blue Cielo was not visible. Arun Kumar said, "Inspector VPN Singh is posted in Ghaziabad; I will tell him. He will come from here; he knows the routes here very well."

Everyone quickly moved forward on the roads from Greater Kailash 2 to Vasant Kunj. Arun Kumar called VPN Singh and told him the whole thing. VPN Singh said that he is still on the Delhi-Ghaziabad border. He is coming in the opposite direction on the same road on which you people are coming. If that car is seen on the way, he will inform us.

After a while, VPN Singh called and said, "Sir, that car has just entered Ghaziabad. I have told some of my people. They should talk to the traffic people; they will keep telling the location." By then, two cars with Arun Kumar had entered Ghaziabad. After a while, I met VPN Singh there. He said, "Sir, let us go to Indirapuram Road and block the road. It has turned in that direction only.

All the people stood on the Indirapuram road and parked their cars diagonally. A blue Cielo was seen coming straight on the deserted highway. The sub-inspector driving the Delhi Police jeep stopped his car twenty meters ahead in the middle of the road; there was no way for the Cielo to escape. Avinash Mishra said, "If he tries to reverse his car and run away, to stop him from doing that, it's better to park a vehicle behind his car in a diagonal position."

The other vehicle accompanying him was quickly backed up and parked diagonally on the road. Seeing the Delhi Police vehicle in front, the blue Cielo slowed down slightly, and Shri Prakash left the driving seat. Rajesh Pandey and Satyendra Veer Singh pounced on him as soon as he got down. Shri Prakash wore the same shirt and pants that the PCO guy had suggested. But he immediately fired two shots at Rajesh and Satyendra Veer, sat on the driving seat, and started backing the vehicle. Avinash Mishra saw from a distance that he was backing up the car, so he hit his truck and began firing heavily on the vehicle's tyres. Shri Prakash and Anuj were also firing from inside the Cielo.

Arun Kumar said, "There is no need to be afraid; just surround him like this; he has only small weapons. He has already sent the big weapons to Ranchi by vehicle. He will not be able to withstand it for long."

Meanwhile, Sudhir and Anuj opened the car door and tried to run towards the jungle on the side of the road. Shri Prakash stopped Avinash Mishra from behind and Rajesh Pandey from the front by firing individually. By then, Shri Prakash was shot by Satyendra Veer Singh; he also tried to run towards the jungle but fell there. Then Rajesh Pandey went a little ahead and fired several shots at Shri Prakash, Avinash Mishra, and Tewatia followed Anuj and Sudhir for some distance from behind and kept firing bullets; in a short while, both of them also fell.

Shri Prakash was lying down, but it was not clear where the bullet hit and whether he was alive or dead. Arun Kumar also went ahead and fired two or three shots, then when everyone went closer, and saw that Shri Prakash was almost dead. Arun Kumar congratulated everyone. Arun Kumar said, "First, search all of them to see if they have hidden a pistol or revolver somewhere."

Everyone thoroughly searched Shri Prakash, Sudhir, and Anuj. Shri Prakash had a diary, a digital diary, and some cartridges. Anuj also had his diary, some papers, and air tickets for all three to Ranchi on the 22nd; similarly, a diary was found with Sudhir.

Arun Kumar looked through the papers and told Rajesh Pandey that everyone's diary and digital diaries and papers will remain with you. Hand over the rest of the cartridges and the revolver found with them to the local police right now; they will be sealed. Rajesh Pandey kept all the papers and diaries in his pockets and said he would keep them in a safe bag after reaching Lucknow.

Arun Kumar immediately informed ADG Law and Order, Ajay Raj Sharma, that Shri Prakash and his two companions had been killed in Indirapuram. Ajay Raj Sharma immediately informed the Chief

Minister's Principal Secretary and Principal Secretary of Home, Naresh Dayal. Naresh Dayal informed that the Chief Minister is currently in a special session of the Assembly.

Today, on 21st September, a one-day special session related to the budget has been called; as soon as the Chief Minister comes out, he will be informed.

Naresh Dayal did say this, but he went straight to the official gallery of the Assembly and from there wrote on a slip of paper that Shri Prakash and his two associates had been killed in Indirapuram, Ghaziabad. Taking this slip, the employee of the Assembly reached the table of Chief Minister Kalyan Singh, and this slip was kept there. At that time, Chief Minister Kalyan Singh was speaking in the Assembly. After a while, when he read the slip kept in front of him, he requested the Assembly Speaker to stop the proceedings of the House for two minutes as he wanted to give vital information to the House.

Assembly Speaker Keshari Nath Tripathi permitted the Chief Minister to stop the proceedings of the House and give the information.

The Chief Minister said, today, I am happy to inform this House that the STF of Uttar Pradesh Police has just killed notorious criminal Shri Prakash Shukla and his two associates in an encounter in Indirapuram, Ghaziabad.

All the members of the House welcomed this announcement by thumping the tables, standing up from their seats, and congratulating each other. There was a queue of people congratulating Chief Minister Kalyan Singh. After a while, the Chief Minister himself stood up in the House. With the permission of the Assembly, he announced that for this heroic act done by the STF, this government announced a cash reward of Rs. 1 lakh and an out-of-turn promotion to each police officer in the STF team.

The news of Shri Prakash Shukla's death spread like wildfire in the forest, and many journalists from many TV channels and newspapers gathered there. Indirapuram police came and sent the bodies of all three to the hospital, and from there, all three bodies were sent to

Ghaziabad for postmortem. Arun Kumar, along with his entire team, came to the office of SSP Ghaziabad. There was a massive crowd of press people, all their questions answered, and everyone went to the hotel. In the hotel, everyone's telephones were getting repeated calls; everyone wanted to know how it happened. What happened? The phone was not going silent even for a second. Lucknow repeatedly told me that everyone should return to Lucknow. It was decided that everyone would go to Lucknow on the evening flight.

In the meantime, Arun Kumar said, "Everyone must inform their respective families. If their families get the news from here and there, then all kinds of questions will come to their minds, so everyone must inform their families." Rajesh Pandey said, "First, the call came from the family members." Satyendra Veer noted that I have also spoken to them; no one there is ready to believe that we have killed him. On hearing this, everyone started laughing. Tewatia said, "The situation is the same with everyone."

Then Arun Kumar received a call from Rajiv Ratan Shah, "Where are you all? I want to come and congratulate you. This STF was formed after my efforts, and it has been only six months since its formation, and within six months, you people have completed the work for which the STF was formed."

Arun Kumar said that we were leaving for the airport, everyone would return to Lucknow this evening, and the family members were worried. Rajiv Ratan Shah wished everyone well and asked, "Where is Shri Prakash Shukla's body kept? My wife and I want to see it."

Arun Kumar said, "All three bodies are kept in the postmortem house of Ghaziabad. I will tell SSP Ghaziabad to send someone to show you the bodies if they have not been sealed yet." Rajiv Ratan Shah said, "Okay, we have left from Delhi. We would like to see them first after reaching Ghaziabad; if you guys meet us at the airport, we will come there and feed you sweets." Arun Kumar immediately called SSP Ghaziabad and told him about Rajiv Ratan Shah's wish. He also said the credit for forming STF goes to Rajiv Ratan Shah. So, if the bodies have not been sealed, show them at any cost.

Everyone put their luggage in the car and left for the airport; then Arun Kumar said to Rajesh Pandey, “Rajesh, today is the second day of Navratri, and you are also fasting. While coming from Lucknow to Delhi, you said we would do this work during Navratri, and Vindhyachal Maa would bless us.” Rajesh Pandey said, “I have a lot of faith; you know that I visit every Navratri with my family. I have decided that after reaching Lucknow today, I will leave with my entire family tomorrow morning to visit Vindhyachal.”

Arun Kumar said, “Tomorrow, the Chief Minister has called the entire team to be felicitated at the Chief Minister’s residence at 11 am, and in the evening, the Governor has called everyone to be felicitated at the Raj Bhavan.”

Rajesh Pandey said, “Sir, I will go to Vindhyachal early in the morning; upon returning, I will apologize at both places, but I will go to Vindhyachal tomorrow first.” Arun Kumar said, “Okay, I will tell the Chief Minister and the Governor. After finishing the program at the Raj Bhavan, I am also going to Shirdi Sai Baba with my family for darshan. I have made my reservation at Pushpak in the evening.”

As soon as the conversation ended, a call came from Lucknow on Satyendra Veer Singh's phone. After a while, Satyendra Veer Singh started getting very angry on the phone. After the call was disconnected, Arun Kumar asked, "Who are you angry at today?"

Satyendra Veer said, "There is Lucknow. DG AK Gupta's team has spread the rumor that the person they have killed is not Shri Prakash. Shri Prakash's location is currently in Singapore. That's what I was saying; first, let's send him here and show him his face." Arun Kumar said, "Let it go; what does it matter if he says so? This is not the first time wrong information has been given about us. Everyone will understand, and everyone will know the truth. Later, they will feel ashamed. No one should spoil their mood today; everyone should reach home; there is no need to go anywhere else."

After a while, everyone reached the airport, and then DCP Airport Security's call came on Arun Kumar's phone, and he started congratulating him. On this, Arun Kumar said to him in an angry tone,

"You did not help at all? You kept saying Joint CP, Joint CP in everything. Did you think that if you do not help, then this work will not be done!"

He kept apologizing to Arun Kumar from the other side. After the call was disconnected, Satyendra Veer asked Arun Kumar, "You were telling me not to get angry with anyone on this day, and were you getting angry yourself?"

Everyone, including Arun Kumar, started laughing. Arun Kumar said laughingly, "He is the same DCP, the airport one, who repeatedly told me that he would not let anything happen. He had called to congratulate you; you must have seen it on TV somewhere."

The whole team reached the airport, and Mulayam Singh Yadav and Lalu Yadav also traveled in the same plane. After some time, the aircraft landed at Lucknow airport. The wives of Arun Kumar, Satyendra Veer, and Rajesh Pandey were at the airport waiting for them to arrive.

SSP Lucknow Rajni Kant Mishra and all the officers of Lucknow Police were present at the airport. The STF team was garlanded with flowers. A crowd of thousands had gathered as soon as they exited the airport. TV and newspaper people were shouting slogans of 'Police Zindabad!'.

None of the team members had imagined such a scene. At least ten to fifteen groups of band players were also present. While coming out, SSP Lucknow, Rajni Kant Mishra welcomed and hugged everyone. The crowd was so huge that it was challenging to sit in the vehicles. After a lot of effort, everyone was able to sit in their cars, and when the vehicles left from there, it seemed as if the crowd had come to the airport from nowhere; it took an hour to get out of the airport.

Late at night, everyone reached their homes. There was a massive crowd of journalists outside everyone's house, too.

(The STF team involved in encounter of Shri Prakash Shukla, upon their return.)

(Grand welcome of STF at the airport, with several band baaja celebrating the victory of STF.)

With great difficulty, everyone was able to get home after convincing them. Everyone's family was eager to know the whole story. After talking till late at night, everyone went to sleep. The next day, all the newspapers had big news on the first page, with only the news of Shri Prakash's death and photos of all the team members. There was a continuous stream of people at everyone's home to congratulate them. All the members received calls from the Chief Minister and Governor's office and were invited to the Chief Minister's residence and Raj Bhavan at the scheduled time.

People from Lucknow's Vyapar Mandal organization also kept calling everyone repeatedly and telling them about the dates of the felicitation ceremonies. Rajesh Pandey left for Vindhyachal Darshan in the morning with his wife, two children, and mother, and Arun Kumar went with his family in the evening to visit Shirdi Sai Baba.

SSP Ghaziabad called Arun Kumar Sahab and told him, "The postmortem was done on the same day, but no one has come to take his body till now. Once the information is given to his family, although Indirapuram police station informed his family in writing through the police in Gorakhpur, no one has come till now."

Arun Kumar asked, "Did Rajiv Ratan Shah come to see his body at night?" SSP Ghaziabad said, "He had come with his wife, and the station head had opened the postmortem house and showed his body. The work of sealing the body was started only after that." Arun Kumar Sahab said, "As per the rules, wait for his family for another 72 hours; if no one comes, then perform the last rites of his body as per the rules."

When asked if anyone had come to take the bodies of the other two, SSP Ghaziabad said that their relatives had come and taken away their bodies. When asked, "Where will you perform their last rites?" they said, "We will perform their last rites here in Ghaziabad itself."

Arun Kumar said, "Okay, it is also possible that they might have taken them to their home district." Three days later, when everyone gathered in the office again, in the evening, former DGP of Uttar

Pradesh, Shri Shriram Arun, came to the office on foot with a box of sweets. It was evening, around seven o'clock, when he told Arun Kumar, "I have been trying to find out for two days, you people were not in the office. Today, I learned that you people are in the office, so I want to feed you sweets myself. During my tenure, he troubled the police the most, and there was a lot of pressure on them. You people have done a courageous act!"

Arun Kumar said, "Sir, there was no need for you to come; if you had informed us, we would have come ourselves. Reaching your house would have taken less than two to three minutes. We all would have reached there ourselves and taken your blessings. Everyone has gathered today only." Still insisting, Shri Shriram fed sweets with his hands to Arun Kumar, Rajesh Pandey, Avinash Mishra, and Tewatia, who were present there and blessed them.

The next day, Chief Minister Kalyan Singh's office informed us that one lakh rupees were being sent to everyone participating in the encounter team and should be given to everyone. The next day, everyone in this encounter gathered in the office and discussed how scared people were. Lucknow's businessman, leader, police officer, and commoner lived in the shadow of fear for many days. While roaming in the city, one can feel the people's happiness. Everyone told their experiences of how the people who were tormented and tortured by him came to everyone's house to thank them.

Satyendra Veer told how Sanjay Seth, Sarana, and his colleagues came to his place running and panting and kept asking whether he was killed or not. Their happiness knew no bounds. Arun Kumar said that Arif was also calling me again and again and asking whether he was dead or not. His joy, too, knew no bounds.

Rajesh Pandey said Minister Raja Bhaiya had called and expressed his wish to come to the office residence and feed sweets. Apart from this, the Principal of Karamat Inter College went to the office with sweets, and she also thanked him a lot; many such people have expressed their happiness through different mediums.

If the pace of this criminal had not stopped in time, history would never have forgiven the police force. Such a notoriously ambitious person who nurtured the dream of conquering the entire state in the battle for supremacy and had done a lot for his Godfather- Surajbhan Singh, who also nurtured the ambition to bring the whole state of Bihar under his grip, had crippled the political forces and posed a grave challenge to the entire political force of the state. He had almost succeeded in his plans.

Only one person's willpower and determination to crush the crime and the confidence of small police team members successfully killed the crime cobra with a hundred heads ready to swallow the system at its will. The terror tale of the monster ends.

.... And this book, too, comes to an end.

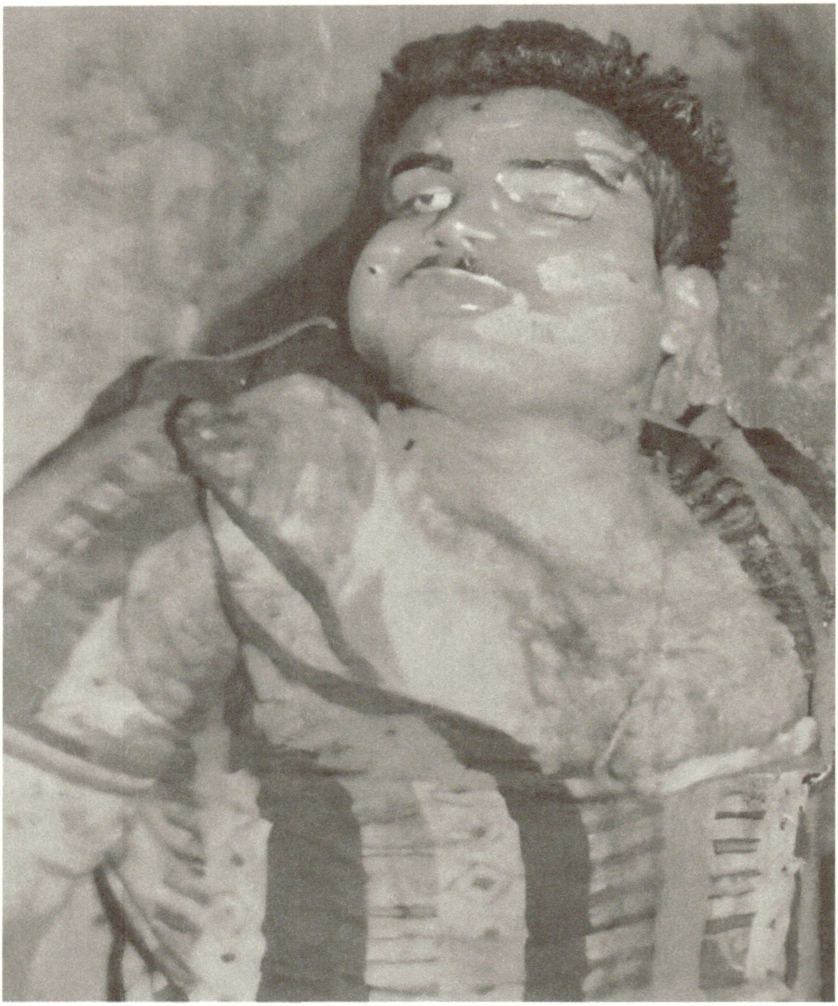

(Post encounter, body of Shri Prakash Shukla.)

(Various newspaper reported in detail about the encounter of Shri Prakash Shukla.)

www.ingramcontent.com/pod-product-compliance
Lightning Source LLC
Chambersburg PA
CBHW031336230926
51848CB00002B/259
9789364315920